HYPE
WOMEN

ERIN GALLAGHER

Foreword by JAMIE LEE CURTIS

HYPE WOMEN

BREAKING FREE FROM MEAN GIRLS, PATRIARCHY AND SYSTEMS SILENCING YOU

WILEY

Published by John Wiley & Sons, Inc., Hoboken, New Jersey.
Published simultaneously in Canada.

The manufacturer's authorized representative according to the EU General Product Safety Regulation is Wiley-VCH GmbH, Boschstr. 12, 69469 Weinheim, Germany, e-mail: Product_Safety@wiley.com.

Trademarks: Wiley and the Wiley logo are trademarks or registered trademarks of John Wiley & Sons, Inc. and/or its affiliates in the United States and other countries and may not be used without written permission. All other trademarks are the property of their respective owners. John Wiley & Sons, Inc. is not associated with any product or vendor mentioned in this book.

Limit of Liability/Disclaimer of Warranty: While the publisher and author have used their best efforts in preparing this book, they make no representations or warranties with respect to the accuracy or completeness of the contents of this book and specifically disclaim any implied warranties of merchantability or fitness for a particular purpose. No warranty may be created or extended by sales representatives or written sales materials. The advice and strategies contained herein may not be suitable for your situation. You should consult with a professional where appropriate. Further, readers should be aware that websites listed in this work may have changed or disappeared between when this work was written and when it is read. Neither the publisher nor authors shall be liable for any loss of profit or any other commercial damages, including but not limited to special, incidental, consequential, or other damages.

For general information on our other products and services or for technical support, please contact our Customer Care Department within the United States at (800) 762-2974, outside the United States at (317) 572-3993 or fax (317) 572-4002.

Wiley also publishes its books in a variety of electronic formats. Some content that appears in print may not be available in electronic formats. For more information about Wiley products, visit our web site at www.wiley.com.

Library of Congress Cataloging-in-Publication Data is Available:

Names: Gallagher, Erin (Executive), author.
Title: Hype women : breaking free from mean girls, patriarchy, and systems silencing you / Erin Gallagher.
Description: Hoboken, New Jersey : Wiley, [2026] | Includes index.
Identifiers: LCCN 2025018883 (print) | LCCN 2025018884 (ebook) | ISBN 9781394329502 (hardback) | ISBN 9781394329526 (adobe pdf) | ISBN 9781394329519 (epub)
Subjects: LCSH: Self-actualization (Psychology) in women. | Women—Finance, Personal.
Classification: LCC BF637.S4 G344 2026 (print) | LCC BF637.S4 (ebook) | DDC 158.1082—dc23/eng/20250510
LC record available at https://lccn.loc.gov/2025018883
LC ebook record available at https://lccn.loc.gov/2025018884

Cover Design: Wiley
Cover Images: © oxygen/Getty Images, © 4zevar/Shutterstock
Author Photo: © Lena Jackson @lenajacksonlens
Printed and bound by CPI Group (UK) Ltd, Croydon, CR0 4YY
C9781394329502_150825

For Erin.

You saved me.

Contents

Foreword by Jamie Lee Curtis   ix

Chapter 1   Why We're Here   1

PART I   **I Was | A Crawling Caterpillar**   **9**

Chapter 2   Constantly Seeking Chaos   11

Chapter 3   Manipulated by Mean Girls   29

Chapter 4   Solitary Confinement   43

PART II   **I Am | Cocooned and Dissolving**   **51**

Chapter 5   Burning Bridges   53

Chapter 6   Unabashed Hype Women   63

Chapter 7   Serve Yourself First   81

Chapter 8   The Only Way Out Is In   101

PART III   **I Will Be | The Monarch**   **115**

Chapter 9   Karmic Crusader   117

Chapter 10   Take Back Your Body   129

Chapter 11   The Alchemist   161

Chapter 12   Main Fucking Character Energy   207

Chapter 13   Prioritizing Pleasure   219

Chapter 14   Take Up Space   231

Chapter 15   The Goddess of Your Dualities   243

Chapter 16   Where We're Headed   253

Bibliography   *263*
Acknowledgments   *267*
About the Author   *271*
Index   *273*

Foreword by Jamie Lee Curtis

In January 2023, at the Golden Globe Awards, I was there with the rest of my cast and crew from our movie *Everything Everywhere All at Once*. Right before her category was announced, Michelle Yeoh leaned over to me and whispered that she had never been nominated for anything in her life before and she was nervous. One minute later, when her name was called as the winner, I threw my hands up in a joyous gesture of excitement and support and watched in awe as she stood proudly on that stage and spoke her truth.

The next morning, I woke up to an Instagram post by Erin Gallagher talking about Hype Women, hyping other women's successes. Erin's gorgeous post and word anthem of support moved me and people who know me and care about me. From that moment to the publication of this book, Erin has continued to dedicate her life's work to supporting other women and to debunking the narrative that women are not there for each other.

That's just not true, and Erin and her Hype Women Movement and now her book are helping change that trope. I am thrilled to have been the spontaneous spark that has given voice to so much and so many.

Erin's spirit has lifted us all. This moment is our launchpad. Let's build on it. Let's lift together.

JLC

1 | Why We're Here

The moment I remembered who the fuck I was, the spell was broken.

Up until that critical awakening, I had been *actively* abandoning myself, predictably and passively participating in my own demise, my own destruction, and the disappearance of any lasting semblance of self.

I equated my value and my worth with my service to others. And it's no surprise that I did. Women are conditioned to choose themselves *last*, to value their worth *less*, to honor their intuition *least*.

And the numbers prove it: women's unpaid labor is worth $10.9 trillion . . . *every single year*.

This is according to a 2020 analysis by Oxfam of the "unpaid and underpaid care work and the global inequality crisis." Said another way, "Women's unpaid labor 'exceeds the combined revenue of the 50 largest companies on the Fortune Global 500 list, including Walmart, Apple, and Amazon,'" per the *New York Times*.

An entire global economy is built on the backs—and sustained by the sweat equity—of women's unseen, undervalued, and unrecognized worth.

That is, until it isn't.

The day I decided to choose myself *first*, to value my worth *more*, and to honor my intuition *most* is the day I began rewiring my brain. And I never looked back.

It was not an overnight process.
It was not without missteps and backslides and upheaval.
It was not for the faint of heart.

But I had to do it—or I wasn't going to survive.

I spent decades in the background, pouring my human capital into building others' social and financial gains. I surrendered to narcissists, tactically targeted for my empathetic, people-pleasing, ambitious, do-whatever-it-takes modus operandi. I made everyone else look good. I handed over my ideas, my intuition, and my identity in exchange for fleeting and fluctuating praise.

The only thing worse than the ensuing bankruptcy of self is realizing that you never thought to open your own account.

The shame of this reality kept me from asking for help, from telling the truth, from crawling out from under the weight of my own self-destruction. And the trauma bonds that relentlessly tied me to my abusers kept me from falling out of line or ever questioning if I actually wanted to stay.

Like so many women, I was caught in the vice grip of a centuries-old strategic plan to keep women down: a concerted all-out assault by the patriarchy, mean girls (also known as "foot soldiers to the patriarchy"), and systems silencing women.

Breaking free from all three has been the most important work of my life: healing my generational trauma, bringing me back into my body, and reminding me of who the fuck I am.

It's led to the loss of my identity, body, and spirit.
It's led to the re-birth of my identity, body, and spirit.
It's both.

It's why you're here.

Turning 40 broke me down, broke me open, and broke me out of a cycle I didn't realize had become the infrastructure of my life, the lifeblood of my body, the embodiment of my spirit. And that was just the beginning.

When I started sharing my experiences with other women, I learned something that I had never known. They were feeling the same. So many of us were sick and tired of the hand we had been dealt, the burden of misogyny carried by each generation and transferred to the next, and the trauma experienced in our daily life and relived for eternity in the expansive confines of our minds.

We wanted a new way forward.

Enter Hype Women: a global movement mobilizing women's collective power.

It was sparked by a moment between Jamie Lee Curtis and Michelle Yeoh. It was lit by a post I wrote giving this concept—and call to action—a name. It was a flame that we grew into a movement, fueled by you.

Hype Women everywhere are changing the world. We are demanding different. We're transforming.

By the time you are done with this book, you will be in full-on metamorphosis mode, transitioning from a place of only accepting what you "get," to dissolving what no longer serves you, to finally emerging and exploring the space of your unbounded capacity.

This book is for women in *all stages* of their metamorphosis: from being terrified to break out of old habits; to trudging through the muck and mire in the midst of cutting out toxic people, places, and programming; to encouraging others whose journeys have yet to begin; to being on the other side, freer and more full of life than you ever thought possible; and everything and everywhere in between.

When you finally break free, you need support. Cutting cords that are keeping you small and extinguishing your light requires great courage and conviction. It requires coming back home. To yourself. And figuring out who you are once all the false identities, opinions, and lies about who you're *not* are stripped away.

Here, *you* get to define yourself; and that is so rarely just one thing.

This book is divided into three distinct parts, meant to meet you at every stage of your metamorphosis, every time you go through them, as every version of yourself:

Part I: I Was | A Crawling Caterpillar: Holding and forgiving the versions of yourself you had to be to survive.

Part II: I Am | Cocooned and Dissolving: Breaking free from people, places, and programming holding you back.

Part III: I Will Be | The Monarch: Stepping into the power of knowing who you are—and showing the world you've arrived.

This book found you, where you are, in this moment. And it will be with you on your journey to who you're going to be.

On March 25, 2022, I turned 40. And everything changed. I stopped holding all of my thoughts and feelings and intuition inside. And I began writing and sharing and shouting *out* into the world the experiences I've had, the cages I've broken free from, the systems I'm dismantling.

My book is a gift to the Hype Women who have been integral to my metamorphosis and a love letter to the little girl in me who always deserved better and more than she received. When women are able to break free and *fight*—not just for ourselves but for other women—we take back our power.

There are a lot of women out there who are waking up, doing the deep work, and evaluating themselves, their relationships, their careers, and what they are putting their time and energy toward.

But the leap from *evaluating* to *elevating* can be daunting. From identifying what no longer works to stepping into what does. From leaving a comfort zone as a "people pleaser" to serving yourself first. From stopping the inertia in your career or relationships to being honest about why you don't want *that* or *them* anymore.

For me, what broke the spell was a singular phrase that came to me and refused to leave until I paid it the respect it was due:

> *I will no longer abandon myself in service to others.*

There are so many ways we abandon ourselves in service to others:

- Staying too long in relationships whose end is overdue
- Doing unpaid work at our company because we care
- Taking less money for a role than we deserve
- Putting others' wants and desires before ours
- Shouldering an inequitable amount of domestic labor at home

- Volunteering for more than we have the energy to contribute
- Spending time with friends we have outgrown
- Breaking our boundaries in order to "keep the peace"
- Allowing our children's lives to eclipse our own
- Moving our dreams to the backburner, time and time again
- Viewing our worth exclusively through external validations
- Saying "yes" to people, places, and projects when our gut screams "no"
- Taking the back seat in a car we should be driving

When I turned 40, however, I decided enough was enough.

In a matter of months, I resigned from the company I had co-founded two-and-a-half years before.

I created—and communicated—new, important boundaries with family and friends.

I continued to heal my own traumas and the generational trauma I carried with me daily on a cellular level as an oldest daughter and the daughter of an oldest daughter.

I chose myself in big and small ways every single day.

And when people told me I was selfish for doing so, I told them they were wrong.

It has been an exhausting, messy, complicated disaster. People were pissed. Many still are.

That's the thing about change. It rattles everyone—and everything—everywhere to their core. What—and who—is left standing tells you everything you need to know.

Well, guess what? I'm still here.

In *Hype Women*, we are going to learn to hold our dualities with compassionate care:

To be fiercely independent *and* deeply loyal
To be a devoted mother *and* a selfish woman
To be self-aware *and* self-actualized
To be sensitive *and* tough

To be careful *and* carefree
To be a Hype Woman *and* to have Hype Women
To play it safe *and* take risks
To follow the rules *and* break them
To be concerned *and* courageous
To be a builder *and* a disruptor
To work hard *and* rest
To seek joy *and* create it
To be empathic *and* have boundaries
To embrace our masculine *and* our feminine

Because our power lies in our dualities.
All women's power does.

The magic of this truth—of our metamorphosis—continues to create a cultural zeitgeist that is shifting solar systems. The world tells us to bloom where we are planted.

But maybe we never chose this bed we've been forced to lie in.
Maybe we don't believe that we can grow here anymore.
Maybe the roots don't feel like a tethering or a grounding, but instead a strangling from which we are trying to escape.

Women are done with the incremental, crawling caterpillar pace of progress. Women are refusing to be cocooned into spaces and places that are limiting our growth and evolution. Women are walking away from people who tell us we're worth less.

Women. Are. Breaking. Out.

Women are transforming and taking flight toward who we were always meant to be.

Hype Women isn't just a book. It's a noun. A verb. A call to action. A question. An answer. A moment. A Movement.

Hype Women is:
- A seismic shift in the way women view one another
- A decision we've made to stop silencing, side-eyeing, and side-lining her success—and our own

- A commitment to supporting, surrounding, and shouting her name in every sphere of influence we occupy
- Our collective sisterhood

No one gets to tell us:
- Who we are
- What we're capable of
- When we're ready
- Where we belong
- Why we matter
- How bright we can shine

Because when we—as women—*hype* women, we hype ourselves. And that shift is going to change the world.

It all starts now.

LFG.

PART

I

I Was

A Crawling Caterpillar

2 | Constantly Seeking Chaos

I grew up around adults whose unregulated emotions and immature behavior set the tone for the day. They acted in whatever way they felt like existing—and I learned, as a little girl, to adapt and adjust around them.

Whether it's implied or inherent, women are drawn to chaos, not because we enjoy it, but because it's familiar. And so, we repeatedly move toward mayhem, time and time again.

So many of us grew up in chaotic homes that became our homeostasis. We learned how to operate in a space filled with problems that needed to be solved. We were there to rescue everyone and everything except ourselves. We became experts at identifying the key players who wanted to feel powerful and in charge—and we shape-shifted *around* them; we kowtowed *to* them. We understood our roles as regulators of our external world, all the while ignoring how dysregulated we were inside of our own.

Living in a state of fight or flight for days, weeks, years, even decades does a number on your nervous system. It becomes the fabric of your being, the foundation of your existence, the fuel of your always-on engine. The deep, hardened angst that forms a pit in your stomach is the weight—the burden—you dutifully carry, day in and day out.

You unknowingly transform into the canary in a coal mine.

The origin of the expression is literal: canaries were historically used to test for carbon monoxide and other toxic gases in underground mines. If dangerous gases collected in the mine, the gases would kill the canary before killing the miners, providing a warning to exit the tunnels immediately.

The canary's life served as an early indicator of potential danger.

How long have you borne this responsibility? How long have you been used—and by whom? How long have you existed in service to others?

There is no relief from your obligation.
There is no place to hide in the open, vastness of your mind.
There is no way out, alive.

That is, until you disintegrate.

My teacher, Mrs. Barber, asks me to step outside the classroom during the silent reading portion of our day. I am in third grade at Star of the Sea School in Honolulu, Hawaii. I am eight years old.

"Erin, I just wanted to check on you. How are you doing? Are you okay?"

"Mmmhmm."

She kneels down to my level and takes my hands in hers. She looks me directly in the eyes. The undivided attention is unsettling and intoxicating.

"I know about your parents' divorce. And I want you to know that it's not your fault."

I never thought it was my fault.

"Okay."

"Erin. It's not your fault. It's not your fault."

The more she said it, the less I believed her.

This memory is seared into the grooves of my brain—a permanent markered moment making up the long and winding roadmap of my life.

I revisit these places often.

Sometimes with purpose and intention.

Other times, I'm relegated to the passenger seat of the car I *was* driving—pulled onto an off-ramp toward a place I hadn't planned to go.

Our lives are made up of "flashbulb memories."

According to the American Psychological Association Dictionary, "a flashbulb memory is a vivid, detailed, and long-lasting memory of a significant or emotional event. Flashbulb memories are often associated with surprising or consequential events. They are often so vivid and detailed that people believe they are like a photograph taken at the moment of the event."

That moment—standing outside of the closed, sliding-glass door to my third-grade classroom—marked a shift inside of me. It was the beginning of a three-decades-long journey to attempt to control everything happening around me.

I believed that I not only had the *power* to impact every situation I faced but the *responsibility*.

It was my *duty* to see the problem before it occurred.

It was my *obligation* to act in just the right way to ensure the boat didn't rock.

It was my *job* to fix everything before it broke.

I behaved much like a child of an alcoholic—even though neither of my parents were.

But it was in our blood. Both of *their* parents were alcoholics—raising them while drinking socially, surreptitiously, and then superfluously. And so, they carried that pain and shame with them at a cellular level. And they transferred it to me.

According to the Addiction Center, "growing up with one or both parents dependent on alcohol can also result in symptoms of post-traumatic stress disorder (PTSD) in adulthood. These symptoms include hypervigilance, need for control, difficulty with emotions and low self-esteem."

Check, check, check, check.

If only I knew then what I know now. If only they did.

But my grandparents' generation wasn't going to talk about a damn thing. I mean, my God, they are called the Silent Generation for a reason. And they raised my parents in homes where so much went unsaid.

As I dug deeper into the impact of addictions on families, the truth was revealed.

"Alcoholic families are behavioral systems in which alcoholism and alcohol-related behaviors have become central organizing principles around which family life is structured. (The whole is greater than the sum of the parts)."

(Judith Adelson, 2010)

In Claudia Black's book *It Will Never Happen to Me: Growing Up with Addiction as Youngsters, Adolescents, Adults* she talks about the infrastructure that makes up an Addictive Family. There are "house *rules*" and "house roles."

Addictive Family "House Rules":
- **Don't Feel.**

    Due to the constant pain of living with an adult substance user, a child must "quit feeling" in order to survive.
- **Don't Talk.**

    Children of adult substance users learn in their families not to talk about a huge part of their reality—and from this early training, the children learn to not talk about anything unpleasant.
- **Don't Trust.**

    In alcoholic families, promises are often forgotten, celebrations cancelled, and adults' moods unpredictable. As a result, children learn not to count on others.

Addictive Family "House Roles":
In an addictive or depressed family system the disease becomes the organizing principle. The affected person becomes the central figure from which everyone else organizes their behaviors and reactions, usually in what is a slow, insidious process.

Original work regarding family roles was written by Virginia Satir and then adapted by Claudia Black and Sharon Wegscheider-Cruse to fit the addictive family. Here's how Black broke down the Common Roles.

Common Roles:
- Addict ("The Dependent")
- Chief Enabler ("The Co-Dependent")
- Family Hero ("The Responsible One")
- Placater ("The People-Pleaser")
- Scapegoat ("The Acting-Out One")
- Lost Child ("The Adjuster")
- Mascot ("The Jester")

—

In my mother's family of seven children, she is the oldest daughter. While she grew up with two older brothers, my mother shouldered the responsibility of keeping it all together, all of the time—to this day.

It is my belief, based on my own personal research, that she plays the role of the "Family Hero." Here's what I learned.

Family Hero or "The Responsible One"

These responsible children try to ensure that the family looks "normal" to the rest of the world. In addition, they often project a personal image of achievement, competence, and responsibility to the outside world. They tend to be academically or professionally very successful. The cost of such success is often denial of their own feelings and a belief that they are "imposters."

Strengths of the "Hero"
- Successful
- Organized
- Leadership skills
- Decisive
- Initiator
- Self-disciplined
- Goal oriented

Deficits of the "Hero"
- Perfectionist
- Difficulty listening

- Inability to follow
- Inability to relax
- Lack of spontaneity
- Inflexible
- Unwilling to ask for help
- High fear of mistakes
- Inability to play
- Severe need to be in control

—

This describes my mother to a tee.
It also describes me.

Do you see yourself in this list?
Do you hear the people praising you for the strengths laid out here?
And complaining about your deficits?

I check every box.
In the following quote, from "The Problem" adapted from "The Laundry List" from Adult Children of Alcoholics, I see the structure of my mother's—and then my—DNA laid out; the paths and grooves and wiring of our brains; the blueprint for the lives we were forced to live:

> We learned to keep our feelings down as children and kept them buried as adults. As a result of this conditioning, we confused love with pity, tending to love those we could rescue. Even more self-defeating, we became addicted to excitement in all our affairs, preferring constant upset to workable relationships.

Even if we, our parents, or our grandparents aren't—or don't view ourselves as—alcoholics, we are all surrounded by it. It's everywhere in our society.
According to the National Association for Children of Addiction, "More than 28 million Americans are children of alcoholics; nearly 11 million are under the age of 18." Studies have shown that 61% of adults have at least one adverse childhood experience (ACE) resulting from growing up

with an alcoholic parent. And one out of six has at least *four* (Center for Disease Control and Prevention, 2021).

> What do you think happens to all those little girls who grow up to be women?
> What do you think happens to all the family heroes who save everyone but themselves?
> What do you think happens to all those responsible girls and women who don't feel and don't talk and don't trust?

Alcoholism is an epidemic that has impacted generations of families. And I can say, with certainty, that it has impacted mine.

My mom was an officer in the U.S. Coast Guard for 25 years, retiring as a captain following her final tour as the press liaison to the commandant: the highest-ranking member of the fifth branch of the U.S. military. Her entire career was centered around service. Her entire life followed suit.

The mantra for the Coast Guard is "Semper Paratus": Never Not Prepared. Said another way, Always Prepared. Said yet another way: Hyper. Fucking. Vigilant.

I grew up learning to be prepared for anything: heavy rain beginning around 2 p.m.; hunger or dehydration striking in the middle of a hike; a chill that would require a light jacket when the clouds came in; an extra pair of soccer gear to make it through the muddy games of a two-day tournament; an uncle who started in on his second bottle of wine and began telling stories not meant for eight-year-olds to hear; an alcoholic, narcissistic, abusive stepfather whose mood shifted with the wind and sucked the oxygen out of every room he entered in a split second with his rage.

All of my vigilance and preparedness and anticipation of needs was focused on the external world.

> How would I be ready for what was happening out there?
> How would I pay attention to the signs that the energy in the room was shifting?

How would I fix what was about to be broken before it had the chance to break?

I did my damn job, that's how.

I never learned to listen—or tend—to what was happening inside of me.

My needs and my feelings were in service to the greater good. I canary-in-the-coal-mined my way through life, not because I enjoyed it but because I was damn good at it.

I was drawn to people who had problems that needed fixing, whose moods ranged from viscous to vicious, whose volatility made me feel alive.

I could fix them!

I was a fixer!

Fixing was my *thing*!

Until *I* broke.

🐾 🐾 🐾

I'm standing in the carpeted hallway, near the top of the stairs, on the second floor of our home. I'm pressing all 10 fingers in a repeated motion from the top of my forehead to my eyebrows and back. I want the pressure of my hands to alleviate my pounding headache, the constricting tightness in my chest, the panic rising in my body. It's my attempt to self-soothe. It's not working.

My husband asks me if I still want to do this. I can't believe him. How could he *dare* to suggest that I leave what I've created? That I walk away from the blood, sweat, and tears I had poured into turning this from nothing into something? That I quit?

I snapped back, "I don't have a choice! I built this! My whole life is 'have to!'"

This was supposed to be hard. It was supposed to hurt. How did you even know you were alive and making a difference in the world if you didn't feel just a little bit nauseous and debilitated with anxiety while you were doing it?

Those were signs that it was working. That you were in it. That you were doing the damn thing.

At least, that's what I had grown up thinking—and had been taught was what it felt like to be a woman with a career in Corporate America.

You were supposed to feel a little (or a lot) like shit after you received feedback.

You were supposed to have your stomach flip when an email popped up in your inbox.

You were supposed to feel like the floor dropped out from under you when your phone rang.

What felt like Brian's judgment, lack of confidence, and disappointment in me was really his deep devotion, love, care, and protection. He saw what was happening to me before I did. He watched as a I turned into a different person; as I turned on myself. I was too deep in it—was too far gone—to view and assess what was happening with any level-headed lucidity.

I went back to my daily hell. But his question stayed with me. It gnawed at the sleeping bear that was beginning to awake from a coma deep, deep down in the pit of my gut.

Growing up as a hypervigilant, self-motivated, people-pleasing perfectionist made me the ideal worker when I entered the "professional" world. I was an expert at anticipating other's needs, of seeing around corners, and of identifying a potential problem before it happened.

What it looks like from the outside is a person who has it all together and is ready for anything.

What it feels like on the inside is running on a treadmill—whose speed and incline continues to increase—while catching and juggling balls that are flying at you, from every direction, with varying intensity and increasing weight.

I loved a good crisis. It made me feel alive. It made me feel needed. It made me feel valuable.

I turned 40 on March 25, 2022. Six days later, I publicly resigned from the company I had co-founded two-and-half years before.

I walked away.

I quit.

I "opted out."

It was the first time in my life that I said, "Enough."

And oh, did it feel shitty.

I had failed. I had given up. I was weak. What had become of me? All of the flashes of faces of the naysayers telling me I "didn't have what it takes," "wasn't ready to be the boss," and "couldn't do it my way" flooded my mind and stole my spirit.

I stayed in bed for three days.

But what felt like the end was really the beginning. I was disintegrating the version of myself that I was finally ready to release to become one I had never had the space or permission to envision.

Disintegrate is defined as "to break up into small parts, typically as the result of impact or decay."

The four months that followed my resignation were deeply unfamiliar. For the first time in my life, I wasn't moving. And moving is what keeps you from coming home to yourself, from sitting with your thoughts, from feeling what you need to feel in order to let go.

For the first time in my life, I sat on my couch. Without a purpose. For no reason. I stopped myself from getting up to "do something" at least 10 times in the first four minutes. I had to actively immobilize my inertia-driven operating system.

It was So. Fucking. Uncomfortable.

I felt suffocated in my own skin.

I wanted to scream from all the quiet.

I couldn't shut up—or off—my mind.

Was this meditation? Fuck this. Who could live like this?

I had never learned to just *be*.

My mother never sat. She was always doing something: working, cooking, cleaning, organizing, comforting, consoling, helping, rearing, leading, building, creating, preparing, planning, rescuing, rescuing, rescuing. As a single mother, she did it all. She had to.

The Family Hero never sleeps. She abandoned herself in service to others.

So, I followed suit.

Sitting was for quitters.
Slowing was for weaklings.
Stopping was for the dead.

Without my service to everyone but myself, without external validation, without solving something somewhere for someone, what was I even worth?

One of my best friends, Neha O'Rourke, said two things to me over the course of our relationship that changed my life:

1. Be where your feet are.
2. You are worthy simply because you exist.

When she first shared these messages with me, they described my personal, fresh hell.

"Be in the moment" and *not* preparing for what's next? Well, that sounds like a nightmare. And it will be. Because of the not preparing part. Sure thing. I'll just sit here and wait for the impending fire to engulf me.

And I'm worthy *just* because I exist? That was some woo-woo shit that even I—as an astrology-loving, universe-believing, witchy woman—had a hard time getting behind. Yeah, yeah, yeah, self-love. Great. Cool. But what am I *doing* to matter?

Chaos made my skin tingle.
Calm made my skin crawl.

Until I shed it.
Until I disintegrated.
Until I dissolved into goo—and left the body of a crawling caterpillar to cocoon.

I started to create small rituals that taught my nervous system—that taught my body—what calm felt like, and why it was a good thing.

I lit candles.
I watched the flames flicker and the wicks burn.
I inhaled the jasmine and blonde wood and tuberose.

I took baths.
With steaming hot water.
And Himalayan bath salts mixed with crushed purple and pink flower petals.

I played music.
And I sang loudly and let my body move.
I was transported by the lyrics and the beat and the stories.

I sat, often.
Wrapping myself in dusty rose-colored, faux fur blankets—surrounded
    by fuzzy pillows.
I wore sweatshirts and socks and stretchy pants that made me feel held.

I read books.
Not to learn about history or public figures or current events.
But for pleasure.

I used lotion.
Tokyo Milk's "Gin and Rosewater" and "Dead Sexy."
I noticed the silky feel on my hands as I held my own hand, rotating
    one into the other repeatedly.

I drank tea.
Magic Hour's "Goddess" and "The Moon" and "Aries."
I steeped the leaves in beautiful mugs and cupped the warmth
    in my hands.

I sprayed sacred mists.
The Sacred Wild's "Goddess"—jasmine, tuberose, and Ylang Ylang—in
    the morning.
And "Energy Cleanse"—mint and sage—early and often.
And "Grounded"—clove, sandalwood, lavender, and vetiver—at night.

I wore perfume.

My *special* perfumes that I previously saved *only* for special occasions, when I would be in the presence of other people: Lilac Path by Aerin Lauder, Rebecca Minkoff by Rebecca Minkoff, and Intimissimi—a perfume I bought on Capri during my honeymoon in 2014.

I sprayed them on my wrists, my neck, and the soft spot above my hard ribcage.

I created a daily routine that told me I was safe. I cared for myself in the way I so freely and diligently took care of others. I taught myself to seek calm over chaos. It took me a long time to get there—to actually enjoy these experiences versus feeling like I was in a bullshit bootcamp of my own making, begrudgingly trying to survive the slowness and the silence.

It wasn't all sunshine and roses.

I sucked at each of these things over and over and over again. I failed to do them well. I kept getting drawn back into the chaos vortex—creating my own drama when it didn't find me fast enough.

And that's to be expected.

Redesigning an operating system that has kept you alive for 40 years takes *effort*. Actually *following* that new operating system takes *time*. Planting the seeds of your growth is a process that requires patience. You can't will a plant to grow faster than the time it takes for the sun to pour its light into the earth, for the rain to water the roots taking hold, for the soil to nourish the potential of what could be.

You must wait.

One of my favorite places on earth is Saugatuck, Michigan. I didn't choose for that to be the case. Saugatuck chose me. Every time we drive to the eclectic, lakeside town on the west coast of Michigan, my entire body exhales. We round the curve over the bridge connecting Douglas to Saugatuck and the 10-foot-high sign—with a painter's palette and brush—welcomes you to this magical destination. And I'm transported.

For the past few years, we've spent my birthday week in Saugatuck. This week just so happens to coincide with my boys' spring break vacation. While most families seek warmer backdrops to break up the winter months, I've convinced my husband and two sons to spend ours in the often wet, cold, overcast sleepy off-season "beach" town.

The weather doesn't matter to me. The peace does.

I've started my own birthday ritual there.

I wake up early, while the rest of the house is still asleep.

I drive to Isabel's Bakery—a beautiful women-owned bakery and specialty food store.

I order the largest cinnamon sweet roll inside of the glass display case and the tallest, hottest Americano.

I drive to Oval Beach. If it's rainy or snowy or too cold, I park in the upper lot, overlooking Lake Michigan. If it's sunny or temperate or unseasonably warm, I walk out and sit in the sand.

I turn on whatever music I'm loving at the moment.

I take a long, slow sip of my piping hot Americano.

I pull off a piece of the soft cinnamon-dusted pastry, smothered in cream cheese frosting, and I close my eyes as I take that long-awaited first bite.

I inhale deeply.

I exhale freely.

I open the notebook—where I write my thoughts and ideas and to-dos and aspirations and goals these days—and I write.

I write down who I'm grateful for.

I write down what I want the next year to be.

I write down where I want my life to go.

On March 25, 2022—the day I turned 40 (and six days before I was set to publicly resign)—when I arrived at Isabel's, I noticed something.

Maybe I had seen it before.

Maybe I had read it quickly while rushing to get in the front door.

Maybe I had missed it entirely.

It's a quote painted in charcoal black and deep red letters that power-fully pop against the creamy white brick exterior:

Judge each day not by the harvest you reap, but by the seeds you plant.

Isabel's Eatery, Saugatuck, Michigan.

My whole life had been about the harvest.

What did I have to show for my work?
What could I hold up to prove I was valuable?
What would the world say about what I had done with my life?

The harvest was proof of worth.

The seeds were unseen, underground, underestimated. They required patience and love and care and time.

This quote met me in a moment when I needed it most. This was the mantra I needed to carry with me into the next decade of my life.

Because what if I didn't need to keep planting *new* seeds in field after field after field?

What if I recognized that I've spent the last almost 40 years planting little seeds everywhere? And now, it was time to stop planting? To stop running? To stop moving?

What if the harvest coming my way wasn't just from the seeds I'd planted? But also from the seeds planted by my mother? By my grandmother? By my Hype Women?

What if I could stop judging every day by all of the things I busily did for others in my external world and I could start admiring all of the growth happening beneath the surface, inside of me, ready to break through?

What if now was the time to receive the bounty coming my way?

What if now is your time, too?

Five Shifts to Move from Chaos to Calm

1. **Identify your chaos triggers.** What are the experiences—and who are the people—that cause you anxiety and distress? You are not required to set yourself on fire to keep them warm.

2. **Rewire your roadmap.** Identify the patterns of your life that draw you to chaos. Investigate where these sequences stem from and shift your behaviors away from this structure. Start small and build from there.

3. **Move through the discomfort.** Overhauling your operating system will not be easy. If you are uncomfortable with the changes you're making, good. It's working. Keep going.

4. **Create your daily rituals.** To teach your mind and body a new home base and foundation for your life, you must create new habits. Test out new rituals throughout the day and keep coming back to those that calm you.

5. **Shift from *survive* to *thrive*.** As you heal your nervous system, you will leave your constant state of fight of flight for a new homeostasis grounded in peace, gratitude, joy, pleasure, and contentment. Take your time. Get to know this new place that could be home.

3

Manipulated by Mean Girls

I've spent a significant portion of the last five years unlearning what women who were threatened by me told me about myself.

Mean girls tell us: we're worth less; our vulnerability is a liability; we're not ready to be the boss; our ideas are too risky; our voice is too much; telling our truth is damaging to our reputation; that we're not doing enough (i.e., everything they told us to do); that opting out of their bullshit makes us quitters.

And it's no surprise that they exist. The patriarchy created them. And they obediently act as foot soldiers *to* that patriarchy. Often organized under the archetype of toxic straight, white, cis-gendered women, they exist in our companies, communities, families, and culture. They are powerful pieces of a system intent on perpetuating the status quo—and minimizing those whose voices have been silenced for far too long.

The opportunity for women looking to live a freer, healthier, more fulfilling life is to have a clear way to identify the mean girls and create an action plan to break free from their stronghold. Because if we don't, they will grind us down to dust. And we will continue to live *our* lives on *their* terms.

You know this vortex of destruction all too well.

There is no escape from their vice grip.
There is no space in your life that they refuse to occupy.
There is no version of ourselves that will ever be good enough for them.

That is, until you ascend.

I am 14. I am a new student at Punahou School in Honolulu, Hawaii—a high school freshman at President Barack Obama's alma mater, attempting to navigate my way through a sprawling 76-acre outdoor campus of 44 buildings and 5,000 students, faculty, and staff.

A group of girls, standing in a circle, are gathered near a banyan tree—a fig that develops accessory trunks from adjacent prop roots, allowing the tree to spread outwards indefinitely.

As I walk closer to them, they turn, look me up and down and then turn back to the center of their group.

I keep walking, alone.

I am 41. I am in a Barre Code studio in the suburbs of Illinois—a group fitness studio (founded by my Greenhills School Varsity Soccer teammate, Ari Chernin) that offered a variety of class formats, including cardiovascular conditioning, toning, detoxification, and deep stretching.

A group of women, standing in a circle, are gathered near the door to the class.

As I walk closer to them, they turn, look me up and down and then turn back to the center of their group.

I keep walking, alone.

There are girls and women who stand in closed circles.

And there are girls and women who always make sure their circle is open. It's really that simple.

And while I've *encountered* both over and over and over again—and *stood* in both groups over the course of my four decades—my ability to read these women and determine their intentions before they have a chance to cause impact has gotten so much better over time.

It's 9:21 p.m. We're in a "war room" in our office: a stuffy, stale 16 × 20 square foot space with dozens of 8½ × 11 pieces of paper taped to anything with a surface. The only items not covered in our ever-evolving printed PowerPoint deck are the harsh fluorescent bulbs overhead and the six of us suckers who truly believe we're in battle—and not the poorly designed conference room we're in. Jimmy John's sandwich paper, half-eaten bags of Doritos and salt and vinegar potato chips, stacks of empty Diet Cokes and La Croix cans, and the discarded wrappers from a bowl of someone's old Halloween candy litter the conference room table.

We've been working on building a huge agency initiative for months. Late nights, long hours, revision and revision after revision. Most of the "do-overs"—I now realize—so superfluous, so meaningless, so irrelevant.

The font we chose isn't "inviting" or "authoritative" enough.
The thickness of that line is too thick.
Why did we use that color for our background?
The photo of that smiling woman is too "smiley."
Why is the woman in that photo not smiling?
You know that video we spent 55 hours storyboarding, casting, producing, film-ing, editing, and cutting into five different versions? Meh. Let's cut it.
Are those companies listed in alpha order? If yes, why? If no, why not?
Why aren't those exec's photos featured in reverse chronological order based on the year they graduated from high school?

Damn, if I could get all those wasted hours of my life back. But that's how "leaders" ensure that you know that you're not the one in charge, right? You must be reminded that you're not good enough; that your "mistakes" must be fixed; that you must learn that their way is the "right" way—the only way.

You fall in line. Or you're shipped out.

We follow our marching orders.

It's the day of our big event. As our "leader" takes the stage—and all of the credit—my colleague leans over to me and whispers, "That should be you up there." As my clipboard rests on my five-months-pregnant stomach, my eyes widen at her in shock and Stockholm Syndromed disbelief.

I look around the room at what we've created. The women who line row after row of folding chairs are locked in; they are ready for something different. One of our male Exec Board members lays sprawled out on a blush-colored velvet couch, completely disengaged, scrolling through his phone. It is the perfect depiction of what we are up against.

I couldn't see myself up there. I had been told too many times to stay down here, to know my place.

It's the day of our big event. As our "leader" takes the stage—and all of the credit—my colleague leans over to me and whispers, "That should be you up there." Again. As my clipboard rests on the lingering remnants of my two-time postpartum stomach—conducting the symphony from the bowels of the beautifully staged room—I audibly guffaw.

I look around the room at what we've created. The people here today are different. But I am the same.

Like any good, trauma-bonded foot solider, I don't question the "leader." I don't ask *why* we're executing a mission. I only inquire: when, where, and how do you want me?

I complete the mission!

I'm here to complete the mission.

According to ChatGPT:

Trauma bonding is a psychological response where a person forms a strong emotional attachment to someone who is abusive, manipulative, or harmful. This bond develops through cycles of abuse, followed by intermittent kindness or affection, making it difficult for the victim to leave the toxic relationship.

How Trauma Bonds Form:

1. **Intermittent reinforcement:** The abuser alternates between cruelty and affection, creating confusion and dependency.
2. **Isolation:** The victim is often cut off from outside support, making them more reliant on the abuser.
3. **Gaslighting and manipulation:** The abuser distorts reality, making the victim question their perceptions.
4. **Fear and survival mode:** The body and mind adapt to an unsafe environment, prioritizing connection over self-protection.
5. **Low self-worth:** The victim may believe they deserve the mistreatment or feel incapable of leaving.

Examples of Trauma Bonding:

- A person staying in a physically or emotionally abusive romantic relationship
- A child remaining loyal to a neglectful or abusive parent
- A hostage developing sympathy for their captor (*Stockholm Syndrome*)
- An employee staying in a toxic workplace due to occasional praise or small rewards

Do you see yourself in these descriptions? Do you recognize others' mistreatment of you? Do you feel like you can't break free?

I have experienced this stronghold in every facet of my life.

So much of my life, my job, my role, my worth has been in the sacrificing-of-myself for the greater good—in crawling on my hands and knees to the spot where people wanted me—so they could step on my back to take themselves higher.

Somewhere along the way, I lost myself. I forgot who I was. I abandoned myself in service to others.

I tried to leave so many times.
I got so close.
I even said the words out loud: "I'm leaving."

The captors changed guard many times over 20+ years. But the reaction to my attempt to walk away was always the same:

They couldn't believe I was willing to leave them.
They were terrified of how they would exist on their self-righteous pedestal
without me constantly fabricating the scaffolding around their house of cards.
They were desperate to stop me from realizing my power and finding my
voice again.

Every time was the same: they pulled me back in.
It was the telltale of an abusive relationship, where the victim finally works up the courage, the wherewithal, and the plan to leave, but the captor destroys the path to freedom with a single breath.
Abuse of power comes in so many forms.

Sometimes it happens in your personal life.
Sometimes it's in your work world.
Sometimes it's a combination of both.

Have you ever been so close to walking away that you could taste it?
And then, they turn everything upside down and inside out, and you don't know which way is yours anymore. All you know is that your captor is in a good mood again. And that is good. It is always easier when they are getting their way and you are doing what they say.

Here's what I've discovered: women fall somewhere under five archetypes. And you should view engagement with them as you would a traffic light. Because your life depends on it.
The first are "Predators."
Predators are "red."

Predators:

Travel as a pack of wolves, looking for a wounded deer to devour

Surround you when you're shiny and abandon you when you appear dull

Pull your feet down from the rungs above them as you both are climbing the apodictic ladder

Crush your fingers with a grinding heel as you grip the edge of a glass cliff, holding on for dear life

Assault you with love bombs and trauma bombs—never sticking around to witness the destruction they've left behind

Are narcissistic, egomaniacal, attention-seeking, self-worshippers—stealing every mic and light and stage and ounce of oxygen in the room from the women who have earned them

View you as a threat, here to be destroyed

See you as their competition, meant to be defeated

Tell you that you aren't good enough

Gaslight you

Make you feel like shit

Make you question your own experience

Make you question your own existence

Walk—no, run—far from these women, as fast as you can.

These women have a scarcity mindset. They want it all. And they want *you* to have none.

At the end of every interaction, you will feel bankrupt. They will rob you of everything, every time.

The second are "Pretenders."

Pretenders are a "flashing red."

These women are either passively acting as followers to the Predators, unsure of themselves or what they believe, or they are actively passing the venom of the bite from the head of the snake into their victims.

Pretenders:

Are afraid of the mean girls

Tell you that the mean girls are talking shit about you—but fail to stand up for you in the moment when they do

Waddle after mean girls like lost little ducklings

Pretend to be on the side of the mean girls when in their midst

Pretend to be on your side when they're in yours

Are foot soldiers to the Predators, be it through action or inaction

Don't realize that they also are the prey

Proceed with caution. Once you've stopped, look both ways before flooring it the fuck outta there.

The third are "Projectors."

Projectors are "yellow."

While I believe that at their core these women are well meaning—and that they don't intentionally set out to hurt you—it's their *own* hurt, their *own* unresolved trauma, and their *own* lack of self-confidence that causes them to project onto you, often. While you live your life, they view actions you take as reflections of their own insecurities.

Projectors:

Ask you if you're mad at them, all the time

Tell you that something you did or said (that had nothing to do with them) hurt their feelings

Are ready to share a story about themselves the second you finish the sentence about yours

Send a feeling of anxiety and dread throughout your body when their names pop up in your phone log, text thread, or email inbox

Make you feel like you can never get it right with them

Make you feel like you're never doing enough

Are never fully convinced that your friendship is real

Can drain your energy in an hour—or a minute

Tread lightly, with an exit plan, as you walk the path with these women. Some are doing their best with the tools they have, while others are on their way to Pretender or Predator status, because they are drawn to those energies. It's important to protect *your* energy, time, and efforts with them. Because too often, the return on your investment can make you feel like you're perpetually swimming in overdraft fees.

The fourth are "Promoters."

Promoters are "green."

Promoters care about you and love seeing you succeed. When asked or directed, they are there to hype you. But they're still learning to be more active in their support and to show up on their own.

Promoters:

Want you to succeed

Show up for you, when you ask

Share their social, human, financial and political capital, when you need it

Celebrate you, when you share your wins

Promoters are important women in your life. They truly want what's best for you. They may not always be the first to raise their hand to help or their voice to hype, but that has so much less to do with you and more to do with the journey they're on, the phase of metamorphosis they're in or their current capacity. Empathy and compassion for—and inclusion of—these women is vital to our collective evolution.

The fifth are "Protectors."

Protectors are "green."

Protectors:

Are active in their support of you

Say your name in rooms where you are not

Defend you

Are your ride-or-die

Will pick you up from the airport *and* the police station

Stand up to the haters who come after you in the dark

Celebrate your wins as if they were her own

Hype you

Believe *in* you

Believe you

Are a soft place to land

Know you're not perfect

Give you space to fail

Meet you with understanding, not judgment

Know that you can achieve anything you set your mind to

Fan your flame
Are the first people you tell when something good happens
Are the first people you need when it all falls apart

Run toward these women, sit with them, build your life around one another. These are the women who will help you heal. They believe in abundance and so you are both invested in pouring into one another, while never forgetting to pour into yourselves.

Your relationship will feel like you've won the lottery.

Some women exist in between these archetypes. And over the course of your life, some of these women will progress toward green or regress toward red, based on their own growth or decay. Some will shift between these groups based on *yours*.

And now, get ready for the hardest truth of all: all of these archetypes exist inside of *you*. All of these archetypes exist inside of *me, too*.

It's not our fault. It's our conditioning. So, when you feel the feelings rise up, pause, take a breath, and release what you no longer want to have control over your life. Conditioning is not our fault. But awareness—and a change in behavior—is our responsibility and our greatest opportunity.

I've had a mean girl start an underground smear campaign about me because I ended our working relationship.

I've had a mean girl tell lies about me "having a thing" for her husband— because she can't handle the fact that I just don't like her.

I've had a mean girl ask me to speak at her upcoming event and then, after I set boundaries, disinvite—and remove—me from the published programming.

These three incidents happened to me in just the past year alone. As a 42-year-old woman. And this is, by no means, an exhaustive list. What they all have in common is the fact that I recognized that these women were not who they said they were—and I cut off their access to me. What mean girls hate more than anything is when you stop giving them attention. It drives them crazy. When they lose their power, they are left sitting with themselves, which is a truly dark place to be.

If these examples sound like something—with slightly altered details—that a middle school girl would do, it's because it's true. Mean girls are petulant playground bullies all dressed up in heels and suits, clutching their white pearls.

Because here's the most important truth to absorb:

Mean girls don't grow up to *hype* women. They grow up to *hate* women.

As you continue to move through life and break free from the mean-girl grip, pay close attention and assess how you feel often. Your intuition is everything. She knows. And she will tell you who the mean girls are—through the way they make you feel, through the way they receive or reject you, through the way your body responds to their very presence.

Maya Angelou—poet, singer, civil rights activist, and author of the famous autobiography *I Know Why the Caged Bird Sings*—has written about this deep knowing time and time again.

Angelou's brilliance is a gift to humanity.

Everything she's written is pure gold. But there's a particular line from her sixth autobiography, *A Song Flung Up to Heaven*—which chronicles her life between 1965 and 1968—that has stuck with me: "When someone shows you who they are, believe them the first time."

We could all stand to sit with this wisdom and take it to heart.

And the second quote of Angelou's that is imprinted on my soul is "I've learned that people will forget what you said, people will forget what you did, but people will never forget how you made them feel."

Think of the women in your life right now: family, friends, colleagues, women you encounter often in your social circles—both personal and professional.

How do they make you feel?

Who did they show up as the first time you met them? And every time since?

Where do they fall under the archetypes of Predator, Pretender, Projector, Promoter, and Protector?

Now, what do you want to do about it?

It's taken me more than 40 years to be able to identify where these women lie.

It's taken me more than 40 years to build the courage to walk away from many.

It's taken me more than 40 years to believe that I deserve better.

It is not our responsibility to convince other women that we matter. The more you have to, the less they believe it. The less you will. Well, fuck them. They aren't worthy of you.

The moment you take your power back from the energy vampires who have been draining you dry, *their* power disappears.

Poof.
Gone.
Vaporized.

Today is as good a day as any to do a little spring cleaning.
Time to take out the trash.

Five Shifts to Break Free from Mean Girls

1. **Unfollow, mute, block, repeat.** Every time you engage, respond, and react, they win. Don't let them. Protect your peace and your spirit. Stop engaging.
2. **Identify the Predators, Pretenders, Projectors, Promoters, and Protectors.** We all have them in our lives. Who falls into each category for you? And how much access do you want to continue to give them?
3. **Walk away.** If a mean girl makes you feel like shit every time you see her, stay away. Remove her from your life in all of the ways possible.

4. **Be patient with yourself.** Lifelong patterns don't change overnight. Conditioning can stir up mean girl feelings in *you*. The goal is to recognize them, forgive yourself, and make a different choice. Recognize, respond, release.

5. **Break the cycle.** Mean girls grow up to hate women—and to raise the next generation of mean girls. Pay attention to who your kids are befriending and who is unfriending them. Because they deserve better. Just like you did.

4 | Solitary Confinement

The times when I have felt the most alone in the world, I was surrounded by people.

Because *being* alone and *feeling* alone are two very different experiences.

As women navigate the different roles they play over the course of their lives—good girl, successful student, obedient daughter, ambitious worker, loyal friend, dutiful wife, adoring mother—they also carry the weight of the expectations for how they should show up as each of those people.

There's no playbook or right or wrong way to be. But that latitude doesn't always look, or feel, like freedom.

And when they become someone they never thought they could—or wanted to—be, the isolation and dissociation from self can take over.

There are so many women who feel alone in their experiences and trapped inside the self-critical spaces of their minds.

> There is no internal compass that always points you in the right direction.
> There is no map guiding you through the rough and rocky terrain.
> There is no light illuminating a path to freedom.

That is, until you escape.

On June 19, 2022, I posted a photo of myself, on LinkedIn, breastfeeding. Yeah, you heard me: *breastfeeding.*

Have you ever breastfed in public and felt uncomfortable?
Have you ever looked at someone breastfeeding in public and made *them* feel uncomfortable?

Well, I decided to take both situations head on in a place I never dreamt I'd show this photo or have this conversation: the world's largest professional network on the Internet. As of June 2024, LinkedIn had more than 1 billion members in more than 200 countries.

The mission of LinkedIn is simple: connect the world's professionals to make them more productive and successful. In the beginning, LinkedIn was a digital résumé: a place to find a job or hire a person. Over time, it became so much more. For me, it became a content publishing platform, and a place for me to create connection with some of the world's most important, impactful, and influential people in business and community.

So, why the hell would I want to bring my breasts into *that* room?

Well, first of all. I bring my breasts with me *everywhere.*

They are attached to my body. I don't get to leave them at home or put them on a shelf when I don't feel like acknowledging, addressing, or attending to them. And if you are ever in a stage of life where you are breastfeeding or pumping (or both!), you know that those breasts that you could sometimes forget about or ignore become the center of all of your attention. Your 24-hour day becomes a battleplan for a military operation— where your world narrows to two-to-four-hour shifts where you lead the troops in to do their job (and they succeed or they fail) and then you retreat to prepare for their next mission.

And the second reason I brought my breasts into the conversation on LinkedIn is because in the summer of 2022, the United States faced an infant formula crisis.

According to the National Institute of Health, the nationwide shortage of baby formula in the United States was caused by a combination of factors, including a product recall, supply chain issues, and increased demand. In May 2022, the in-stock rate for formula was only 47%. In June 2022, some major retailers reported in-stock rates as low as 19%. The shortage caused panic-buying and uncertainty for parents and caregivers.

I don't think the word "panic" is strong enough for what parents with infants who needed formula felt at that time.

I was not one of those parents. My boys were 6 and 3½ in the summer of 2022, well past the formula or breastfeeding stage for me.

But here was the problem. The "solution" being slung around the Internet, in social circles and yes—"at work"—was, "No formula? Just breastfeed! Problem solved."

I felt the rage bubble up inside of my chest, a hot fire fueled by pain and shame I had deliberately shoved so far down inside of me, I never thought I'd have to face it again.

Well, I was wrong.

Here was the post I wrote on June 19, 2022:

> To all the folks telling women with babies to "Just breastfeed! It's free!" during the formula crisis we are facing in modern-day America, I share this:
> Breastfeeding almost killed me.
> Emotionally. Spiritually. Psychologically.
> It never came easily. It wasn't the "most natural thing I ever did." My ability to do it, to enjoy it, to survive it had nothing to do with my love, care, and devotion for my children.
> This picture is from April 21, 2016, when my firstborn son Will was five days old. And my heart breaks for her. I can see the exhaustion, uncertainty, and hopelessness on her face.

My first-born, Will (five days old), and me.

When I went back to work 12 weeks after giving birth and needed to
pump, things got exponentially worse. It was one of the loneliest and
most isolating times of my life. Every pumping session—in between
meetings, deliverables, and high-stress responsibilities—was an exercise in self-worth.

Did I produce enough? Too little? Stress and anxiety created a drop in
supply. A drop in supply created stress and anxiety. It was a never-
ending cycle of hell.

I set my alarm multiple times in the night to try to pump enough for
the next day, desperate to give my baby breastmilk exclusively.

To. What. End.

The pumps (yes, I tried five different brands) injured me, and because
you can never "take a day off," I never healed.

Two and a half years later with my second, Charlie, I was in such a physically and psychologically damaged place, I weaned off breastfeeding
and pumping so quickly that it sent me like a runaway train into a brick

wall of postpartum depression and anxiety. My prolactin and oxytocin levels plummeted at warp speed into a black hole. And I was in free fall. I spent the day after Christmas in the psych ER.

Please don't shame women into breastfeeding. Please don't assume you have *any* idea what their story really is all about. Please don't project your experiences on to her.

For the women who had—and are having—joyful experiences breastfeeding, I'm happy for you.

For the women who experienced—and are experiencing—trauma, despair, and pain, I *am* you. Sending you love and so much empathetic compassion.

Corporate America, society, and culture has had its cake and eaten it too for far too long . . . at the expense of women.

If you want us to carry, birth, and raise babies so badly, support us in our personal, professional, and passion endeavors to do so.

And for those who feel this photo or topic doesn't belong on LinkedIn, I remind you that we take our bodies with us from boardroom to bedroom, from cap table to dining table, from Wall Street to Main Street, from leadership happy hours to kindergarten teas.

Conversations about our health, rights, and freedom belong everywhere.

I couldn't have predicted—or prepared for—what came next. Women (and men!) came out of the shadows *everywhere*.

Women in their sixties and seventies shared their own breastfeeding stories with stunning detail and raw emotion; they were right back in that room with their babies—babies who now had babies of their own.

Women currently breastfeeding, pumping, and struggling couldn't believe that they weren't alone, that there wasn't something wrong with *them*, and that we were allowed to say we hated this.

Women who loved breastfeeding and had a wonderful experience sent love and support and compassion.

Men talked about the struggles of their wives and partners and how they watched them become shells of themselves.

People with zero experience breastfeeding, pumping, rearing, or raising children showed gratitude for the window into this unknown part of life. They said they would view it all so differently now.

They had no idea this happened to mothers.

They had no idea how breastfeeding or pumping worked.

They had no idea their friends and co-workers were struggling in silence.

The comment section was flooded with empathy.

Because remember, shame dies in the light. Once I brought my story, this inherent truth, out of the dark, the shame. fucking. died.

And of course, there were the haters—the foot soldiers to the patriarchy (both men and women)—who came to my post to try to shame me; to tell me that this conversion didn't belong here; that this photo didn't belong here; that I didn't belong here.

Well, I no longer gave a fuck. Because that's just not true.

Six months later, my post was named one of LinkedIn's 100 Most Influential Posts of the Decade.

More than two years later, people are still commenting on that post, sending me direct messages and sharing it in their feeds. As of January 2025, my post had been viewed more than six million times, with 47,338 reactions (of like, love, and support), 4,062 comments, and 659 reposts.

To give you a sense of why the breadth of that impact matters, I share these stats: based on an AI overview of available data, the average number of reactions (likes) on a LinkedIn post is around 23, with many posts receiving between 1 and 10 likes, and only a small percentage getting over 100 likes; the average number of comments per post is usually around 3. Most LinkedIn posts see only a small number of reposts, with the average likely being below 10.

It looks like my breasts *did* belong on LinkedIn, didn't they?

How do you like *them* apples?

Sharing shatters shame.

Sharing shatters shame.

Sharing shatters shame.

I can't say it enough. When you, your grief, your hurt, your pain are placed in the solitary confinement of your own body and mind, the poison festers. And it can destroy you.

Tell someone your truth. The more you speak the words, the less weight they hold, and the less weight you carry.

How that person reacts will tell you everything you need to know about them—and who they should or shouldn't be in your life.

Do they respond with:

I'm so sorry.
You never should have had to experience that.
I understand.
Me too.
How can I support you?

Or do they use your vulnerability and honesty and truths against you? Do they:

Judge you?
Question your experience?
Betray your confidence?
Center themselves?
Weaponize what you've exposed to their advantage later?

Pay close attention. Because the difference between your decision to keep or release each type of person in your life will determine how you heal, grow, and live a life fully out loud.

When we speak our truth to the world, when we share our experiences and our thoughts with other Hype Women—women who have our back— our collective power will heal the generations that came before us and the many who will come after.

Five Shifts to Escape Solitary Confinement

1. **Find community.** You are not the first—or only—person in the world to have this experience. Trust me. Google it. Find others who have walked a similar path and learn how they found their way out.

(continued)

(continued)

2. **Write it out.** Speaking your truth into the world can be very scary. So, don't start there. Write down what you're feeling. Give your thoughts another place—and medium—to go. Get them out of your head.

3. **Share your truth to shatter your shame.** Who is a trusted, safe person in your life? Tell them the thing you've been carrying for far too long in silence, with shame. Feel the relief as it leaves your body.

4. **Seek support.** You can't do it alone. And sometimes, you can't do it without a professional. Therapy can change your life. Find a therapist with a style that works for you.

5. **Start a new story.** You are not one choice, one moment, one version of yourself. You have infinite possibilities inside of you. If you're not living the story you want to tell in 5 or 10 years, start a new one. It won't happen overnight. But every journey begins with a single step.

II

I Am

Cocooned and Dissolving

5 | Burning Bridges

"Don't burn bridges."

We've all heard it before. Hell, I used to dole it out as road-tested advice.

Historically the phrase has been used to mean: no way to return if a course of action is pursued or a current action continues. The term originated in the military to describe the act of intentionally cutting off one's own retreat (burning a bridge one has crossed).

But when used in the context of 21st-century careers and corporate experiences, the suspended structure crumbles under the weight of our reality. Why *would* we want to allow people and places—of which we have no intention of returning—to have access to us? If we know we've left a toxic workplace *and* toxic people, why wouldn't we want to further commit ourselves to a new course of action?

It's because the advice isn't meant for us.

It's meant for the system.
It's meant to maintain the status quo.
It's meant to silence you.

And following it holds us down—and back—from moving on to bigger and better.

There is no escape from the cyclical path that keeps leading you back to the place you tried to leave behind.

There is no protection from the encroaching army, intent on thwarting your forward progress.

There is no retreat—from the enemy forces or toward a safe, protected space.

That is, until you burn.

In 2009, I moved to Chicago, alone and without a job. I was a product of the economic crisis impacting employment for so many. The company I had worked for in Michigan the previous few years shut down completely. I was ready for a fresh start, a big change, a new life.

Chicago was where I wanted to be. I spent months applying for jobs in Chicago while living in Michigan and driving back and forth for hour-long interviews here and there—all while scouring the Internet for apartments I could afford as I rebuilt my life.

After this multistate, remote hustle and grind, I made the decision to move to Chicago before I landed a gig. It would be more efficient to job hunt on the ground, in the city where I was seeking employment.

I project-managed my job search like a woman on a mission. And I was. I created a 100-row, multi-tab spreadsheet to organize and track every step I took; tapped into the University of Michigan Alumni Network to chase down every possible connection I had and lead I could create; went to a dozen networking events a week; and interviewed for jobs that I had no business throwing my hat into the ring for and those I had no intention of taking if offered.

My job hunt *felt* like a full-time job, unpaid.

Then, in the span of one week, I was sexually harassed by two men two decades older than me at two companies during two interviews.

Power is one hell of a drug.

It makes the person with the power feel invincible, self-righteous, and entitled. And it makes the person without the power feel helpless, trapped, and paralyzed.

One of the men was a senior vice president at one of the largest advertising agencies in the world. The other was a senior principal at a multibillion-dollar global recruiting firm—one of the Big Five, universally known as the SHREK executive search firms: Spencer Stewart, Heidrick & Struggles, Russell Reynolds, Egon Zehnder, and Korn Ferry (The Economist Editorial Team 2020).

After one interview with each of them, they both took my phone number from my résumé and began texting me lewd, sexually suggestive messages. One texted me from his family's summer home in Michigan. I bet his wife and kids were playing in the water 20 feet away, smiling back at him as he preyed upon me. The other was at the airport heading to a tropical location. They both told me they wished I were with them.

I was 27 years old.

I was stunned, shocked, paralyzed.

I didn't respond.

I tried to pretend neither happened.

I never got second interviews.

This had happened to me before, to varying degrees, with different details to round out the horror stories. But having two men, 20-plus years my senior—with profound power and the ability to open or close the door of opportunity to build my career at either of those companies in a city where I was determined to do it—turn an interview into a sexual solicitation in the same week made me question a lot.

It was almost as if this was a playbook that these men had used before.

Based on our age difference, I could be their daughters. But what's more important than the age gap was the power chasm.

They had it all.

I had none.

Who was I going to tell? Who would believe me? And what would happen to my chances at getting a job in this town if I was labeled as a trouble-making woman who couldn't handle a few "complimentary" texts here and there?

While the 42-year-old me today would react differently (trust me, you do not want to fuck with me now), the 27-year-old me blamed and shamed herself.

What had I done to make them think I was interested in them?
When and how had our professional conversation turned personal—and then leaped to sexual and romantic?
Was I overreacting and making this a bigger deal than it was?
Were they joking?
Was *I* the joke for thinking I had a chance of working there?

And since this, *by far*, wasn't the first time I had been sexually harassed or assaulted—and sadly, nor would it be the last—I started to wonder if this was just the way the world worked. Maybe being an ambitious woman in an industry with broad influence meant fending off the men who worked there: wolves, fueled by the power of the pack, hunting you down, circling your body, ready to pounce and devour you at any given moment.

I didn't tell anyone what happened. What's worse, I didn't slam the door shut in *their* faces.

While I never responded to their texts, I didn't block their numbers in my phone or block their email addresses in my inbox. I allowed them to retain access to me. I was afraid to burn the bridge.

What if I wanted to work at one of those companies one day? If I pissed them off, they could blacklist me. These Chicago-headquartered companies had power and influence not only in the city where I was trying to build a new life but also in the industry where I was working to build a name for myself.

I couldn't.
I shouldn't.
I didn't.

On September 3, 2024, Rebecca Stewert published an article in *Adweek*: "Two Students File Sexual Assault Complaint Against Ad Industry Consultant in Cannes."

In the public garden of the Carlton Hotel in Cannes, this ad industry exec not only groped these two women but also told them they must learn to accept men's "forwardness" if they wanted to succeed in the advertising field.

These women were prepared to go public with their account but decided not to after each received a letter from the man's company threatening a lawsuit, including threats sent to one of their home addresses.

Sound familiar?

Man harasses and assaults woman.

Woman stands up to man.

Men surround the predator to silence the woman.

Reading this piece—and knowing that this was still happening *every. damn. day.* to women everywhere—filled me with such rage that I finally confronted one of the men who sexually harassed me almost 20 years before.

The advertising agency guy.

It remained clear that the agency world is a cesspool of vultures weaponizing their power to dehumanize young women.

It's important to note that the ad agency guy, who sent me the sex text during my interview process, had the audacity, the gall, the pure privilege afforded to so many straight, white, cis gendered men to request my connection on LinkedIn a few years later; he congratulated me on a promotion I had received at the agency where I worked at the time.

And I accepted his request to connect.

Here's the part that someone who hasn't been assaulted or harassed doesn't understand.

Power fucks with you.

It makes you do things you don't want to.

It makes you think that what *did* happen didn't.

It makes you feel crazy and afraid.

Since that request to connect years ago, he went on to publicly comment on my LinkedIn posts (praising me for speaking out against sexual harassment!) and sent me multiple private messages on LinkedIn.

All those years later, every time I saw his name, I froze again.

Until September 3, 2024.

The courage of those two women in Cannes compelled me to take back *my* power and to send him the message he deserved to receive almost 20 years before.

> Brad, don't know if you remember sexually harassing me with lewd, sexually suggestive text messages when I was 25 [sic] YEARS OLD and you were INTERVIEWING me for a job at [redacted].
>
> But I'll never forget.
>
> Don't ever message me or comment on my posts ever again.
>
> STAY AWAY FROM ME.
>
> And stay away from ALL young women.
>
> I hope your children never experience a predator like you.

Then, I blocked his profile on LinkedIn and his number in my phone (yes, you read that correctly! It was still stored in there!). Trauma bonds are hard to break.

More than 20 years later, these two young women broke something open in me.

And it began the healing process of almost 20 years of stored trauma.

I'm sick of women being brave.

I'm sick of women being blamed for existing.

I'm sick of women being summoned to share our traumas publicly.

But if we don't, who will ever know they happened?

We must stop blaming women.

We must stop excusing men.

We must stop defending misogyny.

On September 4, 2024, I wrote about this experience on LinkedIn, with more than 100,000 people viewing the post in the days that followed.

I made something very clear to anyone who read my story.

If they came to my post to . . .

. . . pressure or shame me for not publicly outing him by name

. . . blame me for accepting his request all those years ago

. . . make any attempt to defend the man who sexually assaulted those women at Cannes

. . . I would block them immediately.

Unsurprisingly, people did all three, publicly in the comments and privately in direct messages. The majority of these people were women. Of course they were.

> Women are taught to shame and blame ourselves when we are violated.
> Women are taught to shame and blame other women when they are violated.
> Women are taught to violate the sacredness of self in the name of self-preservation.

That sentence should be as confusing to read as it was for me to write—as it is for women to live. The power of a patriarchal system that dehumanizes women is the poison we are all forced to consume.

It's killing us.

But we *can* stop it.

Stewert's piece in *Adweek* had this warning under the title of her article: "Sensitive content: This article mentions sexual assault. Help is available through the National Sexual Assault Hotline at 1-800-656-4673."

It made me think: that same warning should be served up to any woman who plans to exist in the world. Because we are forced to face this behavior every day of our lives.

It took me 20 years to work up the courage to face one of my predators. And I have dozens and dozens and dozens of other men in my life who I may never face. Some, I don't even remember because my memory has erased the experience to protect me from reliving it.

So, I know how hard—and sometimes impossible—standing up to, walking away from, burning the bridge with the predators of our past and present can be.

It's not possible for every person.
It's not safe in every situation.
It's not a one-size-fits-all solution.

Corporate America is complicit in the sexual harassment, assault, abuse, and discrimination of women. It's always a silent bystander and often a willing co-conspirator. And our personal lives, relationships, and experiences are intertwined.

When we don't burn bridges that we are destined to destroy, we stay trauma bonded to those who have harmed us.

We're told to return texts, calls, and emails, perpetuating the detrimental cycle.
We're encouraged to continue to interact, virtually and in person, against our instincts.
We're not allowed to completely heal and move forward.

I fully appreciate that everything surrounding burning—or not burning—bridges is complex, complicated, and inequitably structured. But inequitable paradigms can only be dismantled by removing their power, one brick at a time. You don't have to live in that house forever.

And so, bridges we must burn. Because if we continue to operate inside of systems that weren't built for—or by—us, we are unintentionally enabling them, keeping their structure intact.

New system. New rules. New path.

Let's stop *asking* others for directions to places they've never been.
Let's stop *taking* directions from others to places they'll never go.

Let's build our own bridges. On our own terms.

I've gone back too many times—to people and places that have burned me; I've put my hand into the fire again and again thinking that maybe, *this* time, it won't be so hot. I've slipped back while climbing my way out of quicksand because giving in felt so much easier. I even taught myself that it actually felt good.

When we always keep one foot behind, wedged inside this mythical "door" that must remain open indefinitely, we never fully move forward.

It's time.
Close the door.
Walk away.
Burn the bridge.
Build a new bridge.
Cross it.

Holy shit, it is so hard the first time you do it. But with one step at a time, you can.

"Burning bridges" isn't self-destructive. It's an act of self-preservation. And you will always be worth saving.

Five Shifts to Burn and Build Bridges

1. **Walk away, with both feet.** If you're constantly keeping one foot in the past and one in the present, you'll never fully be able to march toward your future.

2. **Stand for your boundaries.** Create, communicate, and comply with the boundaries that you need—and require that those who you allow in your life do the same.

3. **Protect her.** Who is the version inside of you who wasn't—or isn't—safe? Now, go to her and tell her that you know a way out. Lead her there, hand in hand, and don't stop until you get to the other side.

4. **Build your own bridge.** We spend a lot of time running to the next thing. Stand at the peak of your in-between. Look to the left at where—and who—you've been. Look to the right at where you're going, at who you're meant to be. Thank her, the you of *this* moment. She deserves to be celebrated.

(continued)

(*continued*)

5. **Walk to the other side.** Your new bridge is built. The decaying and diseased bridges are burned. It's time to keep going. To live the life you've always deserved. She's waiting for you.

6 | Unabashed Hype Women

In 2023, I wrote a LinkedIn post that changed my life. It was the fruit borne from a seed I had planted and continued to water and care for and tend to decades before. In fact, it became this book you're reading right now.

I wrote my "Unabashed Hype Women" post after I saw a photo taken at the Golden Globes the night before, when Michelle Yeoh won Best Actress for her role in *Everything Everywhere All at Once*. In the moment, Jamie Lee Curtis is doing something we so rarely see women doing.

She's hyping Michelle.

Jamie's excitement, joy, and passion for Michelle is visible. You can *see* it. Her energy, her fire, her power is visceral. You can *feel* it.

The day I wrote the post, Hype Women was born.

But we both know that's not entirely true. Hype Women have always existed.

Standing next to you on the playground.
Sitting with you in the conference room.
Showing up for you, in the good and the bad.

Hype Women are an act of resistance.

Women are taught from the time they are little girls to view other women as their competition, to see them as threats, to view a light shining on her as casting a shadow upon you. But it's a trap meant to distract us and to keep us keeping each other down.

There is no way to escape the cycle of self-destruction.

There is no way to outrun the encroaching envy.

There is no way to unlearn the generations of programming encoded in your DNA.

That is, until you disintegrate.

I'm shifting my weight on the dark, midnight blue velvet bar stool at Beatrix Market. The coffeehouse side of the neighborhood restaurant in Chicago's West Loop on Fulton Market is unusually busy for 7 p.m. I'm meeting one of my best friends of more than a decade, Asia Star Day, for dinner.

And I'm early. Which rarely happens.

I pull out my phone and start scrolling through Instagram.

And this image stops me in my tracks:

Jamie Lee Curtis hyping Michelle Yeoh.

My heart rate increases.

Goosebumps spread from my wrists to my shoulders, from my ankles to my thighs, like a tidal wave picking up strength and pace.

Adrenaline floods my body like a shot of epinephrine.

I feel like Jamie is in the room with me.

The moment took place at the Golden Globes the night before, when Michelle Yeoh won Best Actress for her role in *Everything Everywhere All at Once*—the comedy-drama action film, which began a limited theatrical release in the United States on March 25, 2022—the day I turned 40.

In the moment, Jamie Lee Curtis—who went on to win an Oscar for her role as IRS inspector Deirdre Beaubeirdre in the film—is screaming for Michelle.

Full. Body. Screaming.

She represented something we so rarely see as women: a woman celebrating another woman's success as if it were her own.

I stared at the image in stunned silence. And then I took a screenshot and saved it to my phone. I opened my LinkedIn app and started furiously typing, "*Ladies, this is your vibe for 2023: Unabashed Hype Woman. Full on. Full out. Full force.*" The words poured out of me: cathartic, painful, raw, igniting.

I wrote about what it was like to see Jamie supporting Michelle in that way, how it made me feel, and how I know women so often feel about another woman's success. I talked about conditioning and patriarchy and a new way forward. I wrote it. I reread it once. And then I attached the photo of Jamie hyping Michelle, posted it to my feed, and closed my app.

Asia arrived a few moments later, and we had the best dinner, catching up and sorting through life together, as we always do. On my Uber ride home, I listened to music and didn't look at my phone again before bed.

When I woke up the next morning, everything had changed. My "Unabashed Hype Women" post had gone viral.

Here's the post in its entirety:

Ladies, this is your vibe for 2023: Unabashed Hype Woman.
Full on. Full out. Full force.
This photo was taken last night at the Golden Globes when Michelle Yeoh won Best Actress for her role in "Everything Everywhere All at Once."

Look at Jamie Lee Curtis.
Look. At. Her.
You can feel her energy, her fire, her power.
Her excitement, joy, and passion for Michelle is palpable. The photo moves. It vibrates.
If you saw this photo without context, you may think that it was actually
*   *Jamie* who won.*
Ladies, this is your vibe for 2023.
Hype. Other. Women.
When she wins, fight the urge to question . . .

. . . Who does she think she is?
. . . Why is she getting attention?
. . . Did she really deserve it?
. . . Is she really that good?
. . . What about me?

Guess what? The world has sold you a lie.

Her success doesn't detract from yours.
Her wins don't create your losses.
Her joy can't steal the joy that's meant for you.

De-condition and unlearn what you've been wired to think: that women are
*   your competition.*
It's a trap. Meant to distract us. And to keep us keeping each other down.

Find your Jamie.
Hype their Jamie.
Be her Jamie.

My LinkedIn post had 1,249,699 impressions; 23,439 likes; 1,004 comments; and 2,444 reposts.

But it didn't stop there.

Jamie Lee Curtis's friend saw my LinkedIn post and sent it to her. TO JAMIE. And then, she posted it—with a message—to her 5.6 million Instagram followers at the time.

Jamie writes:

> I was sent this today. I'm so moved by it. I got the chance to play Heidi in Wendy Wasserstein's, the Heidi Chronicles for TNT and the last line of her big speech at the women's luncheon WOMEN WHERE ARE WE GOING? she talks about the fact that even though the women's movement was about UNITY, it now, years after, sadly was just about competition and beating the other girl out of jobs, men, and clothes. She says at the end "I thought the point was that we are ALL in this together."
>
> WELL, WE ARE! @everythingeverywheremovie @michelleyeoh_ official

The day was a blur. Texts, calls, and messages flooded my phone from family and friends I've known my whole life and from people I've never met. My post was showing up in Facebook groups on the other side of the world; in text chains between college girlfriends and on mom threads; circulating between colleagues in offices and discussed on Zoom calls in every time zone.

It was everything, everywhere, all at once.

And then, Ms. Jamie Lee Curtis herself, responded to my DM. She wrote: "You moved me, and people who know me and care about me. Thank you. It was, as you saw, a moment of pure joy. I'm WITH YOU."

We messaged back and forth about the frenzy around this photo and my post. Then, she shared her cell number, and we began texting.

It was proof to me—yet again—of a *Sliding Doors* moment.

Do you know the movie? It's the 1998 romantic comedy-drama starring Gwyneth Paltrow. When Helen (Paltrow), a London ad executive, is fired from her job and rushes out to catch a train, two scenarios take place. In one, she gets on the train and comes home to find her boyfriend, Gerry (John Lynch), in bed with another woman. In the second, she misses the train and arrives after the woman has left.

In the movie, these two parallel lives play out simultaneously.

Every time I watch that movie, I'm taken on an existential journey that questions why the mundane becomes the momentous—why a choice to turn left can upend your universe. It's as simple as a train missed, a train made. Can you imagine? That one moment impacting everything? Leading to life or death, more or less quickly?

Even more daunting—and thrilling—than each choice you make changing *your* life is the idea of the ripple effect; that each of our individual, tiny decisions determine the menagerie that makes up the story of our *collective* lives.

I'm obsessed with the idea that every small choice I make sets my life on a different course. The preciousness, fragility, *and* monotony of every decision meaning *something*.

Sometimes a door opens and invites you to walk—or not walk— through. Other times, a door closes and removes the choice altogether. Regardless, how you move forward after the choice is made becomes the story of your life.

Good and bad things happen in life to tell us something, if we're willing to listen.

I trusted my intuition to write the post and put it out into the world. And if I hadn't, I wouldn't be texting with Jamie Lee Fucking Curtis from my living room on a Friday night in January.

Think of all the times you have an inkling to do something; maybe you even start it, but you leave it unfinished—a call from deep inside, left unanswered; an urgent message, left unread. Life gets in the way (kids, work, distractions). Or *you* get in the way (fear, imposter syndrome, limiting beliefs). It has happened to me thousands of times before I wrote this post. And it's happened to me hundreds of times since.

You won't be able to give into, or see through, every thought or idea that comes to you. That would be impossible, and also hard to capture when driving or taking a shower (why does all the good stuff hit then???). But there will be times where you know something is different. You feel it. The idea doesn't come out of nowhere, disconnected from the rest of your life. It feels like a solid period on the right side of a run-on sentence you've been trying desperately to complete. It feels like effortless flow. It feels like solid ground.

This experience happened, at that moment, for me. I had been planting the seeds for what became the Hype Women Movement for years, decades, centuries. I had been watering and tending to what I knew was growing under the surface. I couldn't see it yet, but I *knew* it was there. I believed.

Too many times, I've been 5, 10, 20 fields over—planting more and more seeds. Willing something, *anything*, to grow. And I'm sure I've missed moments where my dream finally came to the surface, where it pushed through into the light of day for someone else to witness other than my mind's eye. And I wasn't there. The moment passed. The potential, without care and consideration, died on the vine.

This time, I was paying attention. I was standing in the field where the fruits of my labor reaped my most surprising and soul-filling harvest yet. Hype Women has always been inside of me. And I believe that it's always been inside of you, too.

Following the first 24 whirlwind hours of my post going viral, I wanted to further fuel the fires we were lighting and reigniting inside of women everywhere. They were waking up to the Hype Women inside of them— and celebrating the Hype Women surrounding them.

So, I did the next logical thing one does when your message goes viral: I made a shirt.

I created and featured the "Unabashed Hype Women shirt" on my company website within an hour. And Jamie, without being asked or expected, hyped me again.

She posted an image of the shirt I created with the following caption:

> THIS IS HUSTLE! THIS IS HYPE! THIS IS EVERYTHING EVE-RYWHERE ALL AT ONCE ON ST(HER)OIDS! I am quite stunned that a moment of pure JOY on Tuesday night is now a T shirt and a movement on Thursday! Proud and humbled and EXCITED! Thanks @erin.gallag.her and all hail @michelleyeoh_official.

Her co-star in the film, Stephanie Hsu commented on Jamie's post: "SHUT UP I WANT ONE."

Everything was moving at warp speed, and my hands could hardly keep up with the ways I wanted the impact of this moment to continue to grow.

I sent my designs to a women-owned print shop in Bucktown, T-Shirt Deli. I asked if they could turn around shirts and canvas bags in two hours, versus 24. Of course, they made it happen. They're women, after all. I grabbed two badass women notecards from my home office and drove downtown, stopping at my favorite coffee shop, Ipsento, to still myself for a moment to hand-write notes of gratitude and admiration to Jamie and Michelle.

I swung by one of my best friends and Chicago-based designer Christina Karin's flagship store and picked up two "Faces" scarves, a piece she designed to showcase the beauty of the diversity and collective power of women, to include in the boxes.

I worked with my high school friend Emily Rose (now a Hollywood exec whose company produced the *Everything Everywhere All At Once* film) to plan to courier over to Jamie and Michelle Yeoh the boxes filled with my handwritten notes, personalized Unabashed Hype Women shirts, and "Be Her Jamie" canvas bags, with Christina Karin's Faces scarves tucked inside of them.

The containers were filled with so much love and hype . . . for women, by women.

And then, Jamie posted again.

I'm still stunned that a moment of natural exuberance and joy became some sort of symbol for women supporting other women. @erin.gallag.her highlighted it with her gorgeous post and word anthem of support and somehow from Tuesday night to Friday night it became a T-shirt and was left outside of my home with a dozen everything bagels from my @everythingeverywheremovie family. I was COVID sleeping and today after my shower I proudly wear it. #FRIENDSSUPPORTING-FRIENDS is a perfect squad goal for 2033 [sic] Thank you Erin and all who are expanding it and amplifying the message and CONGRATU-LATIONS @michelleyeoh_official YOU ARE EVERYTHING EVE-RYWHERE ALL AT ONCE!

A few days later, Jamie mailed me all 12 of the children's books she's authored over the years—with hand-inscribed notes to my then six- and four-year-old sons, William and Charlie. We continued to send handwritten notes and gifts to one another in a showing of sisterhood and solidarity.

We never held back in our support—wondering if the other would reciprocate. We didn't keep a tally or a scoreboard of whose hype went further or farther. We operated from a place of abundance, not scarcity.

We volleyed hype back and forth to one another in an unwritten, unsaid, unsigned agreement to make the moment count. But, in truth, it was never meant to be a *moment*. It was always going to become a Movement. *Our* Movement. The world told us this was true.

Over the next three days, more than 15 global publications wrote articles about my post, the meme, and the shirt, including *The Today Show*, HuffPost, *People* Magazine, *The Guardian*, Yahoo, *Parade*, *Los Angeles Times*,

Us Weekly, Daily Mail, AsiaOne.com, Upworthy, and Page Six/*New York Post,* and shared in the feeds of FEMINIST, George Takei, and GOOD Worldwide Inc., to name a few.

But, I was frustrated. Because none of the stories really went deeper than the surface-level headline stated. The story wasn't about a post or a meme or a shirt. It was about a cultural zeitgeist, a shift in the way women *want* to view one another. The majority of women—the best of women—*want* to hype other women. We *want* to see other women succeed. We are tired of fighting each other, tearing each other down, and draining our energy trying to unseat those who have fought for what they've achieved.

And then came the backlash. Because . . . of course it did.

What started as a genuine moment of pure joy for Jamie, hyping her friend and co-star Michelle Yeoh's win, became a twisted narrative around me centering a white woman in a moment meant to honor an Asian woman; of media focusing on Jamie's celebration of Michelle more than Michelle's win; of Jamie standing under a spotlight that cast a shadow on Michelle.

The cavalry came for me. And they came for Jamie, too. And that counternarrative started to creep into the minds of women everywhere. It started to wear on the pure heart of Jamie, too.

Here's how I know.

On January 18, I received confirmation that my package for Jamie had finally been delivered to her home.

I texted her: *"Please say they finally delivered my gift to you last night."*

She replied: *"Yes. A lovely gift. I am not posting about it because I don't want to take away from Michelle. It has certainly been picked up everywhere and I am grateful to you, but I'm also just going to let it go right now so that the focus can continue to be on her work. Thank you."*

Before I share my response to Jamie with you, I want you to sit with this moment.

Have you been there?

Have you been ridiculed for the way you showed up in the world by the critics throwing stones safely from protection of their glass houses?

Have you been made to feel like you were competing with another woman when that was never your intention?

One of my favorite scenes from a movie is food critic Anton Ego's monologue, reading his review of Gusteau's French restaurant, in the 2007 Pixar animated movie *Ratatouille*.

It's—in my opinion—a play on Theodore Roosevelt's "Citizenship in a Republic" speech, which he delivered in Paris on April 23, 1910. The speech is popularly known as "The Man in the Arena."

In the scene, Ego shares:

> In many ways, the work of a critic is easy. We risk very little, yet enjoy a position over those who offer up their work and themselves to our judgment. We thrive on negative criticism, which is fun to write and to read. But the bitter truth we critics must face is that, in the grand scheme of things, the average piece of junk is probably more meaningful than our criticism designating it so. But there are times when a critic truly risks something, and that is in the discovery and defense of the new. The world is often unkind to new talent, new creations. The new needs friends. Last night, I experienced something new, an extraordinary meal from a singularly unexpected source. To say that both the meal and its maker have challenged my preconceptions about fine cooking is a gross understatement. They have rocked me to my core. In the past, I have made no secret of my disdain for Chef Gusteau's famous motto: "Anyone can cook." But I realize, only now do I truly understand what he meant. Not everyone can become a great artist, but a great artist can come from anywhere.

The critics came for Jamie—they came for me—because we were doing something different. We were embracing something new. And it scared them.

Jamie was accused of competing with Michelle for attention . . . for simply showing up and supporting her friend.

This is not a new or novel example. How many times have you been ridiculed, scrutinized, accused of competing with another woman for a job? For an award? For a friend? For a love interest? For money? For worth? When it was *never* the case. The worst part is, the two women who were never competing always end up fighting or broken in the end.

So, when I saw this reality come through in Jamie's text, I had a choice to make.

I could say I understood and wish her the best.

And our relationship—and this moment—would likely end there.

Or—to a globally recognized, acclaimed, and (soon-to-be) Oscar-winning actress, activist, and outspoken advocate for justice, equality, and equity—with careful consideration, compassion, and respect, I could say *this* (which is exactly what I did):

> The gift was not meant for you to post. It was meant as an expression of pure gratitude and admiration. I sent the same gift to Michelle.
>
> I honor and respect any decision you make around this moment and Movement. That is yours and it's valid.
>
> The world tells us that it's about Michelle winning OR you supporting her. And I just won't allow that narrative to win anymore.
>
> It's both. We deserve both. Women want both.
>
> And I will continue to fight until they stop pitting us against one another and making us choose whose light is worthy (as you have always done).
>
> Forever in solidarity.

I refused to be scared or shamed into silence. I refused to let the scarcity mindset win, yet again. I refused to let the system pit Jamie against Michelle, to again create conflict between women that never existed.

Jamie responded with: *"Yes, forever in solidarity. You and I are just beginning. I think we are going to do things in the world."*

Over the next few weeks and months, I continued to post, repost, and share any and all messages dedicated to Hype Women. And the only article that got to the heart of the message from my original post—and the response from women around the world—came almost two months later, written by Rachel Bowie for *PureWow* and published on March 6, 2023, International Women's Day: "So Long Mean Girls, 2023 Is the Year of the Hype Woman."

Rachel begins her article:

> *It was the clip shared 'round the world: During the 80th Golden Globe Awards, Michelle Yeoh—who waited 40 years to land a lead role in a Hollywood film—finally (finally!) got her due, winning the Golden Globe for Best Actress in a Comedy thanks to her performance in* Everything Everywhere All at Once.

Yeoh's moving acceptance speech went viral, of course, but later that
night, another moment surfaced. It was the split-second reaction of
Yeoh's costar (and fellow nominee from the film) Jamie Lee Curtis.
How to describe it? Erin Gallagher, CEO and founder of gender
equity company Ella, put it best: Curtis—who lost in her category
for what it's worth—was Yeoh's "unabashed hype woman."

Gallagher's LinkedIn post on the topic also went viral, but she credits all
this virality to the look on Curtis's face—her "excitement, joy, and
passion" for Michelle was "palpable." If you saw it out of context,
you'd actually think it was Curtis who won, she was that genuine in
cheering on her colleague and friend.

Gallagher's call to action? "Ladies, this is your vibe for 2023. Find your
Jamie. Hype their Jamie. Be her Jamie."

The article goes on to feature other women and the way they hype and
are hyped. After all, "Hype Women" is both a noun *and* a verb. It talked about
the epidemic of mean girls and the antidote in Hype Women. And then, the
journalist Rachel asked *me* who *my* Hype Woman is.

I knew I needed to be so careful, thoughtful, purposeful, and powerful
in the way I answered it. It needed to be true *and* it also needed to be a call
to action. Because when you're given a platform to continue to evolve a
moment into a Movement, what you say must stand the test of time.

Here's the truth.

There is only one consistent Hype Woman I can—and always
will—count on.

She doesn't care how old I am or where I work.

She doesn't judge whether or not I have children or who I can intro-
duce her to.

She never questions why I started a company or left a friendship.

She supports my boundaries, my dreams, and my ambition and she
doesn't see them as challenges or threats to her own success.

She isn't perfect.

She doesn't always get it right. But she does acknowledge her faults, and
she works to repair what is broken.

She is willing to let me fail and learn and grow.

She forgives the versions of myself that I needed to be in order to survive, while evolving into the woman I will be—who will ultimately allow me to thrive.

She is *me*.

This is the way I answered the question. My Hype Woman is ME.

I'll admit that after I said it, I paused for a moment, worried that those who read my answer might think I'm selfish or egotistical or missing the whole point. But that is the exact reason I *had* to choose—and hype—myself. Because it's high time women stop making themselves so small that we disappear into the ether.

How you *talk to* yourself sets the foundation for everything else. How you *show up* for yourself tells people how you want to be treated. How you *tell the world* about yourself inspires others to do the same.

If you can't hype yourself first, no one will ever be able to truly hype *you*.

Our Movement is as much about committing to hype *other* women as it is about hyping the women *we* are. When we do, our Hype Women will hype us, and the circle of hype continues forever. This didn't happen for me overnight. It took years of moving through life on autopilot and doing what I was told; never stopping to look around and ask: Is this all there is? Is this all I'm worth? Is this all I'll be? But once I did, there was no going back.

In January 2024, one year after my "Unabashed Hype Woman" post went viral, Jamie Lee Curtis was on the daytime talk show circuit for her 13th children's book *Just One More Sleep: All Good Things Come to Those Who Wait . . . and Wait . . . and Wait*.

In every interview on *The Today Show*, *The View*, and *The Kelly Clarkson Show*, the hosts asked Jamie about my Hype Women post and the Hype Women Movement.

And in every answer, Jamie hyped me. She said my name in rooms where I am not. She continued to fan the flame of our Movement and to act as the genuinely unabashed Hype Woman she always has been and always will be.

You may have noticed who penned the foreword for my book?

❦ ❦ ❦

Two nights before 2024 arrived, my first-born said something to me that healed more than two years of hurt. It wasn't lost on me that my seven-year-old Will asked this on the night of the last full moon of 2023—a time for closure, endings, release.

In the pitch black and as I was putting him to bed, he said, "If you were driving and you had to hit an old person *or* a young person, what would you do?"

My first two thoughts were: "Fuck. He needs therapy." *and* "I'm changing the settings on YouTube (again) in the morning."

As I started to lecture Will on why I didn't like this question and ask where he heard it, he cut me off.

"You hit the brakes, Mama!"

"Ahhhhhhhhh," I responded. {Enter forced laugh.} "Good one!"

Then came, "Would you hit a Zombie or a spider?"

"Zombie, obviously."

And then came the one that took my breath away.

"Have Her Back or Ella?"

My second-grader was asking me, of the two companies I've founded, which one would I save?

He was plucking out of the night sky—from the cosmic pull of the year-ending full moon—a question about Have Her Back: the company I had co-founded four years earlier, left two-and-a-half years later, and closed two months after my departure.

He was asking about Ella: the company I had founded, alone, after four months of liminality—a period of cocooning, of transformation, of rebirth, of second chances, of 13th chances, of taking risks and betting on myself and having my own back and knowing that after birthing my two boys into the world, Ella was my only chance to be the mother of a girl.

But in truth, in launching Ella into the world, I was mothering the girl in me who deserved so much damn better.

Will's question stunned me. It was out of nowhere. Or was it? My hopes, dreams, risks, successes, failures, wins, losses, and grief compounded. All tied up in that first company. All transferred to my next. It was like a ton of bricks and a weightless feather smashing and swirling in my chest.

I knew my answer.

"Well, Have Her Back is gone. So, I would save Ella."

And Will said, "Yeah. Because Ella will never die."

And he's right. She won't. Because Ella was born from the depths of my soul, the phoenix rising from the ashes. From Ella came The Fairway, then Hype Women. Our collective power continues to build and spread.

It has taken me almost two years after leaving my first company to feel closure, to cut chords, and to heal. The healing will be a lifelong process. The hurt never goes away. It just occupies less time and space.

But going forward, I am focused on all the pieces and parts of me worth saving. And I am releasing the parts of me that are already gone.

It's time for you to be the Hype Woman you've always needed and deserved, too.

Oh, and here are a few of my favorite photos of Jamie and me—taken by the ridiculously talented Chloe Jackman—at one of my Hype Women events in Los Angeles We're at Jamie's favorite restaurant, Dear Jane's—owned by one of her best friends, the beautiful and brilliant Patti Rockenwagner.

These photos taken of us together were two-and-a-half years after I wrote that LinkedIn post. Still supporting. Still loving. Sill hyping.

Jamie and me at my Hype Women Brunch at Dear Jane's in L.A.
Photo credit: Chloe Jackman

Jamie and me at my Hype Women Brunch at Dear Jane's in L.A.
Photo credit: Chloe Jackman

Jamie and me at my Hype Women Brunch at Dear Jane's in L.A.
Photo credit: Chloe Jackman

Seven Shifts to Unabashed Hype Woman Status

1. **Forgive yourself:** Forgive yourself for thinking that women are your competition, for resenting their success and for minimizing versus maximizing your moments that deserve(d) hype.

2. **Audit your survival-mode kit:** Focus on what's worth saving. Recognize what you've outgrown. Release the rest.

3. **Create—and communicate—new boundaries:** You are no good to yourself or others without identifying and relaying your expectations.

4. **Grieve the endings:** Give yourself permission to grieve the versions of yourself and others who are not a part of your future.

5. **Identify those who Hype Women:** Surround yourself with women (and men and nonbinary folks) who celebrate your wins and the wins of women everywhere.

6. **Hype yourself first:** Celebrate *your* wins, big and small. And share them with the world.

7. **Reprogram your brain:** Actively celebrate other women's successes out loud.

7

Serve Yourself First

I spent the bulk of the first 40 years of my life putting everyone else's needs above my own. I did this in big and small ways, for individuals and groups, with friends and family, for companies and communities. And then, I began to notice a truth—occurring with increasing frequency and growing intensity—that had been hiding in plain sight all along: to serve others, I must abandon myself.

When the majority of your life—your worth—has been defined by your service to others, the moment you *stop* serving, where do you go? Who do you become? And how do you begin, again?

We are taught that the ultimate archetype of a woman to be admired is one who is *selfless*. "Selfless" is defined as: "concerned more with the needs and wishes of others than with one's own." There is a degree of this that is healthy, that can be positive, that balances the body.

But when you are selfless every day, in every way, with everyone, you disappear. There is nothing left of you—because you forgot to care that she exists, too.

Selflessness is upheld as altruistic. But I call bullshit. I want that word to undergo the pejoration it deserves; to pay penance for the perpetual purgatory in which it's trapped women everywhere. Selflessness destroys women and it teaches our children that women exist for everyone else. They grow up watching women drained of depth and desire.

And then, they become them.
Or they exploit them.

You forget what hunger feels like when you forget you need to eat.
You forget what desire feels like when you forget you need to satisfy.
You forget what lusting feels like when you forget you need to want.

That is, until you satiate.

It's June 1, 1992. My aunt Rosanne is watching my sister and me at her condo in Nu'uanu Valley in Honolulu, Hawaii. I am in fourth grade. I am frustrated. So, I write a note on a three-hole-punched piece of white lined paper to my aunt—who is sitting in the other room.

Thirty-two years later, my aunt put that letter back in my hands. She saved it. I've included a photo of the original. And I've typed out the copy, word for word, here:

> June 1
>
> Dear Rosanne,
>
> You, like others, are always making and telling me to do things for others! Here I am making <u>my</u> sandwich and <u>my</u> snack while you sit, relax, and say, "Erin cut ~~her~~ Meaghan's sandwich in half!" She doesn't want it cut in half! Why don't you ask her?
>
> I'm sick and tired of doing things for others and giving myself nothing. My mother and sister are constantly blaming and putting me in the position of guilt! I haven't done anything.
>
> I'm sorry if I have said anything rude but I'm so frustrated at everybody. I think you also owe me some "sorrys"! I've always dreamed of a place in the mountains under waterfalls where I can be alone! Please appreciate me as if I were an adult! I'm 10!
>
> Erin Turner
>
> P.S. Try to be nice!

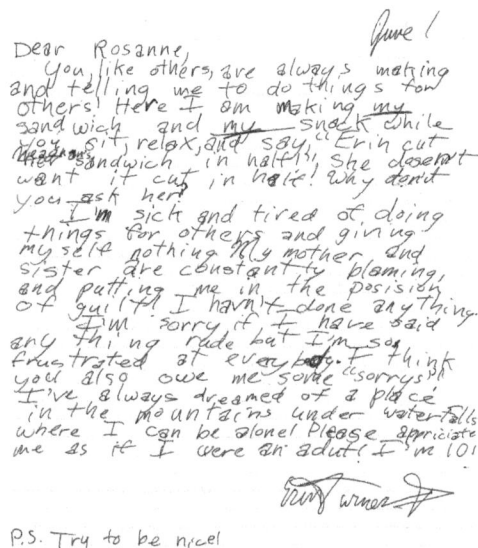

Dear Rosanne,
You, like others, are always making and telling me to do things for others! Here I am making my sandwich and my snack while you sit, relax, and say, "Erin cut her sandwich in half." She doesn't want it cut in half! Why don't you ask her?
I'm sick and tired of doing things for others and giving myself nothing. My mother and sister are constantly blaming, and putting me in the posision of guilt! I havn't done anything. I'm sorry, if I have said any thing rude but I'm so frustrated at everybody. I think you also owe me some "sorrys"! I've always dreamed of a place in the mountains under waterfalls where I can be alone! Please appriciate me as if I were an adult! I'm 10!

P.S. Try to be nice!

My handwritten letter, age 10.

Damn, I love her. I wish I could talk to her right now and say, "Girl, you are *right*. Keep trusting yourself. Don't let the world tell you to give everything you have to others. Don't you *ever* forget that you are the most important person in your universe."

Research suggests, according to a study conducted by Ypulse, in collaboration with authors Katty Kay and Claire Shipman for their book *The Confidence Code for Girls*, that girls' confidence levels fall by 30% during ages 8–12. This period, known as middle childhood to early adolescence, is when societal pressures, self-consciousness, and gender expectations start to have a stronger influence. Between the ages 8–10 girls still exhibit confidence, but peer comparisons increase, and they start picking up on gendered expectations.

This was so clearly happening to me at age 10, when I wrote this letter. I was feeling the pressure to be a "good girl," to serve others, to abandon myself and my own wants and needs. And I was angry about it. I felt like no one was listening to me.

I firmly believe that because my mother and my grandmother were never allowed (or never allowed themselves) to feel or express their own rage that they transferred it all to me.

On Mother's Day in 2020, I left my children and husband in Michigan and drove to Chicago. Alone.

Yeah, you read that correctly. And please, spare me your shock and shame.

I have my reasons.

Every mother does.

Here. I'll explain.

Sunday, May 10, 2020, was Day 58 of the pandemic lockdown.

Two months earlier, on March 13, we picked up our boisterous four-and two-year-old boys from their Montessori School in the West Loop of Chicago at 4:30 p.m. And we drove back to our classic Chicago-brick condo, on busy North Avenue, in Bucktown.

There were rumors going around. People were getting sick. Cities were getting nervous. Companies were shutting down. And then, the reality started to hit us. An email landed in our inboxes shortly after we arrived home on Friday the 13th (you can't make this stuff up!) from the Montessori Academy of Chicago. Beginning Monday, our kids' school would be closed—indefinitely.

I'm sorry, *what*?

As a parent of young children and someone who worked in an office outside of the home, being told that the childcare you count on has—poof!—disappeared into thin air without notice or knowledge of when it would return, feels like you just ran full speed, headfirst into a classic Chicago brick wall.

We panicked. How the hell were we going to do this? We immediately went into crisis-planning mode. Okay, where could we go? Who could help us? How would we get there?

The most obvious answer was to drive to mom's house in Michigan. She was newly retired, had a four-bedroom home with a fenced-in yard, and was an amazing grandmother who our boys loved. My mom wanted us there. She wanted to help. And we needed her.

The plan was set. We would start packing that night and hit the road for the four-hour drive to Michigan (closer to five-and-a-half hours when you travel with small children) first thing in the morning.

By 10 a.m., we had jammed everything we could squeeze around our two boys and 90-pound Golden Retriever that we thought we might need for the next two weeks. I mean, this would go on for two weeks max, right?

Maybe we'd be back before the following weekend. We were *sure* that by even going to Michigan we were overreacting.

I have a vivid memory of driving down Division in Wicker Park, the Chicago neighborhood just south of us, as we headed east toward Interstate 90. Our white Jeep Grand Cherokee was at capacity.

I looked out the passenger-side window at the restaurants and bars decorated with green, orange, and white streamers; three-foot green glitter shamrocks; life-size leprechauns holding frothy, overflowing beer steins. The people inside were smiling and sweating and laughing and dancing, their shiny beads swinging from their necks and flimsy plastic novelty hats precariously perched on their heads, daring to make a leap for the sticky, beer-soaked floor—soon to be crushed under the weight of the carefree crowd. Oh, to be young and celebrating Saint Patrick's Day in Chicago. As was always the tradition, on the Saturday that fell closest to the actual March 17th date, the Chicago River was dyed green, and the parades and bar crawls were in full force. I had been them before.

"God, I hope they're using hand sanitizer," I thought to myself.

Fast-forward 58 days, and we had spent nearly every waking (and sleeping!) hour inside of my mom's four walls.

And we were one of the lucky ones. But it was still hard as fuck. No one is meant to spend that much time alone together.

At that point in our lives, my husband and I had been together for eight years and married for six. *We* had *never* spent this many consecutive 24-hour days together.

It. Was. A. Lot.

So, the Mother's Day of 2020 felt like a cruel and counterfeit celebration, as so many of us mothers not only continued to bear the bulk of the burden of the unpaid, unseen, unrecognized, and undervalued labor of our lives at "home," but now had no relief from it; there was no separation of work and family. We were drowning.

I didn't want more time with my children.
I didn't want more time with my husband.
I didn't want more time with *my* mother.

I wanted to Get. The. Fuck. Out.

The day started with my boys climbing into bed with me, yelling "Happy Mother's Day" at the top of their lungs and jumping American Ninja Warrior style onto my legs and lungs. This quickly devolved into slow but steady, picking-up-steam powerhouse meltdowns.

Me with my sons Will (left) and Charlie (right) and our dog Lincoln (butt in bottom left corner) on Mother's Day 2020.

Next up: my "breakfast in bed" request delivered with 62% accuracy. Followed by my children eating 87% of what was on my plate. And then, more toddler meltdowns.

So. Much. Joy.

But, wait, that's not all. My mom had scheduled a Zoom with her *seven* siblings. And their children. And their children's children.

We were asked to sit in front of the camera with smiles plastered on our faces and "update" everyone on what we had "been up to" the past few months.

A GLOBAL FUCKING PANDEMIC, THAT'S WHAT!

Wow, almost five years later and I can feel my nervous system dysregulating as I write this. Do you feel it too? Do you remember what that time was like?

This shit is still real raw.

I felt like a ticking time bomb.

There was so much talking, so much touching, so much yelling, so much, too much. *Way* too much.

I needed air.

I stepped outside into my mom's driveway—one of the only outdoor places we could go unmasked and unbothered. Six seconds later, my boys were pawing at my legs.

"Mama! Mama! Mama!"

I felt like I was going to lose it. Like, really lose it. And not in some cute, contained "you crazy kiddos are driving me cuuuuuhhhhhhrrrrrrayyyyyy-zeeeee, you silly buns!" version. More in a "I'm going to get in the car and drive until I reached Mexico with no intention of coming back" kind of way.

My boys climbed inside of the bed of my brother-in-law's truck parked in the driveway. They were part of our "pandemic bubble." Remember those? They had driven over from their house a few miles away for our Mother's Day "party."

I tried to let the boys do enough to entertain themselves, but not so much that they'd damage his truck or their brains.

But I was on the brink.

My husband came outside expecting to see me . . . actually, I don't know what he expected to see. He had seen what I had been going through all day—what I had been dragged through the past two months. I was a shell of myself, a car driving on autopilot, fueled by fumes.

He looked at me staring through my children as they jumped in unison with maniacal glee and my arm blocked them from falling out of the back of the truck. He said the first words that came to his mind that he thought could offer any relief.

"You should just drive to Chicago and take a few days for yourself. You need a break."

I snapped out of my trance.

"Really?" I stared at him with disbelief and desperation.

"Yeah," he said matter-of-factly.

"Okay!"

I ran through my mom's front door, letting the glass door slam behind me. I sprinted so fast up the stairs I almost tripped on two of them. I threw my meds and skincare in a bag I found on the floor. I wasn't going to waste time packing clothes. Fuck 'em! I didn't want to let enough time pass for Brian to change his mind.

I hoofed it back downstairs and said, "Okay, I'm headed out. I'll let you know when I get to Chicago!"

My whole family stood there with their mouths open. Was I fucking SERIOUS? I was leaving? Leaving *them*? For *myself*? What kind of a god-damn monster had I become? I mean, Brian *had* made the offer. But that's all it was supposed to be! An *offer*!

I was supposed to do what all good girls should do when offered some-thing they deserve: be grateful for the gesture and politely decline. Their judgment, their disapproval, their disgust with my decision was palpable.

But I didn't care. I *literally* did not care. Nothing could stop me from saving myself.

I had seen the light peeking out at the end of a very dark tunnel. And I was going to drive with my foot on the gas—pedal to the floor—until I found it.

I hugged and kissed everyone goodbye and told them I'd be back in a few days. I jumped in the driver seat of my car and gripped the wheel. I was breaking out. It was the first time I had truly exhaled in months. It was the first time I had felt relief. My skin prickled with goosebumps up and down my arms and legs. I felt fucking alive again.

I reversed out of the driveway, put down the passenger window and waved one last goodbye.

My family stood on my mom's front lawn half-heartedly waving with furrowed brows.

As I drove down the street, I felt pure joy in my body. Giddiness. Tears started to stream down my face. Not from sadness or guilt or shame, but as a release of everything I had been holding together these last 58 days. I started to free the deep grief that had begun to form a pit in my stomach and allowed myself to feel good—like really, really good—for the first time in too long.

I turned up the music. *My* music. All the way. I sang at the top of my lungs. I screamed the words until I lost my voice, until my throat hurt from the pressure I freed without limits, without judgment, without anyone watching.

I let go.

When I arrived at our condo in Chicago, it felt like I was walking into a museum. It smelled dusty, like an antique shop or a consignment store where you know items had lay dormant for weeks, months, maybe years. Nothing had been used or touched or moved since that fateful morning when we fled to Michigan. I pushed through the eeriness to embrace the fact that I was alone. All alone! It was quiet! No one needed me!

Ohmygod what was I going to order for dinner? Sushi, for sure. Coast Sushi. Spicy tuna, dragon roll, two pieces of salmon sashimi (and because I was a beloved customer, they always gave me at least five pieces. Would they still remember me?). And I was going to get to eat all five pieces. *No one* was going to swipe a piece here and there when I wasn't looking. My two-year-old Charlie was my stealthy salmon sashimi stealer.

I cracked a bottle of my favorite pinot noir, McBride Sisters, that had been waiting for—and likely missing—me from our wine fridge. I put the half-full glass on the side table and left it unattended—without worrying that a ball would fly at it, sending the red liquid everywhere, shattering glass into a million pieces.

I lit candles around the room—unafraid that my babies were going to burn themselves or our house down.

I turned on *Workin' Moms*, Catherine Reitman's brilliant brainchild on Netflix about four very different thirtysomething working-mother friends trying to balance their jobs, family lives, and love lives in modern-day Toronto, Canada. I was ready to be entertained by my favorite ladies—delivering the most realistic, raunchy, and gut-wrenching truths, of what it meant to be a mother with ambitions outside of solely devoting themselves to their children—in my living room, at full volume. I had an entire unwatched season to binge. I couldn't believe how lucky I was.

And then, my menagerie began to crack.

A text from my husband said that he couldn't believe I left.

My high school girlfriends and I had a planned Zoom call that night to catch up. I told them all about my Mother's Day jail break—and my staycation for one taking place in my very own home right then and there!

I expected them to rejoice in my bold decision to prioritize myself and to celebrate a mother choosing herself on the day that is meant to honor her tireless work and sacrifice. I thought I was walking into a room of support and camaraderie and sisterhood.

Their faces looked just like my husband's and mother's and sister's when I told them I accepted Brian's invitation to take a break and some space for myself.

The lightness and the air of my newfound joy and peace were being sucked out of the space that had begun to open, the one where I felt like I could finally breathe again.

Everyone thought I was selfish, even reckless. They thought I had lost my mind.

How could I *leave* my children on Mother's Day?
How could I make this day about *me*?
How could I abandon my family in Michigan and hole up in our home
    in Chicago like a fugitive?

When the call ended and I was alone in the room, the silence was deafening. It felt cold and heavy. I started to question myself in the way that everyone in my life that day had.

Was I a monster?
Had I lost my mind?
What was I *doing* here?

All of my joy was gone.

The guilt, the shame, the judgments of others overtook all of the space I had created for myself. I believed what everyone said about me—to me. And I lost myself, again.

I turned off the TV.
I poured the wine down the drain.
I scraped what was left of my sushi into the trash.

I texted Brian. I would drive back first thing in the morning.

Less than 24 hours after I pulled out of my mom's driveway in Michigan, I pulled back in. Days later, I questioned whether I had ever left. Maybe it was a cabin fever dream? Because nothing about what I thought I remembered feeling was with me anymore.

Five years later, the decision to leave my family on Mother's Day still haunts me. But not for the reasons you may think.

I'm still angry about that trip.

I'm still resentful that I didn't stay in Chicago for more than one night.

I'm still deeply sad and sorry that I didn't stand up for her—for me.

This is what our society, our culture, our system does to mothers. We are constantly reminded of who we're here to serve, of why we exist in our home, and of what is expected of us.

I decided I wasn't going to let the grief that I experienced on May 10, 2020, die in vain. So, I created a new Mother's Day tradition following that fateful one. And I still do it, to this day.

I take the entire Monday after Mother's Day off of work. It's just for me. While I enjoy the time with—and the gifts and plans created by—my boys and my husband on that special Sunday every year, I spend the day after giving everything back to *me*.

I take care of myself. I do all the things that I wished others understood I needed and deserved. I don't hope and wait for it to happen—or become resentful when none of the hints I've dropped have been picked up and handed back to me, wrapped in metallic pink paper with gold ribbon. I give them to myself, in the most perfect way I could ever imagine.

I go to our local coffee shop for a hot Americano and a warmed cinnamon sweet roll.

I sit there and eat it slowly while listening to my music of the moment in my headphones.

I get a massage and a facial.

I enjoy a mani/pedi.

I take myself to lunch, by myself.

I stroll leisurely through the local women-owned boutiques—and I pick out whatever I want, to remind myself how goddam special I am.

I buy myself a bouquet of white hydrangeas and pink peonies and roses.

I take a hot bubble bath.

I curl up in a cozy chair with a really good book.

I light a jasmine, tuberose, and blonde-wood-scented candle.

I sip a mug of lavender mint tea.

I order sushi for dinner. Spicy tuna. Dragon roll. *Three* pieces of salmon sashimi.

I watch my all-time favorite movie, *Under the Tuscan Sun*.

I serve myself first. The whole day. And then I remind myself that this won't be a once-in-every-365-day occurrence. This is my way forward.

When the final straw breaks your back, your spirit—when it breaks you down and breaks you open—it's always surprising.

It's rarely the worst thing that has happened to you along the way. It's actually quite mundane; maybe even the same situation that had already occurred 100 times before—or a version of it. But this time, *you're* different.

I remember one such moment in my career.

I led the redesign and full-blown buildout of our website in partnership with a member on my team and an external agency that specialized in this type of technical and design work—a team that I had built, grown, and deepened a relationship and partnership with over time.

And on a Zoom call following my months of tireless work, I was berated for the work I'd done.

It took too long.

It was too expensive.

The copy was wrong.

The images were shit.

The layout was incorrect.

The fonts were off.
She had to review our website on her Thanksgiving vacation!

Something in me broke.

Remember in the *Barbie* movie when the Barbies are brainwashed by the Kens?

When they go from being the President and Supreme Court Justices and Nobel Prize–winning authors and scientists and doctors to foot-rubbing, snack-fetching, brewsky-beer serving robots who don't even consider themselves anymore?

And then America Ferrera's character, along with her daughter and "Weird Barbie" and crew bring them into the Barbie Ambulance and remind them of who the fuck they are?

The spell is broken.

It was exactly like that moment.

A switch flipped in my brain, and I woke the fuck up.

I tilted my head as I looked at the locked, barricaded, super-glued door and started to consider walking over to the handle. I wasn't ready yet. But the seed of the idea had been planted.

For the first time in years, I didn't just stand there and take it. I didn't simply absorb all the hate and vitriol she spewed from her venomous, twisted mouth.

I fought back.

I took every single one of her pieces of bullshit "feedback," and I destroyed them.

I described the rationale, the strategy, and the reality of each choice and showed her why her argument held no fucking water. I used technical terms that she didn't understand. I talked about what I had sacrificed to pull this off. I could go on.

But that day, I stopped.

I took back my power.

The mean girls on our Zoom video call stared back, stunned.

What had happened to me?
What had happened to them?
Why wasn't *their* strategy working?
Why was I calling them on their bullshit?

After the call, a colleague's name popped up on my phone. I reluctantly answered it. She knew something was wrong. She felt it on the call. She said, "I feel the tension that's been building between us all, and I'm afraid we're going to get to a point where we don't speak to each other ever again."

I responded flatly with, "Oh, we're already there."

On a warm summer day, the *New York Times* Sunday paper is being stacked at newsstands everywhere; tossed from delivery trucks, wrapped in a protective plastic sleeve, onto driveways of subscribers; neatly slid onto long wooden dowels on library racks; opened and consumed by readers on airplanes and commuter trains, in coffee shops and at kitchen tables.

It's June 12, 2020. I'm making my *New York Times* debut.

I'm featured in a photo with my two boys in the "Modern Love" section of a six-page Sunday Times print spread titled "Alone Together."

In the photo, I am unshowered, without makeup, braless, wearing the T-shirt I slept in, looking like I'm on the brink of a mental health crisis. The photo was taken while we were at my mother's house in Michigan on April 25, 2020, day 43 of the pandemic. My boys are crawling all over me, using my body as part jungle gym, part breakfast table, part art studio seat. The roots of my hair are five months past needing a full highlight.

The day this *New York Times* piece comes out also happens to be the day that we are driving back to Chicago—to reclaim the lives we left behind at the start of the pandemic on March 14. Remember when I thought we'd be gone from our home for two weeks? It ended up being three months. Ninety days to the day.

$\equiv$ **The New York Times**   Account ⌄

MODERN LOVE

Together.

After months of sheltering at home, 18 cohabitants on what so much togetherness has wrought.

New York Times Modern Love "Together" cover.

New York Times Modern Love "Together" photo collage.

The series—produced by Jessica Bennett, Daniel Jones, Miya Lee, and Anya Strzemien—opens with this preamble:

It doesn't take a Modern Love column to tell you that relationships can flourish—or wither—in times of stress. Add months of isolation, the physical and emotional toll of a pandemic, followed by global protests, and this period we're living through has the capacity to reshape relationships on a broad scale. Rather than publishing one story this week, we decided to try to capture a bigger picture by featuring numerous voices. We wanted to know how people who are living together—romantically or otherwise—have fared with so much time together. Will this era be more about the costs of claustrophobia or the deepening of love? What about the fights? The annoying habits? The romance? The chaos? Here are 18 stories of isolating together.

My story is featured first.

"I have to lock the bathroom."

Erin Gallagher, 38
Chicago
Living with her husband, Brian, their two sons, as well as her mother and dog.

I learned that space and time away from my husband and children is good for everyone, especially me. My husband has started saying "woo!" to everything in quarantine, and it makes me want to scream. My children are amazing and empathetic and annoying. I have to lock the bathroom or they climb into the shower with me or stand next to me while I'm on the toilet. Small breaks: riding the Peloton with headphones on, taking a bath, solo walks, drives to Starbucks and Target runs.

The video I had shared of my "office" was uploaded to the *New York Times'* Instagram page—for their 18.5 million followers to see. When I took the video, I held my phone in selfie mode showing my 360-degree experience.

"This is my office," I say through an awkward blink-twice-if-you-need-rescuing forced smile.

My two-year-old Charlie is sitting on my lap, reaching for strawberries, I pan left to my husband grinding beans for our morning Americanos. Fifteen more degrees to the right, my mom is vacuuming the living room; in the room directly behind me, my four-year-old Will is sitting in the middle of a 25.8-gallon inflatable pool yelling "Mama! I need your help." The competing cacophonous sounds of the room are jarring. There is no escape. You can feel the hell I'm in.

When you dare to speak the quiet truths out loud, the silenced will judge you.

When you dare to tell the world what you think, the cavalry will come for you.

When you dare to choose yourself first—as a woman—foot soldiers to the patriarchy will show up in force.

People had a lot of feelings about me being so honest with the *New York Times*.

The messages I continued to get from those "closest" to me were: stop, shut up, sit down, stay quiet.

But in contrast, as I shared these thoughts and questions and parts of myself with the outside world—with the people who didn't know me personally (or have a history with me as a different version than my current self)—women everywhere felt seen.

They commented on the *New York Times* video and on my posts on LinkedIn and Instagram, saying how I made them feel less alone, less crazy, less ashamed, less lost. They messaged me and shared my posts in their own feeds, talking about how I made them feel more held and freed and sane and validated and brave.

The more I said the quiet parts out loud, the more I shined a light on the secrets buried away in the dark, the more I spoke inherent truths into existence and didn't spontaneously combust, the less alone we felt, together.

One of my dearest friends, Stacy London, shared a quote with me one time, most commonly attributed to Brené Brown. It has stayed with me: "Shame dies in the light." When Stacy referenced it, she was talking about menopause. But it applies to—well—*everything*.

Here's what was happening: I was changing. And the people who had known me the longest—who had the most access to me personally and professionally—didn't like it.

That's the thing about recognizing your self-worth; about setting boundaries that not only allow you to survive, but thrive; about saying no, without explanation; about refusing to abandon yourself in service to others; about choosing yourself first.

According to writer, broadcaster, and podcaster Emma Gannon: "The only people who get upset when you start setting boundaries are the ones who benefited from you not having them."

A woman who chooses herself—who seeks her joy, peace, and healing over abandoning herself in service to others—is a woman living fully out loud, a woman going against culture's conditioning in order to show up fully as herself. *That* is real audacity. That is living her truth.

How the world reacts to a woman's truth tells us everything we need to know about *them*, not her. Those *without* courage and conviction are the first to attack those who have it.

No one will ever know the full story of a person's life except for the ones living it. Requiring external validation and agreement on all decisions will not only stop you from moving forward—it will hold you back and push you back to a time before you were living an authentic life.

I've had friends who were upset with me for moving my family to a town—our kids to a school—that was better for our life; family members who resented me for setting boundaries, healing generational trauma, and letting go of the traditions that no longer served me; and colleagues who shamed me for leaving a job that did not have my best interest in mind.

Why did these people care so much about what *I* was doing? Especially when the choice I was making had the most impact on *my* life? I've come to learn that it has very little to do with me and everything to do with them.

When you make a choice that they had never considered for themselves, it jolts them; when you make a choice that centers your well-being over their comfort, it disregulates them.

Keep doing it.

When you serve yourself first, you will inadvertently and unintentionally hurt people you care about. Because so much of who they believe you are is tied to how you serve them. This does not make you a monster. It makes you human. It makes you a person who is brave enough to change.

The fragility of every aspect of our existence is the price we pay to be alive. In some cases, choosing yourself first will strengthen your relationships—creating a space for you both to tell the truth and speak what's in, and on, your heart.

In other cases, it will end what you have—creating an immovable block whose strongest desires and actions toward forward progress will be thwarted.

Both are okay.

Not everything is meant to last forever. When you know that you are being truest to yourself, you will find peace—held and freed in the knowing that you matter and deserve love, just as you are.

For anyone who shames you—for leaving, for "quitting," for choosing a different path or a different life, for moving on, for "opting out"—I would flip the question back to them: when were *you* ever asked if *this* is what *you* wanted?

The right people will stay with *you*. They will grow with you. They will understand that change is a part of life. Those that don't will become a stagnant part of your story: the past. "History" with people is sometimes just that: history. Don't let the world tell you that you must stay in a place with people and programming that you've outgrown.

With each life stage and milestone and meaningful moment, a woman is transforming. Sometimes that evolution can take years; other times, a shift can happen overnight. But regardless of the length of time the metamorphosis occurs, the action we so often fail to prioritize is in the meeting of yourself, over and over again, for the first time.

Women are told "you can't pour from an empty cup" and to "put your oxygen mask on first." But those are performative platitudes plastered on coffee mugs and distressed wood signs sold at Home Goods.

How is that helpful when we're the ones buying, washing, and putting the mugs away; when we're researching the best masks, writing and posting the family safety plan, *and* ensuring that the mask bin is stocked; that nothing has expired?

It's not working. We're last on our list—that is, if our names even dare to grace the page. It's time to stop the cycle. You matter. And if you don't serve yourself first, no one else will ever dream of doing it.

Today's the day. You owe it to her. And she deserves everything you have to give her.

Five Shifts to Serve Yourself First

1. **Are you on the list?** When you look at your daily "duties," is your health, happiness, and all-around harmony even on the list?

2. **Change the order.** If not, add yourself. *Now.* If you're there, but you're near the bottom, move yourself up. Take first place.

3. **Define your priorities.** How will you make big and small changes, today, that will begin to flex and strengthen your muscle of self-love and self-care?

4. **Communicate them.** Be clear with the people in your life— both personal and professional—how, where, and when your needs will come first.

5. **Resist the resistance.** When you start to serve yourself first, the "system" will not like it. It will push back. It will make you feel selfish. Good. It means your radical act of choosing you is working. Keep. Going.

8

The Only Way Out Is In

The moment my life serves up a problem, I want to solve it.

Immediately.

The idea of dwelling in the pain, the failure, or the loss sounds far worse than rolling up my sleeves and getting to work strategizing my way out. Maneuvering my mind to move through a situation—rather than to feel all the feelings it brings up—has been my MO for decades. I have sharpened this survival skill scrupulously: out-healing the hurt, correcting the wrong, and filling the hole left behind before my brain has time to compute that anything was ever missing.

And while this trait makes me very useful to *others*, it has kept me perpetually just-out-of-reach from *myself*. My nervous system has operated like a treadmill: set to a speed of sprinting that requires such a focus on form, it leaves no time, energy, or space to consider stepping off.

There is no way to slow down.

There is no emergency Stop button.

There is no way out.

That is, until you fall.

On November 6, 2024, I woke up to the news that VP Kamala Harris would not, in fact, become our 47th—and first woman—president.

I put my eight- and six-year-old boys to bed the night before feeling sick to my stomach. By 8 p.m. the "Red Wave"—expected from the conservative-voting "red" states—was showing no sign of waning. The crimson flood spilling over every battleground territory made the map of America look like the aftermath of a massacre.

I went to bed not knowing the final tally but feeling in my bones that we weren't coming back.

But the story of this race doesn't begin there.

It began 100 days before the election.

VP Kamala Harris entered the 2024 presidential race on Sunday, July 21, 2024.

A few hours later, the indomitable Jotaka Eaddy led her weekly Sunday night Win With Black Women call. Jotaka is the founder of Win With Black Women (WWBW): a collective of intergenerational, intersectional Black women leaders throughout the nation who stand united in support of Black women. That night's WWBW call quickly grew to 44,000 Black women—and then, to more than 90,000 in the hours that followed. They raised $1.5 million for the Harris Victory Fund. It was unprecedented. Zoom was not prepared to handle the power of this collective of women. The platform broke under the weight of their unity, multiple times.

The next morning, I was asked if I would lead a similar call for *white* women.

Without hesitation, I said yes.

What was there to think about? We were going to elect our first woman president! A Black, South Asian woman!

Within two hours, we gathered 20 white women on a planning call to talk about our idea, our strategy, and our goals.

But over the course of that hour, something in me changed. I felt off. What started out as excitement and energy was snuffed out by many of the women on the call who are not strangers to sucking the oxygen out of the rooms they occupy, virtual or otherwise. The ideas I shared were shot down, the strategy the group discussed was old-school and outdated, and the "passion" felt like posturing.

This didn't feel like the power that comes from an authentic Movement. It felt like a forced *mea culpa*—the kind you say because you have to, not because you mean it.

I wasn't sure I wanted anything to do with this effort, as it was being constructed.

I've included the transcript of the voice note I sent following that call here:

> Hey [redacted]. This is my first reaction. And so maybe after a few hours I will feel a little differently. But I don't feel great coming off that call. I think it was an important group to have on. I think the perspectives were deeply insightful and come from so many different experiences. But I'm just expressing my instinct and I didn't feel fired up and excited and ready after that call. I felt like—just—I don't know. I just, I don't have a good feeling. So, I want to figure that out. When I was younger, I didn't trust my instinct and I just . . . I don't feel great coming off that call. So, I want to figure out what that is about. I'm going to try to sit with it.

That, my friends, is where this story should have ended. For me.
But, it didn't.

I didn't listen to my intuition.
I pushed through.
I abandoned myself in service to others.

When I re-read that voice note, it's so clear that I'm in the process of figuring out how to trust my intuition. I even explain the journey I've been on to listen to my gut as I'm trying to uncomfortably do it. What is clear is that I don't feel good.

I also want to focus on the word "just"—which I used four times in less than 60 seconds.

We use that word to soften hard messages, to make solid statements sound more malleable.

According to the Oxford Language dictionary, *just*—as an adverb— means "barely."

But I want to believe that where that word was screaming to break free from in my core was rooted in a much more powerfully defining expression of the word—as an adjective: *based on or behaving according to what is morally right and fair; deserved or appropriate in the circumstances; well-founded; justifiable.*

It was an omen.

No less than a minute from the time I sent that voice note, the woman I sent it to called me. I like to call this tactic "flooding."

When a person floods you—especially in response to your effort to set a boundary, to call out an issue, or to remove yourself from a situation—it is meant to erode the path you've carved out; it's meant to dim and extinguish your exit sign.

When a person floods you, they:

Do not listen to what you're saying
Do not care to understand where you're coming from
Do not respect your feelings

When they see their power—and an opportunity to be the center of attention—slipping away, they throw everything they have at their target.

It is the blueprint of the mean girl playbook.

Damn. I'm 42. Have I not learned?

As one of the four organizers and producers of the "White Women: Answer the Call" virtual event that broke Zoom, we raised $11 million for the Harris Victory Fund in two hours.

We broke all of 13-year-old global virtual conferencing company Zoom's previous records. In 48 hours, 200,000 people registered for our call (more than had ever registered for a Zoom call) and 167,000 joined us live (more than had ever joined a Zoom call live). We broke the Zoom platform during our call. Three times. We were featured on every major news network and online outlet, including The Daily Show, MSNBC, The Reid

Out, Time Magazine, The Cut, The Guardian, The 19th, Politico, Tech.co, Yahoo News, TheGrio, The Hill, and more, as well as featured on the "Kamala Harris 2024 presidential campaign" Wikipedia page.

Our call included iconic women such as P!nk, Connie Britton, Glennon Doyle, Abby Wambach, Megan Rapinoe, Sue Bird, and Senator Kirsten Gillibrand.

So, while that all looks impressive on paper—and while I'm deeply proud of the work I did to support the woman who should have become our president during that week—what I'm most proud of is the cycle I'm breaking free from that reared its ugly head yet again: the mean girl trap.

I've replayed that seven-day stretch over in my head a few times since it happened—from the planning call to the virtual event to the intermittent and post-call drama. I've pinpointed each of the moments where I should have walked away. And what each of those moments have in common is not the thought I was *thinking*, but the feeling I was *feeling*.

When I got off that first call, I felt uneasy.

When I was pressured—against my instinct—to lead the effort, I felt flooded.

When my ideas were shut down time and again, I felt dismissed.

When my work, experience, and expertise were invalidated, I felt degraded.

None of those moments happened because I'm weak. They happened because of my strengths. Mean girls are threatened by the talent, intelligence, ideas, and influence of other women.

They identify and isolate your power with purpose and intent—luring you into a cyclical trap of highs and lows, ups and down, praise and persecution that leave you feeling untethered, questioning your worth, value, and skills.

Here's how I describe their step-by-step plan. It's what I like to call the "6-D Strategy":

- Dote
- Destabilize
- Dismiss

- Degrade
- Deplore
- Distance

Repeat. Repeat. Repeat.

These tactics need not be chronological or have a specific beginning and end. It's a special cycle of bespoke hell, choreographed by the perpetrator and perfected to their liking over time, with experience and where they have succeeded in the fastest, quickest, deadliest kill.

Think about it.

Have you ever had another woman treat you this way? A boss? A co-worker? A friend? Family member?

Let's review a "hypothetical" example of a text from a mean girl and break it down using my 6-D Strategy theory:

> "Hey Erin - I noticed you unfollowed me on social media and then [redacted] and [redacted] sent me your recent posts, which are clearly about me. I'm not sure why you're upset since you haven't told me directly, but I'm more than happy to discuss. It seems like a more mature way forward than passive aggressive and vaguely threatening social media posts, but up to you. I'm incredibly grateful for all of your work on our call and hope the call you have this week is great, too."

If, say, a 50+ year old woman sent this to you, should you:

A. Respond with an explanation, an apology, and an offer to meet and learn all the ways that you, too, can be a person who sends texts like this as an adult
B. Tell her to go fuck herself
C. Block her number so all future texts she sends go into the ether where they belong

Friends, the answer is C. We're grown-ass women! Listen, option B is dope. I do love it. But the moment you engage with a mean girl, you've opened yourself up to further attack. You've put the ball back in her court. You've given her power that is yours to retain. And she doesn't deserve another moment of your time, another ounce of your energy, another square foot of space—rent free—in your head.

When you ignore mean girls and don't give their temper tantrums the time of day, they lose their goddamn minds. It's . . . epic. And sadly, you will have ample opportunities to test this theory.

Mean girls are everywhere, and they prey on powerful, successful, goal-oriented, ambitious empaths. Why? Because we are really good at what we do, we care a whole hell of a lot about what people think, and we're willing to sacrifice ourselves for the greater good.

Even with all of your experience and all of your growth, wolves in sheep's clothing can still pull the wool over your eyes. Beware of the 100-watts-shining set of canines they flash through smiling lips—they're determined to sink them into you.

Those feelings I felt the week surrounding our "White Women: Answer the Call" virtual event weren't in my head. They were in my body.

This is worth repeating, imprinting in your head and heart, and applying to your life. So, put your hand to your chest and say it out loud with me:

These feelings are not in my head.
They are in my body.
And they are not debatable.

People will tell you that what happened *didn't*, that you "misinterpreted" the situation, that you were too sensitive, or that you misremembered. Don't believe them. Don't fall for the trap. Don't be pulled away from your truth.

Trust yourself.

Should we go back to the Maya Angelou quote? *Of course we should.*

"I've learned that people will forget what you said, people will forget what you did, but people will never forget how you made them feel."

You know how *they* made *you* feel. And that's your most important compass.

Two weeks after the "White Women: Answer the Call" virtual event, I launched my own Harris Coalition: Hype Women for Harris. I did things my way. I surrounded myself with Hype Women. I brought in women I trusted who brought our vision to life: Jen Cho and Alexis Voss.

Mean girls were not invited into our orbit. And if they somehow snuck in, I immediately removed them. I launched hypewomenforharris.com and @hypewomenforharris on Instagram. We created daily content with resources, inspiration, information, and actionable ways to Hype Harris to become our first woman president.

We held four virtual events in the months that followed featuring iconic women such as Aisha Tyler, Arlan Hamilton, A'Shanti Gholar, Chani Nichols, Demi Moore, Jamie Lee Curtis, Representative Jasmine Crockett, Jenny Nguyen, LaTosha Brown, Molly Ringwald, Monica Padman, Retta, Sheryl Lee Ralph, Sophia Bush, Stacy London, Yvette Brown, and more.

We were recognized by Vice President Kamala Harris and Oprah Winfrey at Oprah's 2024 "Unite for America" global event, where I attended in person and stood with VP Harris and Oprah as they thanked us for our work in person.

I spent all 100 days of VP Harris's presidential campaign dedicated to getting her elected.

I gave it everything I had to give.

On November 6, 2024, I woke up to the news that VP Kamala Harris would not, in fact, become our 47th—and first woman—president.

$11 million goes nowhere fast when you have 31 million white women—53% of white women voters—working against you. The irony of the insidious mean girl trope permeating throughout the process of us "answering the call" is not lost on me.

As I shared with The 19th the morning after our call, just one week into VP Harris's presidential campaign:

> "We need to own the fact that white women have deeply fucked this up every fucking time. [My] name for this pattern: 'toxic white women.'

Very often, white women are the ones who get to be alone in a room full of men and, because of that, have the power to represent all women. They also get to join only women in spaces and, more often than not, have enormous power and influence over them.

The truth is that there are many places where white women hold more power than white men, and in the wrong hands, that can be so deeply dangerous."

I stand by my statements.

Power in the wrong white women's hands is the biggest threat to our democracy; to achieving gender equity; to deconditioning from a white supremacist, patriarchal society.

And it's time to stop allowing these women to hide in plain sight. We all have our horror stories to trauma bond over: from teasing on the playground to metastasized, confidence- and career-killing swat teams.

What were once biting taunts for *sport* have become gender cannibalism for *spite*.

Of course, mean girls exist in every shape, form, race, and ethnicity.

But I'm talking about the army of mean girls that elected Donald Trump twice: the intersection of the concentric circles comprising white women and Trump voters; 53% of white women, who exist inside of the most powerful voting block of our electorate (white women represent 37% of all votes cast in the 2024 election).

The white women who terrorize other women in the workplace are not a different species than the white women who voted for the Trump-and-Vance racist, misogynist agenda. They're also leading organizations claiming to support women and nonprofits fighting for social justice. They are being awarded and rewarded for being "a woman for all women," when in fact, it's a front. The wolf dressing up as the grandmother in Little Red Riding Hood got her closer to her prey, right?

So, what do we do?

How do we stop them?

And where can we commit to keep these energy vampires from draining our life force?

It's simple.
We must *shift our spend.*

Stop spending *time* with mean girls.
Stop spending *energy* on mean girls.
Stop spending *money* with—and on—mean girls.

The moment you take your power back from them, *they* are left with nothing.

So, identify the mean girls in your orbit.
Categorize your spend.
And commit to shifting it.

Shift your spend to the Hype Women who have your back; to the Black women who have continued to carry and save our democracy; to the public and private sector leaders who act with conviction; to the government officials dedicated to serving their constituents and communities; to the family and friends who fuel, rather than drain, you.

After spending 100 days working to get VP Kamala Harris elected president, I faced the reality that all of our work, time, and effort did not materialize.

This time, I didn't run to fix it. I sat with my feelings of grief. And I didn't put a deadline on them.

We've all been told "The only way out is through."

But that's society's way of telling women: "What just happened was terrible. Blah, blah, blah. Get back in the game."

Buck up, Buttercup.
Brush yourself off.
Get back on the horse.
Pull yourself up by your bootstraps.
There's no crying in baseball.

These are white-washed inspirational poster versions of "hurry up and get over it."

Through will get you places.
Through will move you from where you are.
Through is the opposite of stillness.

But when we focus on what we need to *move from* in order to exist, we're missing the point. Escaping the truth about who—and where—you are is a winding maze with no known exit.

The boomerang of that lesson will come back to knock you on your ass, time and time again, until you stop throwing it away. Trust me, I've tried. You will always land where your feet *are*, never where you want to believe—or pretend—they *could* be.

Here's the truth that is stunningly simple—and terrifyingly complicated:

The only way out is *in*.

I've been in therapy since I was 16 years old. And that lesson only finally sunk in at age 42. For more than half of my life, I've been committed to working through—and past—my pain, my trauma, my hurt, my anger.

I wanted to get *away* from it, to outrun it, to leave it behind. I had fantasies of being on "the other side" of it all, free and light.

But life continues. And without hard work, it will keep happening *to* you. Just when you think you have something figured out—that you're over the thing you've carried with you for days, weeks, months, years, decades—something *else* happens to disrupt and dysregulate all of your progress.

Fuck.

Is this really how it is? Today and tomorrow and the next day, forever and ever, until the end?

Yes.

And no.

The same—or similar—situations will reoccur, regardless of how much you try to control every aspect of your life.

But how *you* exist in response to those situations? Now, that's where the rubber meets the road to growth.

🐾 🐾 🐾

It took me until November 2024 to finally accept that I couldn't out-run myself.

A major astrological event—the lunar eclipse in Taurus—occurred on November 19, 2024. As a cardinal sign (shout out to my Aries sisters!), I was told that this date would hold particular significance for me and my "axis of power."

Where the eclipse fell on the 19th was closely tied to a key area in astrology that has been the focus of major karmic lessons and transformations over the past 16 years.

It brought into focus for me a deep karmic lesson: it's not just about what happens *to* you out in *the* universe. It's about what happens *for* you in *your* universe.

Yes, the macro is important to consider, to contribute to, and to acknowledge your role within. But the micro—oh, how the micro gets forgotten when we're out there trying to change the world. It was time for me to shift from taking on everything happening *out there* to taking in what was happening *in here*: my body, my family, my home, my community.

The eclipse on November 19 forced me to face myself in a new and different way. Not the self that I present to the world or use to serve others or seek external validation. But the self that only I can see and hear and feel deep inside of me.

We—the **cardinal signs** (Aries, Cancer, Libra, and Capricorn)—are the initiators of the zodiac, driven by action, leadership, and new beginnings. We are all about moving, making, doing—out in the world, out in the chaos, out in front.

But, my body was asking me a question: to what end?

How much more for everyone else?
How much less for me?
How much is enough?

Eclipses often trigger major changes for cardinal signs, including releasing old karmic patterns related to security, attachment, and transformation and the emotional, financial, or relational baggage accumulated over the last 16 years.

I was coming to another crossroad, prompted to rethink what I value in my personal and professional life, pushed to let go of outdated notions and habits that no longer serve me, and petitioned to recognize and release the karmic debts I've carried.

In November 2024, I stopped running.

And the *not doing* has been one of the most difficult things I've ever done. When your nervous system is built in fight or flight, it only knows how to operate in chaos. Calm is a state where I've never stayed. But I'm here now. And you can go there too.

We've been told our whole lives that "the only way out is through."

But it's not true.

The only way out is *in*.

Five Shifts to Going In

1. **Sit in stillness.** Movement distracts you from truly hearing and feeling all the signs your body is sending you. Take a moment to be where your feet are.

2. **Trust your gut.** When you feel something in your body—whether it's in reaction to a person, place, or your programming—investigate it. Your first instinct is always worth exploring.

3. **Clarify intentions.** If someone's actions hurt you, tell them. Share how it made you feel and ask if that's the outcome they intended. Good intentions mean nothing if they cause harmful impact.

4. **Examine your operating system.** When you are met with conflict, what is your first instinct? If it's to move through, to solve, to fix, take a moment to focus on what you're *feeling* before you even think or act.

5. **Shift your spend.** Not every event in *the* world or *your* world requires a response from you. Not every woman deserves your time, energy and money. Be selective and intentional about who, what, and where you invest.

PART

III

I Will Be

The Monarch

9 | Karmic Crusader

When I tell you that I listened to Taylor Swift's "Karma" 766 times in 2024 (making me one of the top .001% of listeners of "Karma" on Spotify), it's not hyperbole. It's straight from Spotify's "Wrapped"—an annual campaign that provides users with a personalized summary of their music, podcast, and audiobook listening habits for the year. To me, that data is more accurate than classified government documents left in the loo.

That song has transported me. But it's not for the reasons you may think. Sure, I love a good karmic retribution for a mean girl who has fucked with Hype Women. But karma is about more than someone getting what they deserve, from a place of revenge.

According to WebMD, Hinduism identifies *karma* as "the relationship between a person's mental or physical action and the consequences following that action. It also signifies the consequences of all the actions of a person in their current and previous lives, as well as the chain of cause and effect in morality."

When you are constantly giving, you feel depleted.
When you are constantly sharing, you feel exhausted.
When you are constantly producing, you feel empty.

That is, until you withdraw.

❁ ❁ ❁

As I shared in my "The Only Way Out Is In" chapter, a major astrological event—the lunar eclipse in Taurus—occurred on November 19, 2024.

Where the eclipse fell on the 19th was closely tied to a key area in astrology that has been the focus of major karmic lessons and transformations over the past 16 years. Sixteen years before 2024 lands us in 2008. In 2008, I was 26 years old.

When I was 26, I was at one of the lowest points in my entire life. I had never felt more alone. I had never felt less in control of what was happening around me. I had never felt less power and autonomy in my job, my home, my body, my life. I look back on that time—on that young woman, that version of myself—with profound grief.

She wasn't a "shell" of herself. She was a hollowed-out, walking zombie; a prisoner in mind, body, and spirit.

No one really knew. No one cared enough to ask. No one saw what was happening as something—or someone—they wanted to touch with a 10-foot pole.

And no one came to save me.

To stay alive, I had to save myself.

When I look at my life between the ages of 26 and 42, it feels like I've lived 100 lives. I have disappeared and found myself over and over and over again.

Over the past 16 years, I've been in a viscous cycle of mean girls trying to destroy me and a voracious cyclone of Hype Women determined to save me.

Hype Women are an act of resistance.
Hype Women are an expression of self-love.
Hype Women are karmic crusaders.

Hype Women have saved my life. And I know Hype Women have saved yours, too.

And while, for me, this message around "Hype Women" started a rallying cry to wake women up to who they truly are, it has become something so much more.

The concept of "Hype Women" is a noun *and* a verb.

Yes, it's an identity, a philosophy, a belief system, a sisterhood.

And it is an action, a job to be done, a directive, a direction.

Sometimes, you can't see the women hyping you because you don't believe the person they're hyping even exists.

When someone tells you a beautiful truth about yourself but *you* don't believe it, you think it's a lie.

When someone tells you an ugly lie about yourself and *you* believe it, you think it's the truth.

It's August 23, 2022. I have an email in my inbox from a woman named Victoria Savanh.

The subject line reads: *Publishing at Wiley*.

> Hi Erin,
>
> I'm an acquisitions editor on the trade (commercial) team at Wiley and am reaching out about a potential book opportunity. I came across your profile on LinkedIn and love the work you're doing. Do you or a team member have time next week to get on a call and explore possibilities? Thanks!
>
> Warmly,
>
> Victoria
>
> **Victoria Savanh**
>
> Acquisitions Editor, Trade Business

I re-read it with a confused, furrowed brow. She must be mistaken.

Wrong person. Wrong email. Wrong idea.

I don't believe her. So, I don't respond.

Ever.

It's October 9, 2023. I have an email in my inbox from a woman named Victoria Savanh.

The subject line reads: *Publishing at Wiley.*

Hi Erin,

I'm an editor on the trade business team at Wiley and have been following your work. I'm always looking for exciting new voices to publish and love your content—I'm especially keen on elevating women in the leadership book space. Do you have time for a call in the next couple weeks? I'd like to hear more about your work and see if there might be an opportunity here.

I've cc'd my assistant Trinity here who can find 30 mins for us to chat if you're interested. Thanks so much.

Warmly,

Victoria

Victoria Savanh

Acquisitions Editor, Trade Business

I re-read it with a curious, slightly raised brow. She must be certain.
Right person. Right email. Right idea?
I start to believe her. So, I respond.

It's October 25, 2023. I meet with Victoria and Trinity Compton for the first time. I love them. They are Hype Women, through and through. We talk and share and dream.

I'm inspired. But I'm still not ready. I'm still cocooned. I'm still dissolving. I have no solid ground to stand on because too much of my matter remains stuck in my past. Not enough of me is here, in this moment, to be able to move forward.

On November 14, 2023, I tell Victoria that I will be in touch soon. I do not, in fact, get back in touch.

On January 4, 2024, Victoria reaches out. I don't respond.

On March 4, 2024, Victoria reaches out. I respond. A month later.

As I write and re-read this, I look like a real asshole here.

What is wrong with me?
Why am I being rude?
Why am I being so unresponsive?

Oh, it's just not that simple, friends. It's not a 1 + 2 = 3 kind of equation. This is a 42-years-of-life, divided by past-present-and-future-selves, multiplied by false-narratives-and-conditioning-and-so-much-pain complicated problem. I am being asked to develop a new Pythagorean theorem when I had only been taught to—and told I could—count to three.

My method of measurement for my self-worth was so distorted and dysfunctional that I had to teach myself how to fly when I was still feeling insecure about the way I crawled.

I was so used to chasing and being just out of reach from what I wanted and deserved that this experience with Victoria where she showed up for me, where she didn't run from—but ran toward—me was deeply disarming. Instead of it making me feel unconditionally seen, it made me feel uncomfortably stalled.

I didn't know how to exist or move forward inside of this new way of working. My bosses, my mentors, and my leaders had always told me what was wrong with me first (and most).

That was how people who cared about you spoke to you, wasn't it?
They criticized you.
They critiqued you.
They edited you.

This was different. This was weird. This was wrong.

I don't reach out to Victoria again until May 21, 2024. After working with my book doula Rea Frey for months, I finally have a book proposal that I'm ready to pitch to potential agents.

As a courtesy, a sign of respect, a karmic contribution to the innumerable deposits she had already made, I share my proposal with Victoria before I've even secured an agent.

I don't hear back from Victoria for two weeks.

Well, I've done it.
I pissed her off one too many times.

I looked like I was playing hard to get—when really I didn't even see myself as worthy of being considered. I never even responded to her first email! What did I expect?

This is what I deserve.

And then, on June 5, I have an email in my inbox from Victoria.

The subject reads: *Lots of excitement here!*

> Hi Erin! My team is super excited about the possibility of working with you. I'll have more good news for you later today. In the meantime, we'd love to set up a meeting to introduce you to more members on the team including our associate publisher.
>
> Victoria

Five hours and 11 minutes later, I have an offer from Wiley to publish my book.

Twenty-two hours and 42 minutes after I receive my offer, their entire team—including Wiley's Associate Publisher Jeanenne Ray—has gathered on a Zoom to show me how much they want me.

They want my proposal, *exactly* as it is.
They want my book as their *lead* title for fall 2025.
They want *me*.

My first thought when the call ends is: *is Wiley a good publisher?*

There must be some catch here. Do they just take *anyone*? Why don't they want me to change my proposal? Why don't they want to change *me*?

Their undivided attention should be intoxicating. But it's unsettling.

Damn, conditioning runs deep. The voices of a thousand naysayers rise up when just one believer says something good. It's hard to hear how great you are through the callous cacophony of reasons you are unworthy.

On June 5, 2024, I received an offer from Wiley before I even had an agent. So, instead of negotiating and moving forward with their final and best offer in early June 2024—and recognizing the karmic deposits that Victoria began making almost two years before—I spend the next three months pitching, chasing, meeting with, and getting rejected by dozens of agents, editors, and publishing houses.

They don't want me.
They don't want my book.
They don't want this version of me.
They don't want this version of my book.

Now, *this* I could roll with. This felt normal. This felt familiar. This felt . . . good?

Struggle. Rejection. Criticism.

These were people who really cared. They must be good if they don't want me. Should I change to be what they want? Should I write a different book than the one I believe is right?

And then something in me shifted.

My nervous system didn't want the dysregulation; my body was not drawn toward the rejection; my spirit didn't crave the chaos.

What if I started to want what wanted me?

It's 8:14 p.m. CT on Saturday, February 1, 2025. I'm sitting on the couch in my studio, bent over my computer about to click Send. I tap the rose gold track pad of my MacBook Air as the white gloved hand on my screen hovers over the blue "send" bubble. I draw in a deep breath. And as I exhale, I click it.

I've submitted my manuscript for the first book I will ever write to my team at Wiley. I have spent months, years, decades, centuries laboring over this body of work.

The following morning, my developmental editor Julie Kerr writes back: "Congratulations! I hope you did some celebrating over the weekend. This is a big accomplishment!" She tells me that she will have her full feedback to me by February 18.

Holy hell. In less than three weeks, I will know if I'm good or not. I will know if I'm a worthy writer. I will know if Wiley made a mistake.

Three weeks felt like years. The waiting was hard. The scenario planning in my head was harder.

Here's what I told myself: *Okay, worst-case scenario is Julie comes back and says, "Hey Erin. So . . . you're great. Truly. Lots of fun. I don't quite know what this is, though. Yes, it is a lot of words. But this is not what we were expecting. Nor is it what we want. So, we need to regroup over here and think about whether you are, in fact, ready to write a book. Be in touch soon."*

Yep, that sounds right. I can see that happening. Therefore, I better get myself prepared for this total takedown to occur on the 18th.

On February 17 at 2:51 p.m., I have an email in my inbox from Julie.

My first thought: *Fuck. She's a day early. She didn't want to wait to deliver the blow.*

My body floods with cortisol. I decide not to read the email until after I pick up my kids from school. I can't read what will surely be the destruction of my path to authorship and then go to elementary school pickup. I need to wait until we're back home, the kids are set up with snacks and iPads (*I stand by my choice*), and I can go into my room upstairs with the door closed and receive my death sentence.

At 4:01, I open the email.

I've included an excerpt from her full message here:

Hi Erin,

I've completed reading your manuscript, and you've got a great book on your hands! It's provocative in the best ways.

I don't have much in the way of overarching feedback for anything I'd recommend reworking. The thought you've put into how you've organized the book comes through very well and is a success. The stories and details of your life and experiences and how you present them is quite effective. You have a unique rhythm to the way you write and present material—in all the best ways. And I really like the "shifts" that appear at the end of each chapter.

My body exhales. My jaw and fists unclench. My shoulders drop.

My first thought is: *Ohthankgawd. I really dodged a bullet there. Maybe I am an author. Julie likes my book. They want me to keep going.*

And then my next thought is: *is Julie a good editor?*

There must be some catch here. Does she just take *anyone's* manuscript? Why doesn't she want me to change my book? Why doesn't she want *me* to change?

Her undivided attention should be intoxicating. But it's unsettling.

It is the first time in my professional career that a woman with power and influence over my direction, future, and potential success reviewed my work and told me it was good; no, *great*.

It took me 17 hours to respond to Julie. Because I didn't believe her at first.

And then I had a real, long hard talk with myself.

Erin, how much longer are you going to let the ugly lies you've been told about yourself by mean girls eclipse the beautiful truths Hype Women continue to recognize in you? It's time to put down the baggage. It's no longer yours to carry.

My response to Julie was a love letter to my younger self who deserved to have Victorias and Trinitys and Jeanennes and Julies in her life *long before* she turned 42.

Julie,

    This is one of the most important—and beautiful—emails of my life. I poured my heart and soul into writing this book. And you have received, honored, and celebrated me with compassion.

What if all the karmic contributions, lessons, transformations, and deposits I have made in my life had finally vested? What if now was my time to receive; to reap the harvest; to make withdrawals? What if now is your time, too?

I think of a quote by Carl Bard that I have written out and taped to bathroom mirrors, refrigerators, and computer screens dozens of times: "No one can go back and make a brand-new start. But anyone can start from now and make a brand-new ending."

The idea of beginning again gives me so much hope; the idea that nothing must mean everything.

I am not the same person I was at 26 years old. I am not the woman my husband married. I am not the daughter my mother sent off to college. I am not the mother who birthed my first baby into the world. I am not the entrepreneur with no years under my belt.

I'm different. Because I keep living. I keep failing. I keep going. I keep growing. I hope that I keep wanting everything to mean something, for as long as I want it to. And when that something loses its meaning, I will set it free—and in turn, myself.

Five Shifts to Karmic Transformation

1. **Release the scarcity mindset.** Karma shouldn't feel forced or like a scoreboard. It should feel natural, like flow. If you are afraid to make karmic contributions to other Hype Women because you think there will be less in the world for you, you are missing the point entirely.

2. **Adopt an aura of abundance.** Good karma breeds good karma, forever and ever and ever. You will *always* be rewarded for the karmic contributions you make in the world. It may not be immediate—or blatantly obvious. But it's coming. It's there.

3. **Put down what is no longer yours to carry.** Old patterns do not lead to new discovery. It's the definition of insanity. Going into the same place with the same people using the same programming will land you right back to where you don't want to be.

4. **Don't trust the ugly lie.** When someone tells you—or another person—an ugly lie about who you are, release it, and them, as quickly as you can.

5. **Believe the beautiful truth.** When someone tells you—or another person—a beautiful truth about who you are, receive it, and them, as quickly as you can.

10 | Take Back Your Body

The only person you will spend the rest of your life with—every waking hour and sleeping state, forever and ever until the end—is *you*. Whether you like it or not.

It's not debatable. It's undeniable. It's irrefutable.

You are in your body from the moment you break through into the world until the day you leave this earth. Your body carries you through it all; your forever partner in building a life and legacy that extends far beyond the bounds of your beating heart, sturdy bones, and sentient skin.

And while that all sounds poetic and magical and powerful, let's be real. It's not always sunshine and roses.

Here's the truth: I've been at war with my body for decades.

I've hated it and loved it.

I've been ashamed by—and proud of—it.

I've been told it was fat and ugly, and I've been admired for it being thin and beautiful.

Every woman has.

Growing up in a chaotic environment, I mastered the art of disassociating from my body often—escaping the physical space where I existed through the power of my mind. It was a survival skill that kept me from being permanently destroyed by the demons set on stealing my spirit.

But I've learned the hard way that you can never *fully* leave your body. Wherever you go, there you are.

There is no way to escape.
There is no singular solve to fix what you think is broken.
There is no magic pill that makes your self-loathing easier to swallow.

That is, until you choke.

I started a new tradition for myself in 2023. It wasn't planned. I didn't set out to create it with precise intention. It started out as a moment that I kindled and stoked into a Movement.

The Hype Women post I wrote on January 11, 2023, identified a "vibe" that I wanted women to understand, acknowledge, and embody: "Unabashed Hype Women." (You read the backstory of the Hype Women Movement in Chapter 6.)

A "vibe" is different from a "word for the year because it's actionable. It's a rallying cry; it's a mantra that sets the tone for what—and whom—you want to hold close or free yourself from.

The beginning of a new year often feels like relief to me: an exhale after a marathon, a fresh start, another chance to do it differently.

For years, I've been creating vision boards during the month of December to set myself up for the following year. A vision board brings together a few of my favorite joys in life: collages, art projects, magazines, design, creativity, strategy, messaging, visual storytelling, inspiration, aspiration.

I've evolved these vision boards over time to make them even more effective. Obviously. Because God forbid I create something just for the sake of enjoyment. Why stop there? Turn that fun into pro.duc.tiv.i.ty. (I know. Deep sigh.)

I choose a word for the year to help guide me in my decisions and mindset, work toward goals that I want to achieve personally and professionally, identify changes I want to make to my actions and commitments, and determine what—and whom—I want to prioritize.

So, after coming up with a "vibe" for 2023—albeit a few days into that new year—I took this idea with me into 2024.

My Vibe for 2024: Take Back Your Body

When I decided on this vibe, my two goals were twofold: lose weight and stop hating my body. You know, really easy tasks on a to-do list that I had *never* tried to tackle before. (Please read that sentence as it was written: dripping with—no, drowning in—sarcasm.)

Here's what I didn't know I'd be facing when I committed to this vibe:

A healthcare system that hates women

A doctor who made me feel seen and heard for the first time in my medical life

The uncharted territory of my own perimenopausal physiology

My relationship with alcohol

A rekindling of my love of fashion

A new philosophy around exercise and moving my body

Why I couldn't sleep

But first, back to January 1, 2024.

Here was my creative brief:

It's no surprise that so many women have complicated—and often negative—relationships with our bodies. We are surrounded by marketing, advertising, and messaging that celebrate certain bodies and shame others; we are sold solutions that will make us look younger, thinner, smaller, and taller; we are taught to consider and believe everyone else's opinion of our bodies over our own.

So, after a lifetime of judging and criticizing my body, I am ready to take her back. I'm ready to love her, to be kind to her, to trust her, to listen to what she needs, to make her a priority, to know her worth, to value her wisdom, to be fully *in* her.

Does this resonate with you?

Do you hear yourself in these words?

Have you—like me—tried this before, only to get knocked back down off the proverbial horse time and time again?

I know so many women who desperately want to end the cycle of self-loathing. But here's what the world doesn't want us to know: we can't do it in silos, alone and ashamed of all we have to overcome to understand what lies beneath.

We live in a time and a place where governments have removed our bodily autonomy; where our bodies are villainized and violated, the constant target of voyeurism; where in the same breath we're sexualized and shamed for existing.

And we do it all while traveling the treacherous—and sometimes deadly—journey from menstruation to menopause (for all) and through motherhood (for some).

Our self-loathing and lack of support sustains multiple industries worth trillions every year.

Christina Gough of Statista writes, "The global wellness industry was estimated to be worth $6.3 trillion in 2023." This includes sectors such as personal care, beauty, healthy eating, nutrition, physical activity, sports, wellness tourism and spa, and traditional medicine.

The industry is expected to continue growing, reaching $9 trillion by 2028.

According to 2025 Statista Market Insights, "The global beauty market is expected to reach $673.7 billion to $758 billion in 2025. The market is expected to grow at a rate of 3.35–4.6% from 2025 to 2029."

"The global medical aesthetics market size was valued at USD 82.99 billion in 2024 and is projected to reach from USD 91.58 billion in 2025 to USD 213.19 billion by 2033, growing at a CAGR of 9.7% during the forecast period (2025–2033)" (Straits Research, 2024).

The cycle of analyzing, abhorring, and acquiescing is relentless.

When I think back on my tumultuous relationship with my body, it is with great relief that I can finally acknowledge how much of it is not my fault.

Maybe, like me, you've also spent a lifetime disconnecting from your body as a means of survival and escaping from real and perceived threats in moments where trauma occurred and in the revisiting of those moments in your mind in perpetuity.

My nervous system is shot. And I'm so damn tired.

So, in 2024, I decided that I didn't want to spend the next 42 years trapped in this vicious vortex of self-destruction. Here's how I did it—and how you can do it, too.

Find the Right Healthcare for You

The American healthcare system hates women.

Yes, I said it. And this isn't *just* the ranting of a 42-year-old woman powering through a perimenopausal mood swing. It's a fact-based, ethnographic thesis with more proof points than the page can hold.

Here's what we know.

—

ACCORDING TO *Medidata*

For much of medical history, women were largely excluded from clinical trials, especially in the United States and Europe. This exclusion was rooted in several factors:

- **Belief in gender differences:** Researchers thought women's hormonal cycles, pregnancy, and potential for childbirth would complicate studies.
- **Medical misogyny:** Societal attitudes toward women often led to their treatment as less reliable or capable subjects for scientific inquiry.
- **Legal and ethical concerns:** In the early 20th century, concerns about the safety of including women, particularly in relation to reproductive health, led to exclusion, especially in drug trials.

While there were some early efforts to include women in medical research in the 20th century, systemic exclusion was the norm until the 1980s. Major policy changes in the 1990s and beyond, particularly the National Institute of Health mandate, helped set the stage for more equitable and comprehensive inclusion of women in clinical research, though challenges in achieving true gender parity and understanding sex differences in health still remain in certain areas.

What in the actual fuck?

It took protests and legal battles and feminist movements to convince medical professionals that women's bodies are different from men's? We spent decades pumping medicine into women's bodies with no research to support what that medicine was going to do to them? Women—who create life—were *not* seen as the people to prioritize in medical and scientific studies?

Why has it always been so difficult for the world to give a shit about women's bodies?

As women, on a macro-evolutionary level, we need a combination of generalists and specialists to help us navigate the biological and physiological changes that result simply from living. And then, microbiologically, we must understand how our individual bodies show up in response to our own experiences, environments, and existence.

I've had doctors tell me that my symptoms were in my head.
I've had doctors tell me that I just needed to "live with" the distress
    I was experiencing.
I've had doctors tell me that I didn't know my body as well as they did.

Some were men. Many were women. After all, medical misogyny is more powerful than the gender of the person dishing out the diagnosis.

That is until Dr. Erin came into my life.

I reach for the silver metal handle and open the glass door with ease.

"WomanCare" is stenciled onto the door in a beautiful serif font—possibly Garamond, Baskerville, or a modern Didot-style.

The waiting room is filled with women of all ages. The walls are painted a calming shade of creamy white. The art on the walls is peaceful, inviting. I feel like I've walked into a day spa, not a medical facility.

I have finally found a practice in the town where I live whose entire focus is women. It's an all-women team of doctors, an all-women staff, and an all-women squad of specialists equipped to help any—and every—woman.

I share my struggles with Dr. Erin:

- I've carried around 40 pounds that I *cannot* shake—regardless of diet and exercise—for the past two years.
- I believe I am perimenopausal.
- I am struggling to navigate my symptoms: hot flashes, night sweats, mood swings, insomnia, exhaustion.
- I don't recognize my body—and I hate it.

Dr. Erin listens to me like a friend who cares and wants to help. She acknowledges that everything I am experiencing is true. She shares that I am not alone—and that this is the struggle of so many of her patients. She doesn't respond by telling me that what I'm doing is wrong nor does she bark orders of what she thinks I need to do in order to make it right.

She asks me what I want—and then, she shows me my options for getting there.

I feel seen by a medical professional for the first time in my life. There is no shaming, no judgment, no accusatory questioning. Her philosophy is: *Yes, this is exactly where you are. Now, let's figure out how to get you where you want to be.*

I share that in the previous year, I had such an upsetting yearly checkup with a female doctor who dismissed me that I took a break from the traditional medical profession.

As a die-hard advocate for women-founded and owned companies, I've proudly proclaimed my status as a femtech torchbearer online and in real life. Entrepreneur and author Ida Tin coined the term "femtech" in 2016, which describes all tech and innovation that aims to tackle health issues that only, or disproportionately, impact women" (Hannah Ward-Glenton, 2023).

So, I explored other options.

I signed up for Elektra Health—an evidence-based menopause education, care, and community for the 21st-century woman, founded by my friend Alessandra Henderson.

I signed up for Winona—a women's wellness center and telehealth company that aims to empower, educate, and treat women throughout the entirety of their menopause journey, founded by Dr. Nancy Belcher, PhD.

Through Elektra, I met with a perimenopause specialist virtually. She took the time to educate, validate, and understand me. She recommended that I explore hormone replacement therapy (HRT). And she shared some over-the-counter vitamin supplements to help with my symptoms: B6 for hot flashes and night sweats, magnesium for insomnia, and D3 for strengthening bones and muscles and increasing energy.

Through Winona, I entered all of my symptoms into my profile on the portal and was matched with a doctor who specialized in managing women like me and prescribed an HRT regimen of DHEA, progesterone, and estrogen. Ladies, the patient login page of the Winona app greets you with "Hello, beautiful."

I was on my way out of my own personal hell.

When I met with Dr. Erin, I was six months into my HRT treatment. My symptoms were *just* starting to shift. Dr. Erin reviewed my medication and thought it was spot-on for addressing my hormones. For the weight issues, she felt I was a prime candidate for a medical weight-loss drug.

Let's talk about the first feelings that came up for me when I considered using a weight loss drug:

- I'd be cheating and not losing weight the "real" way.
- I was a failure.
- I was embarrassed that I needed that level of intervention to lose weight.

Guess what?

Every single one of those thoughts is bullshit. They are lies sold to women to shame us, keep us silent in our struggles, and stir up the system's conditioning of us to believe we are less than—and we are alone.

But my desperation for a difference in my current state outweighed any of the negative thoughts that threatened to impede my progress.

So, I started on the injectable weight-loss drug the following week.

Over the next three months, I lost 45 pounds.

For me, it was a bumpy road. There were setbacks and plateaus along the way. My nausea was unmanageable without daily anti-nausea medication.

I fainted twice upon standing (from a lack of calories and low blood pressure): once while alone in a hotel room and the second time in front of my six-year-old on the floor of my bedroom.

It scared me.

But the alternative terrified me more. I could *not* remain trapped in my current state.

So, I stayed the course.

After three months on the weight-loss drug, I weaned off of it with Dr. Erin's oversight. In the three months that followed, off of the weight-loss drug, I lost an additional 10 pounds. And I've been able to maintain my weight in a body that feels like me again. The difference between carrying around an extra 55 pounds and setting it down permanently has changed my life.

I feel freer; unencumbered. I have more energy. I breathe easier.

This was my foundation for a new way forward. But what happened next was going to require a more-than-skin-deep exploration and excavation.

Explore Your Daily Mindless Actions and Habits

My relationship with food, exercise, and alcohol has been a tumultuous one since I started college at the University of Michigan in August 2000.

Before that, I was a multisport athlete with a great metabolism who could count the number of alcoholic beverages I consumed before age 18 on two hands.

My weight had never been an issue. I ate what I wanted and burned it off on the soccer field, basketball court, pavement, and pool.

"Exercise" wasn't something I forced myself to do. It was my way of life.

But as a freshman in college, it was the first time since the age of six that I wasn't on a team playing sports daily. My body took a major hit. The "Freshman 15" was more like 25 in my case. Lack of exercise was only one piece of the equation. Staying up later and drinking beer and liquor led to fourth and fifth meals past midnight.

I felt like shit. I looked like shit. I treated my body like shit.

Since college, I've lost and gained 40 pounds multiple times over. Through both pregnancies with my two boys, that number edged closer to 60 or 70 pounds. The expansion and contraction of the space that has defined my body rears me unrecognizable in some photos.

And the alcohol. Oh, the alcohol.

I was drinking so much—and so often—in college that I took a month off from drinking to "ensure" I didn't have a drinking problem.

Since I was able to do it, I felt confident that I had dodged the alcoholic bullet that hit and destroyed so many members of my family (on both sides of my parents) going back generation after generation—and I ordered a drink to celebrate!

But it took me until age 42 (more than 20 years later) to understand that when assessing my drinking, I was using the wrong method of measurement.

The alcoholics in my family drank every day. And they hid it. So, I always defined alcoholism as an inability to go a day without drinking; drinking too early in—and for too long over the course of—a day, or hiding that you're drinking from others.

When society, media, and movies show us alcohol dependence, they feature people who start drinking at 8 a.m.; who chug vodka from the shitty plastic gut-rot bottle hiding behind cleaning supplies under the sink in their bathroom with the door locked; who destroy their lives, their careers, and their families in drunken stupors; who end up incapacitated in public and private settings.

When I think of alcoholics, I think about actress Meg Ryan in the movie *When A Man Loves a Woman*—and the scene where while taking a shower, wasted, she crashes through the glass shower door. Her nine-year-old daughter (played by actress Tina Majorino) finds her naked on the bathroom floor, laying on shattered glass, bloody and unconscious.

That was *never* me.
That could never *be* me.
That wasn't *my* story.

Or was it?

I continued to push the bounds on my definition of what it meant to be an alcoholic—putting pressure on the guard rails I had set up in my mind to keep me from falling over the edge.

My "special occasions"—where drinking earlier in the day was acceptable—began waxing and waning a glide path down a slippery slope. These occasions moved from being reserved solely for holidays to being acceptable on weekends, when eating out at restaurants, while traveling through an airport, or when having breakfast with a friend, because I deemed the day "special" and a morning mimosa felt right.

Drinking daily became a way to delineate between "work" and "not work." I don't know about you, but this turn took place for me during the 2020 pandemic, when we were all trapped at home—and the lines blurred between what was once clear: office for work, home for play. I now watched the clock for 5 p.m., ready to remove the cloak of heaviness from the weight of my job and replace it with a lighter, more fun and frivolous cape. I wanted to transform myself into a younger version, where I had fewer responsibilities and roles to my name.

I wasn't hiding *the act* of drinking from others. But I did begin to quietly conceal *how much* I was consuming—both at home and in public.

At home:

At home, I would refill my wine glass when my husband left the room.

I started using YETI insulated wine "glasses" to conceal my hefty pours. My alcoholic aunts and uncles poured their wine into coffee mugs. *Those* were people with *real* drinking problems. I was just using a cute, trendy vessel to keep my drink colder for longer. Geeze. What's the big deal?

When a glass of wine here and there over the course of the evening ended up draining the bottle, I tucked the evidence under flattened cardboard boxes and my kids' schoolwork in the recycling bin.

I didn't have a "problem."
I wasn't *hiding* my drinking.
I just didn't want my husband to bother me with his concerns. Those talks were so annoying and suffocating.
I was a grown-ass woman and could make decisions for myself. Damnit.

In public:

In public, I started showing up early to restaurants for dinners with friends to cozy up to the bar for a glass (or two) before they arrived. I told myself this was because I deserved a little "me" time. But we both know that's not true. I was strategically getting a few drinks in before anyone in my party could keep track of my booze count.

If drinking wasn't involved in a "date night" with my husband or a hangout with a friend, I deemed it less fun and sometimes even pointless.

When I ordered a drink at a restaurant, I planned my next one—and if there wasn't enough time to order a second drink, I was visibly irritated.

Seeing a movie with my kids at our favorite full-service theater always included two drinks. I mean, if they were going to serve it, why would I *not* order it?

That right there is what I've now realized was a critical shift in my relationship with alcohol. If alcohol was available, I didn't even consider the option of *not* consuming it. Its mere presence felt like an invitation that would be rude and ridiculous to decline.

It was *so* easy to slide into this gray area because everything in our culture supports—and even encourages—drinking. We are told that drinking is fun, celebratory, and deserved. And anyone who doesn't do it—or tells you that you shouldn't—is a buzz kill, literally and figuratively.

My whole life, I had viewed *dependence* on alcohol as the telltale of a person in trouble.

But what I really should have been examining was the way I *abused* alcohol—and aided and abetted in it abusing me. I didn't need to drink every day. But when I did drink, I needed to have more than one.

That's the truth of the issue I faced. It wasn't about daily dependence. It was about lack of control when given access.

One of the side effects of the weight-loss drug I took was that it completely killed my desire for alcohol. Some of that was due to the constant nausea I experienced. But it also targeted the area of my brain that told me I wanted a drink.

So, without the intention of setting out to search for my own version of sobriety, I ended up going full speed right to its core, to my core.

A year earlier, almost to the day, on August 8, 2023, I ordered a handful of books about society's relationship with alcohol. I had no intention of becoming sober. I was just curious about what was happening with this alcohol-free phenomenon that was popping up in my Instagram feed, friendship circles, social events, restaurants, and stores, and in the form of new businesses and brands.

I bought:

- *Sober Curious: The Blissful Sleep, Greater Focus and Deep Connection Awaiting Us All on the Other Side of Alcohol* by Ruby Warrington
- *We Are the Luckiest: The Surprising Magic of a Sober Life* by Laura McKowen
- *This Naked Mind* and *The Alcohol Experiment: The Essential Books to Explore Your Relationship with Alcohol* by Annie Grace

On Halloween, I bought *It's Not About the Wine: The Loaded Truth Behind Mommy Wine Culture* by Celeste Yvonne.

When I look back at those dates, I don't know exactly why I ordered those books in those exact moments. Like I said, I had no intention of quitting. I even drank wine *while* I read these books. I just had this somewhat salacious desire to be a spectator of the stories, written by—and about—women who stopped drinking. Who *were* these people?

My takeaway? Sobriety was for alcoholics—of which I was not one. I felt deep sympathy for the struggle so many of these women faced. But I couldn't feel empathy because I did not see any part of myself in their stories.

I read the books and shelved them back on my bookcase. "Well, that was interesting," I thought. Now, back to my life.

I wasn't ready for their messages.
I wasn't ready to connect to their stories.
I wasn't ready.

In December 2024, without setting out to abstain, I had gone more than two months without a drop of alcohol.

I had never felt better in my entire life.

Now, now, dear reader. Don't worry. I'm not oblivious to how obnoxious and grandiose this statement sounds. But I do want to make sure you know my intention behind it. I'm sharing my experience not to put pressure, serve up shame, or even indirectly inquire if you want to try this thing I'm trying. I'm sharing it because it's *my* truth.

Whenever sober people talked about their experience on the other side, it always felt a little too preachy, pretentious, and cult-like for me.

It wasn't because I didn't believe them or because I didn't want to also feel that way. It was because I didn't want to imagine my life without alcohol. So much "fun" was built around consumption of alcohol in my mind. And if I removed it, what would happen to me?

But when I really took the time to de-construct it, and to be honest about the details, it wasn't all my imagination had cracked it up to be.

My perpetually rosé-colored glasses were starting to crack under pressure.

Was I ready to do the work of removing the numbing escape that alcohol provided from a world that felt so heavy and a world that made me feel so many feelings?

Many times, I wanted to tell my husband that my drinking was consuming me, that I thought about doing it and not doing it more than I was proud to admit, that I needed to take a hard look at how it was impacting my body and my life, and that I was starting to exhibit behaviors that I would immediately deem "concerning" in others, but I was terrified to admit might be destructive in me.

But I knew the moment I said it out loud, it would become real. And I didn't want the accountability.

It is so hard to start something; to stand at the bottom of the mountain taking in all that lies before you to climb. The only way I was able to do this is because I did not do it alone or without support. My medical professional helped me to tackle *this* problem from a different angle, with a different tool and a different goal in mind. My friends supported me in navigating this new journey—and didn't make me feel like the outcast I was worried I would be. My husband acknowledged and celebrated me as I made a 180-degree reroute from my daily routine.

And while I expected that taking a break from drinking would lead to me being less lethargic, foggy, and irritable, here's what I had no idea I would experience:

Deep joy while sitting in my living room with my husband, Brian, my sons, Will and Charlie, and our dog, Lincoln.

Waking up to my body's alarm clock at 5 a.m. every day (was I becoming an insufferable "morning person"? FACK. Grosssssssss.).

Being transported by that first sip of my Americano every morning—when the luscious layer of froth is still intact and creamy.

The breathtaking beauty of fluffy white hydrangeas in a clear glass vase on our wooden dining table.

Watching the sun rise every day in awe that it was happening—and that I was lucky enough to witness it.

Full body chills when Chappell Roan sings "Casual" on full blast in my AirPods.

Intoxication from my favorite Moxy hotel candle: jasmine, crystal musk, and blonde wood (honestly, I feel like if I were a candle, *this* combo would be me).

The silky feel of ToykoMilk hand lotion in gin and rosewater . . . OMG the smell too. I just can't.

The melodic clanging of my heavy "Grit" and "Grace" gold bracelets from Parker Thatch.

The truly perfect broken-in Flying Monkey jeans in a wash and rise that I'm convinced the universe made for me after many decades of demoralizing and devastating jean-buying excursions.

The way Unhide's fuzzy blankets and pillows make me feel held, safe, and cared for.

Being truly present in every moment.

I'm not trying to sound preachy. Or nuts, for that matter. And as I re-read it, it actually kind of sounds like I'm high. And maybe I am. Not from weed or gummies, but—like—natural endorphins that I spent so many years unintentionally blocking.

I'm operating on a whole 'nother level. My five basic senses are firing on all cylinders. And I've unlocked senses I didn't know I possessed.

Some neuroscientists and philosophers debate that humans may have as many as 22 to 33 senses. And while it is believed that other species have senses that humans don't—such as directional and magnetic senses—I feel like I might be closing in on those too.

Before I turned 42, my nervous system was shot. And it felt like every one of my nerve endings lay exposed, at risk of short circuiting and shutting down my entire body at any given moment.

In taking a break from alcohol, I took the risk to feel all of my feelings—feelings I feared would destroy me if given full access to my body. Instead, I started to feel beautiful, powerful feelings that I had no memory of ever experiencing before.

When I made the decision to take back my body, I stopped escaping my life, my body, my grief, and my joy through alcohol. And I started sitting in all of those places and feelings fully.

Where you are in your expedition with—or without—alcohol is yours and yours alone. No two people experience it the same way. So, my choices at the moment will not be the right choices for every person.

But here's what I do know: I can now admit, say out loud, and put here in print that my relationship with alcohol will always be one where I need to be very present, intentional, and mindful. At the same time, I know myself. "All or nothing" and "forever" or "never" do not work for me. I hate feeling controlled by someone or something else. It makes me feel trapped, held hostage, and without the autonomy I need to breathe, unrestricted.

My natural instinct in those situations is to rebel—regardless of whether it's in my best interest.

Will I ever drink again? A month ago, I would have said "of course, absolutely, without question." Today, I say "I don't know. Maybe not." Tomorrow? It's still to come.

But what I can say with absolute certainty is that my body—without alcohol coursing through it—has made me feel the most grateful, clear, creative, physically healthy, mentally stable, emotionally connected, and spiritually expansive than I've ever felt in my life.

So, I'm going to hold on to that for as long as I possibly can.

Celebrate Your Wins Along the Way

With any goal, there is the place you start and the place you want to finish.

Sometimes, we never get to the end.
Sometimes, it takes longer to arrive than we had planned.
Sometimes, the destination changes along the way.

But one thing I've learned the hard way is that you don't have to wait until the end to celebrate that you *began.*

When I set out to lose 40 pounds in July 2024, it felt daunting. I had achieved this feat, time and time again, over the previous 20 years. But the older I get, the harder it's been to change my body.

Like any good rider of the weight roller coaster, my closet is filled with a range of all the sizes I've been, from 4 to 14.

There are:

Gowns that mimic mumus, flowy and forgiving
Spandex-infused, form-fitting dresses
Shifts that serve the in-between

When I was struggling with my weight (again) from age 40 to 42, I lost my love of fashion.

When you're uncomfortable in your body, clothes are your enemy. They feel tight, ill-fitting, judgy, and constricting. My uniform during this time was black "yoga" pants, roomy tops, and oversized sweatshirts. I didn't want to deal with it—"it" being clothing, my body, my discomfort.

I wanted to blend in with the crowd and not draw any attention to my being.

It's important to note here that as I continue to share my own personal story of *my* relationship with *my* body over 42 years, I want to be clear: there is no one weight, body shape, or size that a woman must be. Besides being physically impossible, physiologically untenable, and psychologically harmful, it's a deeply destructive message that has destroyed and even killed women for centuries.

Every woman is different.
Every body is beautiful.
Every experience is personal.

Culture is finally catching up to these truths and featuring women in marketing, media, and movies who actually represent a broad range of bodies.

I grew up in an era where every magazine geared toward girls, teens, and women featured a thin (often borderline emaciated) woman on its cover, with callouts in varying fonts and sizes telling us to be smaller—literally, metaphorically, cosmically.

Former supermodel Kate Moss is known for her infamous line in 2009: "Nothing tastes as good as skinny feels."

For me—as I took on this "Take Back Your Body" vibe—I wanted to *feel* good again. To get back my energy and strength and sense of self that I had lost along the way.

As I started to lose the weight, my eyes were drawn to areas of my closet that had lay dormant for years. And while I wasn't yet at my goal weight, I was doing the damn work to make change.

I started to shift what "celebrations" looked like in my life. In previous years, popping a bottle of champagne or indulging in a decadent dessert represented a special occasion, an achievement, a reward.

Now, I was marking my moments differently:

- Getting a massage or facial
- Trying a new fun color for a mani/pedi
- Pouring one of new favorite alcohol-free drinks into a pink, glass chalice
- Reading a book while wrapped in my favorite Unhide blush-colored fuzzy blanket
- Pulling oracle cards by candlelight
- Writing my intentions in a butterfly-covered journal with my favorite gold pen
- Manifesting the life I wanted while bathing in the light of the full moon

Sure, these may sound like simple, run-of-the-mill everyday activities that you can experience with—or without—achieving something. But that's the point.

You can go through life seeing the magic in the mundane. Or you can busily hurry past all its beauty on your way to the next. And the next. And the next.

I love Albert Einstein's quote: "There are only two ways to live your life. One is as though nothing is a miracle. The other is as though everything is a miracle."

I choose the miracle.

Do It Differently Than You've Done Before

As a competitive athlete, I knew what hard work looked—and felt—like:

- "Two-a-days" during the off-season, keeping you locked in from sunup to sundown
- Running "suicides" on the basketball court (can we please stop using this term for what is really a ladder drill?)
- Sprinting until I felt like I was going to puke (and did, many times)
- Working to shave time off my mile (a sub-six-minute run was required to make varsity soccer freshman year)

Exercise meant exhaustion. I needed to be dripping sweat for it to count, struggling to catch my breath, or bent over wishing for it to *be* over. It was a competition with myself to "get through it." Not to be in it.

And while I left the cleats and high tops of my competitive playing days behind when I went to college, that mindset of what it meant to be an athlete stayed with me.

But I struggled. I didn't quite know how to navigate the transition from competitive sports to elective exercise. How do you run for fun? What is "going to the gym"? The only athletic endeavors I knew had edge and required grit and were built around a team.

I've tried many forms of exercise over the last 20 years:

- Running outdoors (oh, this sucks)
- Running on a treadmill (ugh, this sucks more)
- Stair steppers (also ugh)
- Ellipticals (honestly, WTF is this machine)
- Personal trainers
- Billy Blanks Tae Bo DVDs (do you remember these?)
- Gilad step aerobics (shout out to my mom for this gem)
- Weightlifting
- Pilates (bar, mat, and reformer)
- Body Pump
- Exhale Core Fusion
- Soul Cycle
- The Peloton bike

- The Tonal
- Barre Code
- Core Power

It's been a journey. And what all of these forms of exercise have in common is that they go hard, they're hard-hitting, or they just straight up *feel* hard.

What I grew up thinking was that you kind of had to hate exercise a little for it to work. If you enjoyed it, you probably weren't doing it right or with enough effort.

It's an interesting philosophy. It worked for me for a period of time. It helped me drop the weight I gained in college, the weight I gained due to depression, and the weight I gained through both of my pregnancies. But this time, it wasn't working.

Going hard five days a week past 40 moved my body, but not my weight.

Yes, I believe that age had *a lot* to do with it. I believe that the hormone shift and imbalance I was experiencing as I entered perimenopause had *more* to do with it. But I think there was an *even more* complicated factor that is rarely discussed in the medical field as it relates to the body, specifically in women: stored trauma.

One of the most influential works on this topic is *The Body Keeps the Score: Brain, Mind, and Body in the Healing of Trauma* by Dr. Bessel van der Kolk, a psychiatrist and trauma researcher. In his 1994 article published in the *Harvard Review of Psychiatry*, van der Kolk discusses how traumatic experiences can alter brain function and physiology, leading to persistent somatic symptoms and emotional dysregulation.

> When the body stores trauma, it refers to the idea that traumatic experiences—whether physical, emotional, or psychological—can have long-lasting effects on the body and mind, even after the event itself has passed. Trauma isn't just something that exists in the mind; it can be experienced in the body as well.

The following is a breakdown of how this process works and what it can look like:

Physical Manifestation of Trauma

- **Nervous system:** Trauma can cause the autonomic nervous system (ANS) to become dysregulated. This can lead to chronic states of heightened arousal (hypervigilance) or shutdown (dissociation).

- **Muscle tension:** People who have experienced trauma may unconsciously hold tension in their muscles, especially in the neck, shoulders, and jaw. This can result in chronic pain or discomfort.

- **Adrenal fatigue:** The body's fight-or-flight response is activated during trauma, releasing stress hormones like cortisol and adrenaline. If the trauma is ongoing or unresolved, the body can become "stuck" in this heightened state, leading to exhaustion, burnout, and other physical symptoms.

- **Post-traumatic stress disorder (PTSD):** One of the most common outcomes of trauma stored in the body is PTSD. This condition involves symptoms such as flashbacks, nightmares, and intrusive thoughts, as well as physical symptoms like a racing heart, sweating, and hyperarousal.

Body Memory and Somatic Experience

- **Somatic memory:** The concept of "body memory" suggests that the body can "remember" traumatic events even if the conscious mind does not. This can manifest as physical sensations, like pain, tension, or tightness in certain parts of the body, that seem to have no clear cause but are linked to past trauma.

- **Dissociation:** Some individuals may dissociate from their bodies in response to trauma, creating a feeling of disconnection or numbness. This can lead to a reduced awareness of physical sensations, sometimes making it hard for people to identify or process their emotional or physical experiences.

Chronic Health Issues

- **Chronic pain:** Trauma can be linked to chronic pain conditions like fibromyalgia, headaches, back pain, and other musculoskeletal issues. These conditions may arise due to the body's response to trauma, which includes persistent tension, inflammation, and altered pain perception.

- **Gastrointestinal issues:** The gut-brain connection is strong, and trauma can affect digestion, leading to issues like irritable bowel syndrome (IBS), bloating, and indigestion.
- **Immune system suppression:** Chronic stress and unresolved trauma can weaken the immune system, making the body more susceptible to illness and disease.

Emotional and Psychological Effects

- **Mood disorders:** Trauma is strongly linked to mental health issues like depression, anxiety, and panic attacks. These can be directly related to the physiological changes in the brain and nervous system triggered by trauma.
- **Behavioral changes:** People who carry unresolved trauma may develop coping mechanisms like overeating, substance abuse, or risk-taking behaviors. These behaviors can be a way of managing the emotional pain or trying to avoid the body sensations that come with stored trauma.
- **Attachment and relationships:** Trauma can impact how a person connects with others. It may lead to difficulties in trusting people, feeling safe, or maintaining healthy relationships. This is often due to the nervous system being on high alert, as a result of previous traumatic experiences.

The Role of Trauma Processing

- **Healing through bodywork:** Approaches like yoga, meditation, acupuncture, massage, or somatic therapy can help release stored trauma from the body. These modalities work by encouraging body awareness and helping the person reconnect with physical sensations, allowing them to process and release tension or pain.
- **Talk therapy:** Therapies like cognitive behavioral therapy (CBT), eye movement desensitization and reprocessing (EMDR), and trauma-focused psychotherapy can help individuals process trauma on a mental level, which can also lead to physical healing.
- **Mindfulness and breathwork:** These practices help regulate the nervous system and reconnect the mind and body. Breathing techniques, in particular, can be helpful for managing the physiological responses that come with trauma, such as a racing heart or shallow breathing.

The Concept of "Unresolved Trauma"

■ When trauma remains unresolved, it can become "stuck" in the body, contributing to ongoing stress responses and the development of physical or psychological conditions. If trauma isn't processed or integrated, it can influence one's worldview, emotional reactions, and even health in the long term.

In summary, when the body stores trauma, it can lead to a range of physical, emotional, and psychological effects. Trauma doesn't just live in the mind—it can become embedded in the body's tissues, nervous system, and energy patterns, creating a cycle of distress. The good news is that trauma can be healed, often through a combination of therapies that address both the mind and body.

Trauma had been stored in my body for decades.

■ The psychological, physiological, and emotional abuse of my ex-stepfather
■ The abandonment of my biological father
■ The rape on Spring Break in Cancun when I was 18 (he's a doctor now, the motherfucker)
■ The sexually and psychologically abusive year-and-a-half-long, hostage-like situation in my 20s
■ The rampant sexual harassment and misogyny in my workplaces in my 20s and 30s
■ The emotionally abusive "friendships" with women I've survived for more than 20 years
■ The psychologically abusive women I worked for—and with—for more than 20 years
■ Men, specifically the toxic shitty ones in my personal and professional life (too many to count)
■ My journey navigating anxiety and depression since the age of 13
■ My struggle through an eating disorder in my 20s
■ My postpartum hellscape filled with postpartum anxiety and depression, labor injuries, breastfeeding struggles, and more
■ My first-born William's chronic, lifelong bleeding disorder, severe hemophilia A

- My husband Brian's chronic, lifelong autoimmune disease Type 1 diabetes
- Brian's emergency open-heart surgery when I was eight-and-a-half months pregnant with our second son
- My youngest son Charlie's respiratory and pulmonology struggles and scares post-COVID that led to multiple hospital and pediatric ICU stays
- The betrayal, theft, and abuse in my first company
- The daily vigilance required to be a woman existing in the world—where our bodies are the constant target of exploitation and attack

This is just what I can remember as I write this. I know my mind has blocked out even more.

I had been pushing through—and past—it all to survive.

What I didn't realize was that going hard at the problem wasn't going to work this time. I couldn't outwork my pain and grief. I had to sit with it. I had to feel it. And then I had to release it.

These were completely new ways of being.

Those "actions" felt *in*active. Like, why the fuck would sitting help? Sitting gets you nowhere. *Literally!*

Ah, but that's the irony. Sitting removes your ability to escape dealing with where you are right now, in this moment.

I know anxiety. It's been part of me for more than half of my life. I am a pro at anxiety. But for those who are less familiar, let me define it for you. Anxiety is an emotion that can be described as feelings of fear, dread, or uneasiness.

The simple way I like to describe it to those who have never experienced the clutches of its death grip is worrying about the past and the future, constantly.

I revisit in my mind the shitty things that have already happened to me all. the. damn. time. And based on the previous list, you can see how much material I have to work with.

I replay them.

I think of what I could—or should—have done differently.

I fume at what *they* should have done differently.

My mind takes my body back to the scenes of the crimes over and over and over and over again. And I feel like I'm there . . . right now. My body tenses, my heart races, my palms sweat, my brow furrows. Sometimes I'm so deep in the daytime nightmare that you could walk in and see me sitting, looking off into the distance at . . . something, and having no idea that I am in the middle of a full throwdown circa 1998.

My body is *here*.
But I'm not.

I've perfected this quantum leap. And I've done it so many times I wonder how much of my matter exists here, with me today, versus in my past.

But this is just half of my struggles with anxiety. The back half. Let's talk about the second part. Why only worry about everything that *has* happened when you can also worry about everything that *could* happen?

The number of potential scenarios I've played out to prepare for what could go wrong—and all of the possible offshoots of said shitty situations—could fill hundreds, maybe thousands, of books.

I've role-played full scenes of dramatic trauma with friends, family, foes, colleagues. They've said—and done—horrible things. Unforgivable things! And the more I imagine them, the less clear I am on what was real and what is imagined.

I'm physically exhausted from the mental gymnastics. And I don't want to do it anymore.

I've wasted a lot of years of my life living in the past and worrying about the future. But it's been the *being* in the present that's the hardest for me to do.

And this all connects back to my body.

You saw on the list of the ways I've exercised how much go, go, go, hard-hitting, pavement-pounding was required to be successful. You saw on the list of traumatic life events how much trauma has been stored in my body. You saw how much space worry-about-what-was-or-could-be has occupied in my mind.

But since I started dropping the weight, releasing the trauma, breaking free from the people, places, and programming holding me back, I've been able to sit in the stillness.

I've sat in the present.
I've stayed where my feet are.
I've stopped running.

I've started practicing—and loving—yoga.

This isn't my first foray into the group of physical, mental, and spiritual practices or disciplines that originated in ancient India, aimed at controlling body and mind. It's just the first time I've respected it.

I always said that it wasn't for me. It was too slow, too quiet, too still. But in truth, I avoided it because of how much I needed it, how much it pulled out of me that I had been trying to escape, and how much it went against all of the fight-or-flight instincts that had helped me survive and kept me alive on some of my darkest and most dangerous days.

I'm giving myself the chance to do things differently, to explore exercise in a new way, to connect with—and to—my body with a reverence and respect that I had never reserved for myself.

It's slow.
It's intentional.
It's healing.

🐺 🐺 🐺

We step out of the freezing cold into the warm, cozy studio. The lighting is low, the room smells of palo santo and burning candles. The drapes separating the entrance and retail space from the yoga studio are parted loosely and fall just right against the worn and loved wood floors.

The Sanctuary lives up to its name.

It's been mine for the past few years intermittently and the past few months intimately.

It's my favorite yoga studio. The owner and instructor, Natasha, is my favorite teacher. She is magical. She has helped me hold on to myself while releasing what is meant to leave my body for good.

The location of the Sanctuary is not convenient to where I live. It's a 30-minute drive on a good day. But this is Chicagoland, folks. So, add in any kind of inclement weather and that number could double. There are plenty of yoga studios closer to me. Hell, I could have my own personal yoga class led by an instructor on the screen of the Tonal in my basement. But it's not the same. It's not even close. The distance I have to drive to get there brings me to an internal proximity I've never been to achieve alone.

Today, for the first time, I've brought my boys with me. It's a "Mommy and Me Aerial Class." The three of us have never done aerial yoga before. So, for those of you who may be as unfamiliar with it as we were, here's a description from Chat GPT:

> Aerial yoga is a modern style of yoga that incorporates the use of a hammock or yoga swing suspended from the ceiling. Also known as anti-gravity yoga, it allows practitioners to perform traditional yoga poses and exercises in mid-air.
>
> The hammock supports the body, enabling deeper stretches, greater flexibility, and often a sense of weightlessness. Aerial yoga combines elements of yoga, aerial acrobatics, and Pilates, offering both physical benefits such as improved flexibility and strength, as well as potential mental benefits like stress relief and relaxation.
>
> It's popular for its unique and playful approach to yoga practice.

Play. For *adults.* What is *that*?

I've been horrible at "play" as an adult. What's the point? Where's the result? Why would you do *that* when there are so many other things you *could* and *should* be doing?

When my children ask me to play with them, I struggle. Not because of *them*. Because of *me*.

I'm not good at the unstructured.
I'm not good at the "unproductive."
I'm not good at the unknown.

As a parentified child—a child who is forced to take on the role of a parent or caretaker within their family, often before they are developmentally ready—I stopped playing long before the length of time I was owed.

So, this is my attempt to try to bridge the gap between who I am and who I want to be more of.

The next 45 minutes are a window into my past, present, and future—through my children.

My Will, my firstborn, my adventurous, headstrong, competitive, precocious eight-year-old, takes to the aerial yoga like a fish to water, like a bird to air, like a moth to a flame.

He jumps into the first move. Literally. He proclaims to the room, "I got this!" "Watch me!" "This isn't even hard!" I try to temper Will's announcements to the group. I tell him he's amazing and so strong and so talented. And that yoga is not a competition. Everyone goes at their own place. There is no winner or loser here.

He couldn't care less. He sails through the moves, doing more than I can. "Look at me!" he proudly exclaims, hanging upside down, arms and legs extended in opposing directions. He looks like the sun, bright and hot and strong and blinding; a burning ball of fire.

Natasha is impressed. "Wow, he's really good," she mouths to me.

Will is a rule-follower. Not only because he is a deep empath and people pleaser—a firm believer in fairness and justice—but also because he likes to win. Show him a rule and he'll prove that he's the best to ever do it.

When Will was six, he came off the soccer field after a game and my husband said, "Did you have fun?" And Will paused, looked him dead in the eye, and said, "I don't play for fun. I play *for real.*"

Will is the sun.

He is the ultimate source of energy. Every second, he produces as much energy as a trillion nuclear bombs exploding simultaneously. Without him, all would be a frozen, lifeless rock. He is a symbol of life, vitality, and divinity. His gravitational pull keeps the planets, moons, and asteroids of the solar system in orbit. Without him, the solar system would fall apart. He inspires awe and is a symbol of strength, consistency, and power.

My Charlie, my youngest, my deeply feeling, self-conscious, creative, powerful, perfectionist, experiences a range of emotions.

He begins, excited and curious. He looks around the room. He watches Will before he begins. He tentatively approaches each instruction. As the moves become more challenging and difficult, he gets frustrated and discouraged. He says he's "not good at this." He's "not good enough."

He opts out. As the other children and adults attempt to follow Natasha's direction—failing and succeeding—Charlie folds himself into the hammock and gives in. He lets the hammock hold him. He's curved like a crescent moon, illuminating the stars around him.

Charlie doesn't give a fuck about rules. They are there not only to *not* be followed but to be actively and purposefully ignored, broken, destroyed, eviscerated.

Charlie is the moon.

His gravity controls oceans, creating tides, crashing waves, influencing every ecosystem. He stabilizes the earth when it tilts. His phases mirror life's cycles—growth, fullness, decline, and renewal. He is a symbol of femininity, intuition, mystery, and transformation. His soft glow can evoke a sense of calm, wonder, and inspiration. Everyone feels more reflective, more creative under his light.

I stand in the middle, torn between who needs more of me and for how long; when to step in and guide and when to step back and let go. It's a physical representation of the tension, turbulence, and tight-rope of parenting.

It's the uncomfortable truth about the tension of my own existence.

How do you help them succeed, while also letting them fail?

When do you step in versus step back?

Where do you guide them or watch as they chart their own course?

My boys know who they are. And they constantly remind me of who the fuck I am.

They are the sun.

They are the moon.

They are the universe.

Damn. My children are me.

They are me in all the stages of who I've been before. Of who I am sorting through who I am now.

They are a crawling caterpillar.

They are cocooned and dissolving.

They are the monarch.

I look to my left. Charlie is lying flat, suspended in the hammock, protected and hidden from the world, with only his precious little face peeking out.

I look to my right. Will is 3 feet from the top of the 20-foot-high ceiling, the gleaming gold satin sheet woven tightly around each of his legs as he takes flight.

Charlie represents the surrender: the soft, the rest, the observing, the slower place.

Will represents the fight: the hard-working, fiercely driven climb and survival of what surely seem like insurmountable mountains.

A river can't be pushed. It can only be observed, respected, and ridden.

I stand in the middle and look down at my own feet.

What if I decided to be here? To let go? To believe that everything had led me to this moment? And that everywhere I'm supposed to go will be revealed to me in time, on pace, at peace?

You don't have to do things the way you've always done them. In fact, insanity is defined as "doing the same thing over and over, expecting a different result." You are not who you've always been. And you're not yet who you will become. Isn't it time to give yourself the space to consider a new way forward?

Just like I said before, "all or nothing" and "forever or never" don't work for me. And you don't have to force yourself into a box either. Who you were yesterday doesn't have to be who you are today. Or tomorrow.

There is deep freedom in just being; in honoring the woman you are in this moment. Because remember, you're going to be with her forever and ever . . . and evermore.

Five Shifts to Take Back Your Body

1. **Pay attention to self-talk.** When you look in the mirror, are your first thoughts love and admiration or loathing and accusation? Walk over to the mirror right now and tell her how beautiful she is. Even though it may sound impossible to do, a 100-mile journey begins with a single step.

2. **Quit Comparing.** No one is an exact carbon copy of you. So, when you find moments where you're comparing yourself to other women, pause and make a shift. You can't stop loathing and lusting after other women's bodies and lives until you start loving your own.

3. **Sit in stillness.** In the quiet of anti-movement, you create space for your soul to send signals about what to do. But you can only hear them if you're still and listening.

4. **Stop doing the same thing.** Have you had the same exercise routine for years? Do your traditions involving food and alcohol still work for you? Maybe it's time to switch it up.

5. **Take the reins.** When you decide that no one else on Earth gets to decide how your body is treated, cared for, held, or freed, you take back your power.

11

The Alchemist

People often witness the results of a scientific experiment and call it magic.

How did they do that?
There's no way that's real.
I can't believe what I just saw.

Yet, society asks us to put science and magic into two separate and distinct categories. One, they tell us, is real. The other, imaginary.

But I don't buy it. I continue to come across the blurred lines. The in between. The inexplicable. What category does *our* reality fall into when so much of it exists in the limitless universe of our imagination?

Take "chemistry," for example. Chemistry is defined as the branch of science that deals with the identification of the substances of which matter is composed.

But it *also* describes the complex emotional or psychological interaction between two people. One can be clearly measured, while the other is an ethereal, unseen intangible.

The same goes for "alchemy." In the realm of science, alchemy is defined as the medieval forerunner of chemistry, based on the supposed transformation of matter. It was concerned particularly with attempts to convert base metals into gold, or to find a universal elixir.

But it *also* describes the seemingly magical process of transformation, creation, or combination.

Words, like people, are deeply complex—and hold a world of meaning if you care enough to explore them.

There is no one way to start a fire.
There is no experiment that must begin and end the same way.
There is no single answer to encompass how every part of every equation will react.

That is, until you explode.

I'm 10 years old, sitting on the cold, hard, plastic, blue government-issued elementary school chair of my art class in Atlantic Highlands, New Jersey.

I spread the thick, hot pink paint on the canvas with a hard, plastic spatula. I take the cardboard "stamp" I've created—made from cutting and gluing other pieces of cardboard onto a 5 × 7 foundation to form an image—and press it into the pool of paint. I lift it up carefully and shift it toward a clean, blank, white piece of paper waiting to be filled. I press it down, hard, experiencing those anticipatory moments before a full reveal.

I lift up the cardboard. A butterfly rising above blades of grass toward rays of sunlight appears.

I have no idea what she'll mean to me.

I've always been drawn to create. My favorite subjects in school—from kindergarten to senior year of high school—were art, music, photography, languages, and anything that fell under the category "English": writing, reading, grammar, poetry, etymology, storytelling. Math and science were harder for me. Or so I've told myself.

According to research published in the journal *Psychological Science*, research shows that girls often begin to lose confidence in math and science as early as age 8, with the gap widening during late elementary school and middle school (around ages 10–13). Here's a breakdown of why:

Early Patterns

- Ages 6–8: Girls begin to internalize gender stereotypes about intelligence and ability, particularly the idea that boys are more naturally gifted in STEM fields.
- By age 9: Girls' interest and confidence in STEM starts to decline even though their performance remains equal to or better than boys.

Middle School (ages 11–13)

- Social pressures, stereotype threat, and lack of female role models in STEM become more pronounced.
- Confidence and interest in math and science often drop significantly, even among high-achieving girls.

Why This Happens

- Stereotypes: Exposure to cultural messages that suggest math/science are "for boys."
- Representation: Lack of visible female role models in STEM careers and media.
- Feedback: Teachers and parents may unconsciously give different encouragement or critique based on gender.
- Peer dynamics: Social pressure to conform to gender norms can discourage girls from expressing STEM interests.

I see myself in these statistics. And I bore the brunt of a system that wasn't built by—or for— girls and women. I was told that I didn't "instinctively perform as proficiently" in these two subjects. So, I was put on the "slow" or "less advanced" tracks in school at an early age.

I hate that we label kids so young—and put them into boxes that not only don't *care* to fully understand the *what*, *why*, or *how* behind a child's experience with a particular subject but also leave very little room for them to grow out of the stigma that the school system stamps on them.

Maybe I wasn't as "good" at math or science because of:

- The teacher
- The style with which the subject was being taught—conflicting with the way I learned best
- What was happening at home
- My experience with other kids, in the classroom and on the playground
- Chaos out in the world
- The system that stereotypes girls as "bad at math and science"

Or maybe I just sucked at them both.

But damn, don't the next generations of children deserve to do it differently, especially when it hasn't worked as well as it should, or could, have for so many of us?

I carried my "slow track" science and math label with me, well past high school and college, into the 42-year-old woman I am today. When my third grader brings home his math worksheets, my anxiety about the problems he'll soon face in middle school instantly triggers me. (And I'm not just talking about the kind that involve numbers on a page.)

So often, what we *believe* we're good at—and who we know ourselves to be—comes from the external validation that begins with our parents and teachers and continues to be enhanced or extinguished by our friends, family, co-workers, and the world around us.

One person's confidence-killing comment can counteract every previous procedure we'd performed to make a discovery, test a hypothesis, or demonstrate the most important truth about our existence: we matter.

When you read that sentence, does someone come to mind for you? Many someone's? Oh, I have my list. And you'll continue to learn about those experiences throughout the book.

It's why I think it's so important to recognize the impact that teachers have on the human race—people who arguably spend more hours with us during our most formative years than our parents, caregivers, coaches, friends, and community outside of school *combined*.

My favorite teachers—from elementary school through college—were my English teachers.

Shout out to Mrs. Young (first grade), Mrs. Lau (second grade), and Mrs. Barber (third grade) at Star of the Sea School in Honolulu, Hawaii; Mrs. Littlefield (fifth grade) and Mr. Bolger and Mr. McCabe (sixth grade) at Atlantic Highlands Elementary School in Atlantic Highlands, New Jersey; Mrs. Laskowski (seventh grade) and Mrs. Steinhauser (eighth grade) at Mark Twain Middle School in Alexandria, Virginia; Mr. Martezki (ninth grade) at Punahou School in Honolulu, Hawaii; Mrs. Dupree (twelfth grade) at Greenhills School in Ann Arbor, Michigan; and Sejal Sutaria and John Rubadeau at the University of Michigan.

Y'all. I can't remember the names of almost any other teachers I've had over my 16 years in the primary and secondary school system. The fact that every teacher I named here taught me the subject of English is very important to the story of my life.

Did these teachers *tell* me that I was a good writer because I *had* talent? Or did I *have* talent because they *told* me I was a good writer?

I would bet all my money on the latter being the leader. Their support of my skillset sparked confidence in me that only made me better. The power of someone believing in you and telling you that you are good enough—even exceptional!—can be the difference between deciding to abandon a dream and aspiring to make it a reality.

These are the voices we hear in our heads when we're alone and struggling to find meaning and purpose.

These are the voices we hear in our heads when we're pushing the boulder up a hill toward the highest peak of what we believe is possible—and falling and failing, over and over and over again.

These are the voices we hear in our heads when our little wins are adding up to something bigger and better than we ever could have believed we'd achieve.

My love for writing deepened with age. The more I wrote, the better I became. And the more I shared my writing, the more I believed I was worthy of calling myself a writer.

That is, until I was told to stop.

❧ ❧ ❧

I didn't start to truly put my writing out into the world, on a broader scale, more publicly—and into the feeds of strangers—until I became a mother.

There is a level of zero-fucks-given that arrives *inside* of you to counter-balance the birth of your baby *out* into the world. It occupies the space that is left behind by the most expansive internal work of your life.

I had so much more room for bullshit before Will and Charlie were born. At work, at home, in all the places. But the complete transformation I experienced during my 10 months of pregnancy, each time, with both my boys—from an individual woman to growing a human being inside of my body to birthing said human out into the world and continuing to count on my body to keep him alive—was the most epic life transition I ever have experienced, or ever will.

That brings me back to **butterflies**.

The internal work here defies logic or science.

A caterpillar crawls along at a glacial pace, barely moving from one point to the next. Then, it decides it's just about had it with this slow shit. So, it creates a cocoon, dissolves into goo, transforms into an entirely new being, grows wings, breaks through the exterior shell, and flies the fuck outta there.

What?

How do they do that?
There's no way that's real.
I can't believe what I just saw.

Talk about transformation.
Talk about metamorphosis.
Talk about magic.

I got my first butterfly tattoo when I was 18—a tiny little blue thing on my left second toe, no bigger than a copper penny. It was easy to hide and rarely seen by anyone other than me.

My *second* butterfly tattoo, more than 20 years later (and my fifth tattoo, so far—sorry mom!), was another, much bigger butterfly on the inside of my left wrist, larger than a Canadian Gold Maple Leaf coin: a blue monarch that you couldn't ignore.

When I was a kid, I drew butterflies everywhere. In art class, on the backs of electricity bill envelopes addressed to my mother, inside of hand-made cards for people I loved, *all over* my math and science homework (take that, slow track!).

When I was 26, I framed an art project that I found in a memory box in my mom's basement from elementary school. It was a series of four butterflies. I had created each of them using the same medium, but with slight alterations and expressions. The method I used yielded four very different results—with varying colors, patterns, and personalities.

You remember me talking about her, right?

I hung them in my first apartment in Chicago—a two-story walk-up on the corner of Southport and Belden in Lincoln Park.

Butterflies are brave.

They're willing to take the risk of leaving everything about who they are behind in the hope of becoming something else. They leap before the net appears.

Metamorphosis—in an insect or amphibian—is defined as the process of transformation from an immature form to an adult form in two or more distinct stages. But it *also* describes a change of the form or nature of a thing or person into a completely different one, by natural or supernatural means.

There goes that science-y magic stuff again.

Motherhood is some serious science-y magic stuff.
Motherhood showed me how powerful I really was.
Motherhood showed me how strong my convictions had become.
Motherhood showed me how much I needed to say.

And then, when I shared my internal voice out loud, the external world showed me how much they wanted to hear it.

I wrote my first post on LinkedIn that intentionally blurred the lines between the "personal" and the "professional" on March 29, 2019. It was seven months—to the day—after I delivered my second son, Charlie, into the world.

I've included this post, in its entirety, here.

Why I'm posting about my "personal" life on a "professional" platform for the first time ever.

Me with my son Will on the "606" in Bucktown, Chicago.

Cute picture, right? Well, here's the whole truth. My firstborn, Will, has been having a tough time lately. You know . . . about to turn three, new baby in the house, I've been traveling for work, I cut his waffles the wrong size. Usual toddler stuff. But it's been REALLY hard on us both. (Ask my team at Golin that sees me arrive at work every day looking like I've been through a Tough Mudder course.)

I asked Will last night if he was sad that we didn't have special time, just the two of us, anymore. He looked at the floor. Then, he looked at me and said "yes." (Cue the ever-present mom guilt. Again.)

So, today, I called an audible. On everything. Except us.

I kept him home from school and we spent the morning together, just us, for the first time since his baby brother was born. Charlie turned seven months old today.

Will eating a donut from Ipsento.

We ate donuts and drank coffee and hot chocolate on a grassy hill by Chicago's 606; we played at the park and he swung on a big boy swing for the first time all by himself; I took him on his inaugural bus and train rides (and you would have thought we were at Disneyland).

Will with a "pupuccino" from Ipsento.

We smiled at each other and held hands and he sat on my lap with no one competing for my attention.

It was a special, magical morning that I'll never forget.

And then he had a total meltdown and made me carry him for over a mile while I pushed an empty stroller, sweating profusely.

But, hey. That's life with a toddler.

My point is, life isn't easy. But this one is mine. And I only get one shot.

I have a big job. At home and at work. And figuring out how to be successful at both is an everyday struggle. I'm lucky to work for a company that embraces #lifetime. But, it's not perfect.

We all have to get better at creating places where people feel supported to fully integrate their personal and professional goals and lives.

We have to get better at acknowledging that "work" doesn't just take place in an office between 9 and 5 and "life" doesn't neatly show up for the day's bookends. We have to get better at proving that we will always #haveherback.

Who is going to be brave enough, bold enough, progressive enough to do it?

To truly change the world?

To unconditionally prioritize the quest for equilibrium?

Why not me?

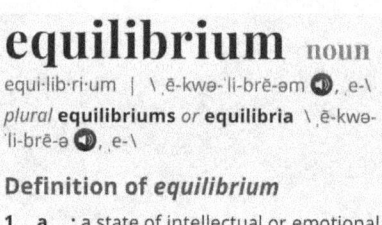

The definition of "equilibrium."

I'm replaceable in a lot of aspects of my life. But I'll never be replaceable as Will and Charlie's mom. So, I damn well better get this role right the first time. Or at least keep trying every day to be better than the day before.

Me with my son Will on the CTA bus.

The struggle is real. The juggle is worse.

I know I'm not alone. My mom tribe tells me as much. Well, guess what? You're not alone either. Together, we can do it differently. Because do you want to know the whole truth? I have a sneaking suspicion that the very best version of each of our lives depend on it.

As I read that post now, six years later, I feel a lot of things.

I want to go back to that exact moment with my two-year-old and hold him and smell his sweet baby smell while his head is resting on my shoulder and the crook of my neck cradles the crook of his neck, forming an infinite loop of love and trust and security.

It breaks me a little just to write out that sentence.

But I also feel the fear in my words. Not fear of what it meant to now be a mother of two young boys, but what it meant to publicly share more of that part of my life on a "work" platform; to talk about how the system—and even my company—needed to change; and to begin to poke the proverbial patriarchal bear.

I feel how much conflict existed inside of me.

I can see it in the title of my article.

I can see it in the way I dropped "work" lingo throughout the piece.

I can see it in the way I debated the idea of "balance."

I was the forever marketer and good girl, ensuring that I plugged two of my agency's internal and external marketing campaigns—"Have Her Back" and "Lifetime"—while sharing the story of my day with Will.

Here I was again, an English major—"bad" at science and math—setting up yet another experiment where I tested a theory; questioned the method of solving a problem; and tried a new and different way than the one I was told to follow, exactly as instructed.

I thought "work-life balance" was bullshit, and I was beginning to find my courage and my voice in saying so, out loud.

I was curious about this idea of "equilibrium."

In chemistry, *equilibrium* is defined as a state in which a process and its reverse are occurring at equal rates, so that no overall change is taking place. But it *also* describes a state in which opposing forces or influences are balanced.

On May 19, 2019, I spontaneously stopped into Metamorph Tattoo on Damen while walking around my Bucktown neighborhood to permanently mark the symbol for equilibrium on the inside of my right foot, below the ankle and above the arch. It was 51 days after I wrote the post that set my life on a completely new course. It was one week after I celebrated my first Mother's Day with two children.

I was just starting to test the waters, dipping my toe in the pool where I would soon plunge headfirst into the deep end.

On April 16, 2016, I became a mother. And I experienced firsthand how fucking hard it is to hold the line of equilibrium between the individual, ambitious, career-driven woman I *was* before having a baby and the cosmically connected creator of a human that I birthed into the world—and continued to sustain using physical, mental, and emotional energy from places that didn't exist before—that I *became*.

So many times, it was too much.

I wanted to give up. I wanted to walk away. I wanted to save myself from what felt like an underwater, viscous vortex determined to drown me.

And I wasn't alone.

I noticed a trend at my agency that concerned me. Some of the most impressive, brilliant, and passionate women were leaving. Some were single 20-somethings who were burning the midnight oil just to cover rent. Others were newly married and deciding when—and if—to grow their families. Most were new mothers, returning from maternity leave (such a bullshit term for childbirth recovery) looking like they had vacated their bodies.

They were struggling. And we weren't doing a damn thing to help them.

Many new mothers were leaving within their first year of returning to work. And I mean *fully* walking away from our profession. They didn't go to a smaller agency or a boutique firm that focused on their expertise. They left the industry. They left themselves.

Some stayed home to raise their children full time. Others switched careers entirely, becoming therapists or interior designers or real estate agents or Rodan + Fields reps, the modern-day Mary Kay. Many wandered aimlessly—because they had no idea who they were anymore. They had no idea where to go.

What was happening? And why were we all walking around pretending like we didn't see it and it was just another Tuesday?

I started asking hard questions. I wanted to know how these women were feeling, what they needed (that they weren't getting at work—or in life), and how we could make it better. I identified about 15 women across varying life stages who I felt could intersectionality represent the issues we needed to better understand and address inside of our agency. And I wanted to gather us to talk about what the hell was happening—and what we were going to do about it.

I took these 15 women to lunch off-site to create a safe space to tell the truth.

Their stories were gut-wrenching, heartbreaking, and oh-so-familiar.

They were stories of discrimination, sexual harassment, subtle sexism, blatant misogyny, unequal opportunity, inequitable pay, the motherhood penalty, the motherhood tax, and the motherhood bias.

My rage continued to build.

And as I do with anything I'm trying to process, to understand, and to move through and forward, I wrote.

I let the feelings stored deep in my gut and lining the chambers of my heart power my fingers to type out 606 words that became the blueprint for a life I didn't know I wanted; one I didn't know I had the authority to ask for or the right to create.

On August 22, 2017—one year and six days after my oldest son Will was born and one year and seven days before my youngest son Charlie was born (damn, talk about being smack dab "in the middle" of it), I wrote the beginnings of a manifesto.

It poured out of me. I didn't know what to do with all that was swirling around in my mind—inside of my body. I didn't know where I was going to put it. But I had to get it out.

After I wrote it, I shared it with my husband, and I sent it to my mom and sister and my best girlfriends from high school, college, and the past 20 years. I emailed it individually to every person with power in my company.

I was testing the waters again—trudging through the muck and mire of conditioning to the deepening and expanding clarity I was feeling about what I must do next. I was gathering the lotuses that skimmed the surface of so much turmoil beneath. They were breaking through everywhere.

"Here's the Problem" is what I called my 606-word manifesto that began with an explanation of what was happening to me.

Remember the day I spent with Will walking along *Chicago's 606*—an elevated trail named after the first three numbers of every Chicagoland ZIP code? It was where I took my Will the morning I started to break free from my cocoon—the day that inspired me to start to tell the truth on LinkedIn.

And it is the exact number of words in the manifesto I wrote that would break me out of Corporate America—and years later, break free from all of the people, places, and programming holding me back.

These are the signs from the universe that show you the way. This, my friends, is some witchy shit.

Here's what I wrote:

Ever since the evening of November 8th, when T⋆ump was elected President, I've felt off; confused, scared, frustrated, enraged, worried . . . as a woman. All of the progress we've made (and the women who came before us have fought for) feels in jeopardy. And all that we've endured—and continue to endure—feels ignored. The flame of this feeling has been fanned by much of what's followed: T⋆ump's egregious behavior since he's taken office, threats to women's rights and reproductive health, the Women's March, conversations with men about the realities of what it means to be a woman (and much of the ignorance that surrounds that), the Weinstein scandal, the #metoo movement, and on and on and on. I feel like something is about to break open on all of this—and there's no going back.

I can confirm that that has, in fact, happened for me.

So, I put my thoughts on paper . . . a bit of an open letter to all of the men who just don't seem to get it; who don't see their role in everything that's happening around them. (See below.)

I don't know what I plan to do with this yet, but hoping it might provide a feeling of solidarity for you if you're also feeling the same way.

—

Here's the problem.

When the conversation starts with, "This doesn't happen in our industry / at our company / around our office / on our team . . ." you don't want to say that, in fact, it has.

When the conversation starts with, "No one has told me that it happened to them . . ." you don't want to admit to the reasons why you stayed silent.

When the conversation starts with, "We have women in leadership positions, so clearly, they are treated equally and have equal opportunity . . ." you don't want to go into the details of the path you endured to get there—sometimes painful, challenging and unjust.

When the conversation starts in any of these ways, it usually stops just as quickly.

WHY do we have to keep starting the conversation with one eye closed, one ear covered and one foot stepping upon the pedestal that we will use to preach our progressive, inclusive superiority; our immunity to the abuse of power; our leading response following an epidemic?

WHY can't we simply ask our women, "What has it been like for you?" And then . . . believe them?

Don't punish them for the times it DID happen to them. Don't punish them for the times they didn't speak up and out against their perpetrator. Don't punish them for the success they've achieved despite the hardship and pretend that the road to leadership looked the same for a woman as it did for a man.

Just don't.

Here's the problem. You're not listening. Again.

This isn't about you for the reasons you're making it. But it should be about you for the reasons you're avoiding.

You've been complicit. Or you've been complacent. But what you haven't been is compassionate.

We're all in this together—whether we want to be or not. So, take the "you versus me," "us versus them," "guilty versus innocent," "men versus women" and throw it out the window.

Because you're as much a part of the problem as you can be the solution. Own that. Think about it. Reflect for a bit.

And then, when you remember that time you said or did that thing or watched someone say or do that thing—and you said nothing—consider the fact that the woman on the receiving end has endured those offenses fiftyfold.

Here's the problem: it might be you.

The responses I received varied.

My husband was supportive. *And* worried. He didn't yet understand—or know what to do with—this ocean of fury surging inside of me.

My mom and one or two of my girlfriends replied in solidarity. I was surprised and disappointed that I didn't hear back from more.

Most of the leaders at my company said nothing. I don't think they knew what to do with me anymore. I had always been such a good little soldier, taking orders and carrying them out without considering the consequences. Now, I continued to question them, the way we worked and society, at large. My inability to just shut up and fall in line began to place me on a track where the destination was not yet clear.

Have you ever seen the movie *Working Girl*? It's one of my all-time favorites. I've probably seen it 50 times.

Here's the plot, per Chat GPT:

> The 1988 film *Working Girl* is a romantic comedy-drama about ambition, deception, and breaking barriers in the corporate world.
>
> Tess McGill (Melanie Griffith) is a smart and hardworking secretary from Staten Island who dreams of climbing the corporate ladder in Manhattan's competitive business world. Stuck in a dead-end job with condescending bosses, she finally gets a chance when her sophisticated and seemingly supportive new boss, Katharine Parker (Sigourney Weaver), takes her under her wing. However, when Katharine breaks her leg on a ski trip, Tess discovers that Katharine has been stealing her business ideas and passing them off as her own.
>
> Determined to take control of her own destiny, Tess assumes Katharine's role and pitches her idea—a lucrative merger between a radio network and a media company—to a major executive, Jack Trainer (Harrison Ford).
>
> When Katharine returns from her trip earlier than expected, she confronts Tess during the meeting, outing her as her secretary and accusing *her* of stealing the idea. Just when it seems all is lost, the CEO of Trask confronts Katharine, who is unable to explain where she got the merger idea. Tess proves that the idea was originally hers. Trask promises to have Katharine fired for her action and offers Tess the job of her dreams.

On her first day at Trask Industries, Tess meets a colleague named Alice, who Tess initially assumes will be her new boss. But it turns out that Alice is actually Tess' secretary. Tess insists they work together as colleagues, showing she will be very different from Katharine. Finally, Tess calls her friend Cyn (Joan Cusak) from her own office to tell her that she has made it.

The film is a sharp, feel-good story about perseverance, self-worth, and challenging societal expectations, set against the backdrop of 1980s Wall Street. It won an Academy Award for Best Original Song ("Let the River Run" by Carly Simon) and remains a classic feminist workplace comedy.

Damn, I love that movie. I love how, in the end, the underdog wins.

I've learned a powerful lesson over the course of my career.

People have ideas every day. At work, at home, with friends, alone, while sipping a glass of pinot noir or a piping hot mug of tea, when out for a walk or a run, while ruminating in the shower or relaxing in a bath.

Ideas are everywhere. But a critical aspect of *action* separates the idea generators. People with ideas who do *nothing* are dreamers. People with ideas who do *something* are entrepreneurs. Women who take credit for *other* women's ideas are mean girls.

I didn't know I was an entrepreneur. I just thought I was a doer. I got shit done. I didn't wait for someone else to do something. I didn't wait to be told to take on a task. I didn't ask how we were going to get it done. I just did it. Every time.

I step on to the stage in the Gotham Hall Ballroom of the Grand Hyatt in New York City. It's January 25, 2019. I am four months postpartum from giving birth to my youngest baby, Charlie. I'm wearing a forgiving black dress with white polka dots. The dress still feels tight and constricting.

But it's not the rayon fabric that I'm uncomfortable in; it's my body. The body that has spent 20 months growing humans inside of it and years trying to recalibrate into the skin of the person, the mother, the woman I've become.

And yet, on this day, January 25, 2019, something broke in—and out of—me.

For the first time in my 10 years with my agency, they put *me* forward for an award: PR News' Top Women in PR.

And I won.

It was the first time in my career that I publicly stepped *out* of the shadows.
It was the first time I was invited *onto* the stage to speak *into* the mic.
It was the first time that those in my world saw who was *really* behind the curtain.

I was named a 2019 Top Woman in PR among a class of women from iconic brands like Aflac, Barclays, Capital One, Cisco, Clorox, Comcast, Delta Airlines, Discovery Channel, Hilton, Hotwire, HP, IBM, IHOP, KFC, MTV, Macy's, Marriott, National Civil Rights Museum, NextDoor, Nissan, PayPal, Proctor & Gamble, Prudential, Rent the Runway, Sephora, Showtime Networks, SoftBank, T-Mobile, UPS, VH1, Visa, and more.

I had CEOs and senior leaders of some of the world's biggest brands and companies reaching out to me to congratulate and connect. They wanted to know more about *my* work. They wanted to be a part of what *I* was building. They wanted to work with *me*.

What was happening?

How did I do that?
There's no way this was real.
I couldn't believe my eyes.

Could *I* be bigger than the increasingly constricting box I had consistently been shoved back into, time and time again, suffocating me quietly, against my will?

🌸 🌸 🌸

It's 6 a.m. Pacific Time. I'm at my hotel in Palo Alto. I am in California to put on a huge event for my agency that night. I reach for my phone on the nightstand and am met with a flurry of texts and emails from my agency's leadership team. The most horrific thing that can happen to a person happened to a woman in our company.

Our colleague was murdered: brutally killed by her boyfriend and buried in her own garden.

She was discovered that morning, on International Women's Day. And the investigation was open and underway.

The devastating irony of learning about this senseless tragedy on a day that "celebrates" women was almost too much to bear.

This had never happened in our agency's 60+ year history. We convened our leadership team on a call. We needed to put a crisis plan into place immediately. And we needed to think about how we would navigate the huge International Women's Day (IWD) Event we had planned in Silicon Valley that night.

Everyone on the call weighed in. The suggestions ranged from canceling and calling off everything to continuing all programming as planned, without a single change.

I felt the anger bubbling up inside of me again. And I couldn't stay quiet another minute.

I felt sick. I felt deep grief. I felt profound sadness. Then, all of those feelings snowballed into one another, creating a rolling, momentum-shifting sphere of sorrow that couldn't be stopped.

I raised my voice on the call to cut through the chatter. I had something to say.

The thing that we continued to claim never happened to any women at our agency had happened. The worst, most final version of the death by a thousand cuts had taken yet another woman away from the world, the flame of her existence extinguished permanently by the whim of a monstrous man.

WHY can't we simply ask our women, "What has it been like for you?" And then . . . believe them?

Where were their responses to my fucking manifesto now?

We needed to first communicate to our staff what happened and how we would support everyone. Then, we needed to cancel all planned social posts. Those planned, light-hearted posts would now be so deeply insensitive and tone deaf. I refused to allow us to act like what had just happened to her didn't happen. With the investigation underway, we needed to put out a statement on social media that didn't announce what had happened to our colleague, but spoke to those who knew. And all live-tweeting of our event that day would not take place. We would continue with the event in the room in Palo Alto, but we would not promote or publicize it more broadly, as planned.

The team agreed with this approach and I drafted our single post for that fateful International Women's Day, where yet another woman in the world—one of our own—was lost to domestic violence:

> "At Golin, we are dedicated to the empowerment, respect and support of all women, every day. But, today, that dedication has never meant more to us. #IWD"

Not everyone was happy with what I said. But my moral compass outweighed anyone else's desired roadmap pointed toward their personal glory.

And the track I had begun to lay for myself was starting to show a new destination.

Devastating tragedy had begun the day 5,421 miles east of Palo Alto. And on the opposite side of the world 12 hours later, we created an experience focused on supporting women that was powerful. The complexity and heaviness of holding both weighed on me more than almost any other moment of my 15-year career. It was the epitome of the dynamic and devastating duality of what it means to be a woman.

The morning after our event—as we waited in the hotel lobby for our Uber to the SFO airport—our agency leaders who were in attendance were beaming in the afterglow.

One of them pulled me aside to congratulate me. And he asked how working with the managing director (MD) of our San Francisco office had been—in preparing for this huge client and prospect event in *his* market.

Before I share my response, it's important for you to know just how strong my relationship with this person was. Over the previous 10 years, I had supported him in his work, and he had been instrumental to my success as I rose through the ranks of our Marketing team, starting out as a new business and marketing associate to now running the entire global department as the executive director and senior vice president. He'd been a true mentor and friend. He saw me as a confidant and genuinely consulted me in many big decisions for the agency.

He was one of the only positive male figures in my life. At that point, I hadn't seen or spoken to my biological father in more than 15 years. This man was someone I went to for advice in life—both personally and professionally.

So, when he asked me how working with our San Francisco MD had been, I told him the truth: the MD was completely useless, didn't deliver on anything he promised, and went MIA until the night of the event where he had the audacity to pull me aside as we walked into our sit-down dinner for 50 people to ask if he should "deliver a speech."

I ended my feedback with a simple statement: "I could do his fucking job."

We got in the Uber and headed to the airport. I had a missed call and voicemail from another senior leader. He congratulated me on an incredible event, praised my leadership and direction in a crisis from the morning before, and said that I needed to be recognized for the work I was doing in new and different ways; there was something bigger coming for me.

I saved the voicemail, put my phone in my bag, and didn't think much more about it.

Until two weeks later.

On Thursday, March 21, 2019, a member of our executive board asked me to meet him at 1 p.m. in the big, private executive conference room. This wasn't abnormal or momentous. I met with him often. So, I walked in thinking we were there to talk about what they needed from me next.

We started out by talking about family and sports and kept it light for a while. And I assumed this was just a casual catch-up. But then he said that the senior leader had shared my comment about our San Francisco MD with him from a few days before.

Shit.

Was I about to be reprimanded? I mean, this wasn't the military. So, I wasn't—like—going to be court marshalled for insubordination. But, what the hell? How could he do me like this? That was a private conversation. And now my confidence had been betrayed. And I was going to get in trouble for it?

He leaned forward and intertwined his hands in a loose prayer position on the oversized wooden conference table.

"Do you want his job?"

I thought it was a joke. A sarcastic "Oh, you think you can do it better" rhetorical kind of question.

But it wasn't. He was serious. "We want you to be the MD of the San Francisco office."

He told me that he had already spoken about this idea with the executive team. They not only *believed* I could do it; they believed I could do it *better* than the guy currently running the show out there.

They had always put people with tech backgrounds in the role—since it was the core of the client work in that market—but they didn't feel like any of them had the leadership skills to truly inspire the staff, drum up the business, impress the clients, and truly establish our company as a force to be reckoned with among all the other heavy-hitting agencies in the Bay Area.

They saw something special in me.

They believed I could lead differently and have success.

They watched how I had been a builder for a decade and wanted to see me build this.

I was stunned.

I had never imagined myself for a role like this. I didn't have any of the traditional background that other MDs did of running a large client account and PNL before taking on the big task of managing an office of people and clients. But they didn't care. Because I had the thing that couldn't be taught: the ability to inspire and lead.

It looked like the leader I had grown to be was kicking my slow-track's ass now, amirite?

I thanked him for believing in me and said I'd need a few days to think about it and weigh my decision. He understood and said he'd anxiously await my response.

He walked out and I stood looking out our 11th floor window at Water Tower, across the street. The people heading north and south on Michigan Avenue looked like little ants in a single file line.

My immediate thought was: am I okay to even consider this opportunity as a possibility?

Ugh. I'm so sad thinking about how much I didn't believe I could do because of all the women who had been my bosses who told me I was less capable, less worthy, and less deserving than I was.

I called Brian, my husband. Holy shit. What was happening?

Was this real?

How did I do that?
There's no way this was real.
I couldn't believe my eyes.

I had been in love with San Francisco for almost 20 years—from when my cool older cousin, Jessica, lived there after college to when my cool younger sister, Meaghan, did the same.

California was in my blood.

I was born in Long Beach, California, and had spent a few summers of my childhood visiting our father there after our parents divorced when I was 7. He was born there too and had spent his entire first 18 years growing up near Solvang in Bakersfield.

I had always been drawn to the ocean, which made sense—since the first 16 years of my life were spent living in five different ocean-side states due to my mom's career as a U.S. Coast Guard Officer.

Was the ocean calling me back to it?

Sure, Lake Michigan in Chicago—that I could see from the 11th floor of our office in the John Hancock Building—*resembled* an ocean (its 22,300 square miles of water was so massive that when standing on a shore, you couldn't see land on the other side). But it wasn't real. It was an illusion.

The two biggest hurdles to clear in order to move our family from where we were established in Chicago to San Francisco were solved by the City by the Bay: Brian's job and Will's health.

Brian worked for Salesforce. Salesforce was headquartered in San Francisco. Problem solved.

My Will has a lifelong chronic illness: severe hemophilia A, a genetic bleeding disorder caused by the absence of Factor VIII, a clotting protein, in his body. If you're reading this, you likely have Factor VIII and don't think twice when you cut your finger or trip and fall or grow taller or build muscle or simply live your life—all actions that cause you to bleed internally and externally to varying degrees.

Hemophilia is extremely rare; there are only 30,000 males with hemophilia living in the United States. And there is a roughly 100% chance that the mother will be a carrier when a son has hemophilia. I am not a carrier. Will's hemophilia was a result of a spontaneous mutation in utero. That's a fancy way of saying that my baby is one in a million. He was, is and always will be.

We had a team of hematology specialists at Northwestern's Ann and Robert H. Lurie's renowned Children's Hospital (two blocks from my office!). Could we really leave them? Well, San Francisco had the Marc Benioff Children's Hospital (named for the incredible donations of Salesforce's Founder and CEO). Their hematology clinic and team were some of the best in the world. Problem solved.

I spent the next few days dreaming with Brian about what could be. A new adventure in both our careers and for our family. We were excited and nervous and unsure and a bit giddy.

And then, the shine started to wear off.

The day that I was offered the San Francisco managing director job and I told the exec that I needed time to think about it, his immediate response was "How long?" This guy was not good at being patient—or reading a room.

I told him on the Thursday of our conversation that I was headed to Austin, Texas, the next day, Friday, to host my sister's bachelorette party through the weekend. I would come back to him the following week with additional questions, concerns, and thoughts that would help me make my decision. He begrudgingly agreed to the plan.

I'm sure he was thinking: Who is this chick? What does *she* need to think about? What's there to consider? She should be *grateful* and jumping to accept the opportunity *we* are giving *her*.

So many men's careers never need to be balanced with anything. Their ambition and professional dreams ride on a completely separate track from the day-to-day realities of their family.

That's the reason that I started to write my second manifesto on my 10:37 flight to Austin that Friday morning.

My sweet giddiness had turned sour, my excitement had an edge, my flattery was becoming deflated.

And as I muttered to myself on the flight, while my fingers furiously typed up what I was feeling, my seatmate glanced over every few moments considering whether she should press the flight attendant call button.

By the time the plane touched down, my latest manifesto was complete.

As you read this, remember that I wrote this on March 22, 2019 (a full year before the pandemic of 2020 completely changed the way we lived and worked).

San Francisco Pilot

A Progressive Workforce

The world has changed. And yet, the workforce hasn't kept up. Advancements in technology, travel, and communication have evolved the way we live and work. But the infrastructures of so many companies remain staggeringly similar to ways they were built decades—and sometimes centuries—ago.

It's time to create a progressive place where men's and women's careers can thrive, not in spite of their personal lives but because of them. A place where people are encouraged to not only bring their whole selves to work, but a place where they feel supported to fully integrate their personal and professional goals.

I propose a "Progressive Workforce" pilot in our San Francisco office centered around "equitable leadership." The inspiration for this pilot considers how caregiver bias and the unpaid emotional labor women so often bear the burden of alone—or in an unbalanced way—affects women's abilities to progress in their careers.

Sure, when women and men "arrive" at the same place in their careers, we applaud those companies who treat them equally—who give them the SAME opportunities. But, are they *really* the same? Are they *really* equitable? Were their paths *really* comparable in any way?

Why, when we offer women opportunities that we offer men, do we act like the choices they have to consider and weigh, the sacrifices they will need to make and the work and family "load" they will be painstakingly tasked with balancing are in any way the same? THEY ARE NOT. So, let's stop acting like what we hold up as "equal opportunities" are in any way equitable.

Progressive companies work to find innovative solutions to move themselves and society forward.

That's what I'm proposing here: a "Progressive Workforce" pilot that embraces and builds an office dedicated to 21st century leadership; a workplace and workforce culture that empowers diversity, inclusion, belonging; and an unbiased infrastructure that makes equitable leadership a priority and a reality.

The struggle is real. The juggle is worse.

The truth is, I can't be the MD of any office at Golin in the way that we currently are structured.

- I can't work 10–15 consecutive hours a day in a row, every day. I need flexibility to consider the structure of each day differently.
- I can't ignore my family's health when it requires immediate, undivided attention. I am not replaceable in my family's unit.
- I can't put my own physical and mental health on the backburner when it deserves to be a top priority.
- I won't miss the important moments of my children's lives, big and small. I don't want to outsource every aspect of raising my kids.
- I won't miss the important moments in my husband's life and our life as a couple.
- I won't be made to feel guilty when I'm living out my defined and clearly communicated life priorities.
- I don't want to look back in 3 or 5 or 10 years and regret any amount of time I devoted to my career or my family.

- I will give the job *everything I have to give it* . . . which—let's be clear—is not *everything* I have to give. *That* would be completely counterintuitive to the mission for this pilot.
- I will have missteps along the way that will lead to better choices, solutions, and results.
- I will fail on this journey, maybe as often as I succeed. But failing forward will lead to much more rewarding and powerful destinations.
- I will attract hard-working, exceptional talent.
- I will win the hearts, minds, and business of evolved, enlightened clients.
- I need the full support of leadership to make this a success.
- I need to be able to offer flexible careers to people who want to work *for* the San Francisco office (if we want to compete in *any* way with the progressive tech companies based in the Bay Area)—notice how I didn't say "in" the SF office, b/c I don't believe that everyone who is right for this work and mission needs to live in the Bay Area.
- I want to forgo the misguided notion of working "longer" or "harder" for working "smarter" and "better."
- I want to build an office that supports this vision for a new way of working.
- I want to build an office that proves our mission to have her back.
- I want Golin to be a career innovator and create an incubator that successfully integrates its employees' personal and professional goals.
- I want to do things differently.
- I want to Go All In on what I believe could be one of the most rewarding adventures of my life.

I pulled together an extensive, thoughtful strategy around my progressive pilot, with additional programs and initiatives to consider, plus a daily work-life integration model. I wasn't fucking around. I was ready to do this. I was *born* to do this.

When I landed back in Chicago a few days later, I was fired up. I was buzzing. I was ready to bring this big idea back to the executive board member.

And then, my seven-month-old baby got very, very sick and was hospitalized.

I had to postpone the meeting meant for Monday. Charlie dropped 20% of his body weight, was hooked up to IV fluids, had an allergic reaction to the antibiotic they gave him in the hospital, and his perfect, tiny body was covered in huge welts and hives. I stayed in the hospital with him for three days until he was discharged while Brian took care of Will at home.

The day he was discharged, Will had a muscular bleed in his thigh, and we rushed him to the ER. He received multiple infusions of factor over the next two days to manage and stop the bleed.

Parenting is a full-body contact sport. Parenting a child with a chronic illness is like playing quarterback in the NFL without a helmet or pads, barefoot.

I was completely depleted. All of the excitement around my new career opportunity—and the energy I felt when creating the idea (and a full-fledged strategy and plan of action) for a pilot in our San Francisco office—was transferred to my children. I needed to give them everything I had. And I did.

When I was out of the office acting as a round-the-clock nurse for that entire week following my conversation with that senior leader, he was fully supportive of me caring for my children . . . at first. Then, as he always did in matters that concerned him, he grew impatient.

When were we going to meet?
When was I going to give him my answer?
When, when, when?

The first day I returned to work after my hellish hospital week a colleague asked me to go to coffee so we could talk in private about what I had decided.

I was exhausted, coming off of almost a full week in the pediatric ER and step-down unit. But I was also excited about this idea I had to create an incubator, a pilot, a better way of working, leveraging my agency's most senior leaders' trust and belief and faith in me to turn around what had been a fledging office for years and to propose something even better and more impactful.

When we arrived at Dollop Coffee, we put our orders in and grabbed a spot on the overstuffed couch tucked in the back. I was going to meet with the executive board member who offered me the MD role the following day to share my idea and to make my ask.

When I started to share my full idea and read directly from my manifesto, the blood began to drain from her face. She turned gray. She looked like she was going to be sick.

And although what looked like disapproval from her began to churn up the acid and anxiety in me, what I realized—in reflecting, years later—is that she was in a state of shock.

When a butterfly is considering breaking free from its cocoon, the exterior that once felt and looked like a hard, metal locked cage begins to reveal itself to be penetrable, as thin as a house of cards.

What happened next had happened a thousand times before—to me, to my mother, and to my mother's mother. It's happened to you. And your mother. And your mother's mother.

For a moment, you experience life on the other side. You test what taking back your power could taste like. And then—with a word, a sentence, a conversation—it's gone.

You stand frozen on the platform, watching the doors to the train you knew could take you to where you want to go slowly close in front of you. The pendulum swings too far in the wrong direction, past the point of no return.

I walk into the coveted tiny executive meeting room with soft seating. I'm finally meeting with the exec after being in the hospital with my sick children for almost a week straight and after having my internal compass redirected.

I close the glass door behind me. And before my ass even has the chance to land on the oatmeal-colored accent chair, he says, "Well, if last week showed us anything, there's no way you could do that job."

[Record screech.]

"I'm sorry . . . what?" is what stumbles out of my mouth, without a filter.

"Well, I mean, there's no way you can run an office and handle clients and new business pitches if you have to take an unplanned week off because of your kids."

A calm washes over me. It's one of those pivotal life moments, where the road converges, and the path becomes clear.

Robert Frost's poem comes to me time and time again when choices are hard—and then easy—to make: "Two roads diverged in a wood and I, I took the one less traveled by. And that has made all the difference."

I take a deep breath.

And I let him have it.

"Hold on. I am here to give you *my* answer. So, you don't get to tell me how this is going to go. *I've* decided not to accept the San Francisco MD role. But it's not because I'm a mother. It's not because I have two small children. It's not because my kids were sick last week. It's because I'm not going to walk into something I'm being told is an opportunity when I know I'm being set up to fail."

It is the plight that many—if not, most—women with children and careers face every day.

1. **We are "given" an opportunity.** Because it's never "earned," is it?
2. **The "opportunity" is shit.** In this case, I was being asked to take over a fledgling office that had not been profitable or successful in a decade. And they wanted me to bring it back to life while raising my two children under age three—with not only a lack of acknowledgment that said children existed but also with an expectation that I would outsource the bulk of my parenting and maternal instincts to protect them to someone else.
3. **If we accept "the opportunity," we *will* fail.** Because remember, the "opportunity" is shit and we are being set up to fail. "See! This is why we don't offer women these opportunities. They don't accept that they don't have what it takes."
4. **If we reject "the opportunity," we *are* failures.** "See! This is why we don't offer women these opportunities. They don't accept them because they don't have what it takes."
5. **Rinse, repeat, forever until the end.**

I've lost count of the number of women I know personally who were hired to excavate a sunken ship. We're so rarely brought in to keep steering the speed boat straight along a placid sea. And whether or not we're able to pull off the impossible (which we often do!), we are still thrown overboard from the ship we captained, left sinking into the ever-expanding gulf of its wake.

All of that is to say that when I stood my ground and said that I didn't want the job, he was pissed.

I wonder now, as I'm typing this, what conversations were had behind my back; who may have said that there's no way I could do the job with two children under three and that I didn't have what it would take?

Regardless, what mattered most is that I had spent significant time in my mind on the other side of the wall that divided my 15-year career inside of a system that wasn't built by—or for—me; imagining and dreaming up a better place for women everywhere.

The gauntlet had been thrown. The line in the proverbial sand had been drawn. The two opposing forces had been identified.

I was leaving Corporate America.

Starting a company, leaving a "safe" job to pursue a lifelong dream, betting on yourself against all odds—none of this is for the faint of heart.

So much is unknown and undecided at every turn.

So much depends on you pep talking yourself into believing, every day, that it's possible.

So much requires you to build the plane while you fly it.

I've made so many mistakes.

- I agreed that I "wasn't ready to be the boss."
- I agreed to be paid less than (and in one case, half as much as) my "equals."
- I agreed to a lower title than the one I deserved.
- I agreed that because I was younger, I was worth less.
- I agreed that I didn't deserve help when I worked up the courage to ask for it.
- I agreed to take on more work than was physically, psychologically, or humanly possible.

- I agreed to have less power inside of a "equitable" partnership.
- I agreed to show up differently than my heart, soul, and spirit wanted.
- I agreed to stay behind the scenes, the curtain, and the "talent."
- I agreed to pour every ounce of human, social, financial and political capital into my work without expecting, or asking, that others do the same.
- I agreed to do the work of multiple people—for no additional compensation.
- I agreed to take a backseat inside of my own company.
- I agreed when my vulnerability was positioned as a liability.
- I agreed to dismiss my intuition as "nervousness" and "misunderstanding."
- I agreed when I was told that I "care too much about people."
- I agreed when I received little to no gratitude for my work.
- I agreed when I received constant feedback about my "flaws."
- I agreed that my market value was directly related to years, not experience.
- I agreed to abandon myself in service to others.

Now now, dear reader, let me be clear: I didn't "agree" to *any* of this.

I didn't begin by abandoning what I felt was equitable, fair, and just.
I didn't start out accepting all of the ways that I would be undervalued, underpaid, and overworked.
I didn't have this experience because I was a person who lacked confidence or ambition or aspiration; I felt this way because I lost all three.

I defeatedly ceded my firm stance, my power, my value, and my worth more and more and more every day because I lost myself along the way.
Here's a critical lesson I learned:

When someone tells you a beautiful truth about yourself but *you* don't believe it, you'll think it's a lie.
When someone tells you an ugly lie about yourself and *you* believe it, you'll think it's the truth.

That is, until you flip the switch.

Until you turn off the lie and illuminate the truth about who you've always been.

I learned more about myself, my worth, my value, my intuition, my strength, my skills, my gifts, and my power from those painful moments I listed out above than almost any other experience. But I still wish I didn't have to be treated so terribly in order to learn them.

I will never get those years back.

I will never regain that time I lost.

I will never be able to go back to those moments with my children, my husband, my family and friends—when I was hurting, distanced, disassociating—and relive them again.

They're all gone.

But I'm still here.

Because I kept going. And you can, too. We don't have to let the past dictate our future. And we don't have to allow it to mean more than we want it to.

I've made so many good decisions:

- I started a company.
- I left a company.
- I asked for—and received—more money.
- I asked for—and received—a bigger title.
- I asked for—and received—help.
- I took on bigger roles than I was ready for.
- I applied for jobs where I didn't meet all of the prerequisites.
- I walked into rooms, where I was the most junior, with authority.
- I sat at the table—and not in the chairs on the periphery.
- I asked for—and secured—meetings with the most powerful and influential people.
- I admitted I was struggling—and the best people stepped in to support me.
- I said no, without explanation.
- I said yes, without expectation.

Even if it feels like it's all too much, start small. Don't think about everything you *need* to do this week, this month, this year. Think about what you *can* do today.

So, whether you're thinking of starting a hobby or a project or an initiative or a campaign or a round of funding or a company, here are some lessons I've learned that I'd love to share with you:

- **Start date:** Today. You don't need to have it all figured out to begin. And you don't need to have everything in place before you share that you've begun. Nothing happens overnight. And just as true, nothing happens until you start.
- **Pay:** Be clear and in agreement about what you're worth. Your *unique experience* (regardless of your age or years in business) is your *product*, *service*, or *offering*. Maybe something only takes you an hour to do it well; but think about the years you spent honing that craft and expertise to complete it that quickly. *That's* what you're assigning the value to. If you're working with others, be clear about what each person is paid and why. This investment determines the bottom line of your business and the power and influence of your people. Do not take this decision lightly.
- **Roles:** Outline every single responsibility that must be accounted for in your endeavor. What needs to be done? Can you do it all? If not, what can you outsource or who can you bring in? Assign each task to an individual. Step back and assess the weight and distribution. Ensure it's realistic, fair, and sustainable.
- **Value proposition:** What is the product or service you are offering? Price it according to its value. You hold all the power here. How you price yourself tells the world what you are worth. And they will value or devalue you based on it.
- **Vision and mission:** Your "vision" and "mission" are not the same. Understanding the difference, and defining and aligning on both, is essential. This is the backbone of your business.

I want to talk a bit more about how "vision" and "mission" are different. Because understanding the nuances and getting detailed and specific about how both show up in your organization are critical.

According to ChatGPT:

The **vision** and **mission** of a company are both essential for defining its purpose and direction, but they serve different roles:

1. Vision Statement (The "Why" & The Future Goal)
   - **Definition:** A vision statement describes what the company aspires to become in the future. It is an inspirational, long-term goal that serves as a guiding star for the organization.
   - **Focus:** Big-picture, future-oriented, and often idealistic.

2. Mission Statement (The "What" & The Present Action)
   - **Definition:** A mission statement explains the company's purpose, what it does, who it serves, and how it operates in the present.
   - **Focus:** Practical, action-driven, and focused on current objectives.

Key Differences:

Feature	Vision Statement	Mission Statement
Focus	Future aspirations	Present-day actions
Purpose	Inspires and sets direction	Explains what the company does
Timeframe	Long-term (5–10+ years)	Short-term to mid-term

A company's *mission* helps achieve its *vision* by defining actionable steps toward that goal. I love the idea of creating vision and mission statements for yourself, too. It's why I make a vision board every single year. So, let's do it together.

Grab a piece of paper. Make two columns: Vision and Mission. Write your focus, purpose, and time frame under each. Use this as your guide for the decisions you make. This will be your written roadmap, guiding your moral compass toward your North Star.

No one can take your North Star from you; and no one can get you there better than yourself.

※ ※ ※

Danielle and I slide into our slate gray Ford Mustang convertible in the Enterprise rental parking lot of the Palm Springs airport. We turn and look at each other and do a little giddy "Ahhhhhhhh!" scream. We made it out.

My best friend Danielle Nelson (left) and me in Palm Springs, California.

Today, we're in Palm Springs, California. It's November 19, 2021. It's the first time we're seeing each other in person in two years because of the pandemic.

It is also the first time either of us are traveling since COVID locked down the world. This is the first time we've left our husbands and children for more than a few hours in that same amount of time.

We feel like Thelma and Louise.

There is no one on Earth like Danielle. Being her best friend has been one of the greatest gifts of my life. We've been through it *all* together.

While the majority of our friendship has existed with us living any-where between hundreds and thousands of miles from one another (4,827 to be exact when I lived in Hawaii Kai on Oahu and Danielle was in Alexandria, Virginia), it never mattered. Physical distance couldn't drive emotional distance between our cosmic connection.

Do you have a friend that simultaneously grounds you and lifts you up—encouraging your high-flying dreams and visions and aspirations that land you among the stars? I hope you do. Danielle has always been that person for me.

When we are together, time stands still. We can go five minutes or five years without seeing each other and it feels the same. There's never any guilt or score boarding in our friendship.

For the next four days, we talk about everything—what we are both navigating in our jobs, with our families, and inside of ourselves.

We drink rosé by the pool, take gummies, and slip into the hot tub, and eat snacks wrapped in sun-warmed towels on the soft seating under white string lights. We buy journals and write our thoughts and feelings and fears and hopes in them while my phone pumps out lo-fi beats to serve as the backdrop to our forward motion.

We bathe in the sun during the day and bask in the moonlight at night. We aren't wives or mothers or workers. We were just us, Danielle and Erin, existing, together.

I tell Danielle everything.

She's shocked. I feel nothing. The scar tissue that has grown over my gaping wounds so many times by now has destroyed any softness to my skin that existed before. It has become a hard, metal shield, abrasive and rough.

We decide enough is enough. We both make life-changing decisions during that trip that irreversibly shift the trajectory of our lives.

We are both breaking generational curses in different ways.
We are both choosing to save ourselves over dying inside of the cages
    where we've been suffocating, trapped.
We are both shedding the good girl cloaks that have weighed us down
    for decades.

I open my computer and see an email from Fast Company's CEO in my inbox.

I can't believe my eyes.
There's no way this is real.
How did we do that?

My company has been named one of Fast Company's World's Most Innovative Companies.

For anyone who's unfamiliar with how awards work, it is rare that a person or a campaign or an initiative or a company wins an award by chance, without their own participation and work.

It's a process. And a money-making one, at that.

You have to find the award program you want to enter, pay the fee for your submission, answer all the questions, and provide all the documents required to be considered and only then, after a panel of judges go through all the entries from all the others, might they consider you worthy of winning.

I had single-handedly pulled together our submission for this Fast Company Award. The email stated that the winners would be announced on March 8, International Women's Day.

On January 14, I wrote this in my journal:

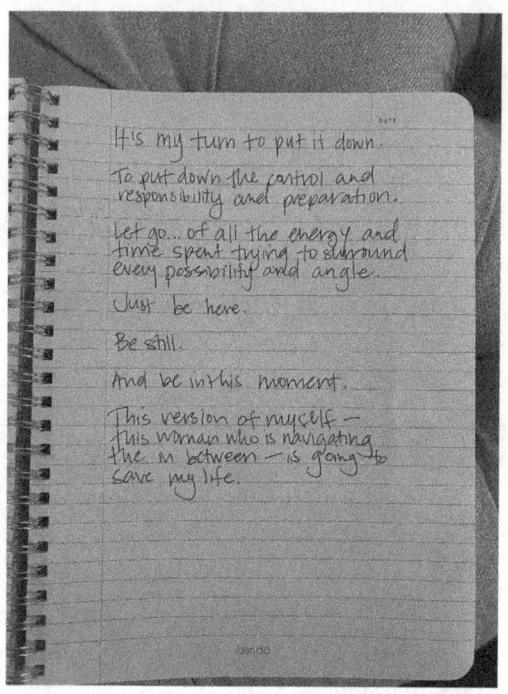

My handwritten note in my journal.

It's my turn to put it down.

To put down the control and the responsibility and preparation.

Let go . . . of all the energy and time spent trying to surround every possibility and angle.

Just be here.

Be still.

And be in this moment.

This version of myself—this woman who is navigating the in between—is going to save my life.

On January 24, I took this photo of my bookcase.

My bookcase in my home office.

What two words stand out to you immediately?
I know. I couldn't believe it either.

Be HER.

Two months after I resigned from the company I had co-founded two and a half years before, Have Her Back closed.

Leaving something you created—poured yourself into, filled with your hopes, dreams, time, energy, spirit, and whole being—does not feel possible.

It feels like a death. Because it is. But it's also a rebirth.

When the world tries to set you on fire, it will fail. The fire won't consume you. It will *fuel* you. You will *become* the fire. And you will walk through and from it, alchemized, transformed from a tarnished penny into lustrous gold.

It's time to remember your value.
It's time to remember your worth.
It's time to remember who the fuck you are.

I did. And I will never, ever forget her again.

My dear friend Michelle Stuntz said four words to me on May 4, 2022, that changed my life. They are words I have carried with me every day that's followed. It was one of the most powerful messages I've ever received about my worth, my value, my power:

"You are the gold."

I remember exactly where we were standing. It was in Anotheroom, a bar on Perry Street in the West Village of Manhattan following my very first Fairway Dinner—before it was a Fairway Dinner. I was consulting for one of my best friends, Jen Cho, CEO of The Wing at the time. So, this was a "Wing Woman Dinner." I was testing out my theory for these Fairway Dinners. I was experimenting with some of my favorite women on the planet.

After our three-hour event at Gelso & Grand, six of us kept the night going in Anotheroom. We drank, we laughed, we shared stories, we told the truth. We talked about what we wanted in the world and how fucking hard it was to get it. I shared what I wanted to build.

I was 34 days out from leaving the company I founded. I didn't take a beat. I never slowed down long enough to feel everything that had happened. I didn't want to. I wanted out of this pain. I wanted to move on. I wanted to get my life back.

I was still transforming from the goo that I had dissolved into. I was slowly becoming what I was going to be next. I was tentatively scratching at my cocoon from the inside, wary of what I would discover when I emerged.

I told the five other women about the 25-page deck I had been build-ing. Hours upon hours, waking up in the middle of the night to keep creat-ing and tweaking until it felt finished. It was my dream for my next company.

I was going to call it Metamorphosis.

It was everything I had wanted to do all those years before. This time, I was going to do it my way.

But I still felt the need for that external validation, for the system to tell me that I was good enough, that my ideas had merit, that I mattered.

I was having serious conversations with massive consulting firms about coming in to build this new practice area, talking to senior leaders across every major business unit about my dream. It was slow moving and layered with red tape.

I shared all of this with the women that night, in the glow of the can-dlelight emanating from every high-top table, with the bass of the 1990s hip-hop matching the beat of my heart.

And then, Michelle looked me directly in the eye. It was one of those moments where the world around you falls away. Everything else becomes muted—a faded backdrop to the spotlit main character of the scene.

"You are the gold."

Her words pierced my cocoon.

She was telling me to stop waiting.

She was telling me to break the fuck out.

She was telling me that everything I was working *toward* existed *right here, right now*, inside of *me*.

I was the alchemist.

The previous 15 years of my life came flooding back.

All the times I was told I wasn't good enough.

All the times I was told I wasn't ready to be the boss.

All the times I was told I wasn't who I thought I could be.

They were all lies. Meant to keep me small and crawling along at a cat-erpillar's pace. Mean girls had always tried to destroy me, to burn me out. But the fire didn't incinerate me. It reignited who I've always been: a phoenix, rising from the ashes of all the versions of myself I've shed and am leaving behind. Through it all, I became the fire. And I will never let another mean girl snuff out my flame.

I flew back to Chicago the next morning and got back in my lab to change the components of my experiment, yet again. The theory I had set out to prove had shifted. The potion I was working to create had changed. The role I was playing had begun to reveal itself.

I was starting my own company.
I was doing it on my own.
I was the gold.

And so, on July 20, 2022, Ella was born.
As the mother of two boys, this was my only chance to have a girl!
All of my hopes and dreams and ideas from the previous 15 years—all of the seeds I had been diligently planting—were poured into my new company.

She was everything I had wanted to bring the world to create change; to challenge the status quo; to disrupt stale, outdated systems. She was feisty and fearless and full of fire.

She was me.

And while I would love to say that I fully realized my role as the alchemist immediately—as the creator of gold and the embodiment of gold itself—rewiring your brain, rewriting your DNA, and reclaiming your power doesn't happen overnight.

This will continue to be the work of my life: to remember who the fuck I am; to realize the power that exists inside of me; to be the main fucking character of my own story.

But the shift had begun. And I was never, *ever* going back.

Five Shifts to Becoming the Alchemist

1. **Believe in your own magic.** The mind has more power than any element we can tangibly see and touch. There is so much magic deep inside of you, desperate to break free. Let it out.

2. **Own the experiment.** Do it your way, regardless of what the rules or rulers around you say. If you keep doing things the way they've always been done, nothing will change.

3. **Embrace your failure.** The only way to avoid failing is to never try anything new. Failure means you're growing, you're changing, you're living. Keep failing forward.

4. **Defend your dissertation.** Even when the world tells you that the theory you're trying to prove out is impossible, irrational, illogical, defend it. You exist at this moment and place in time for a reason.

5. **Don't stop until you've made gold.** When the experiments continue to yield tarnished pennies, keep going. Everything is possible. You are the gold.

12

Main Fucking Character Energy

"If you don't stand for something, you'll fall for anything."

This quote was attributed to Alexander Hamilton. But, let's be honest, it was probably a woman who said it without being credited.

Regardless, it stands the test of time.

Nike went on to use an iteration of this in a campaign in 2018, celebrating the 30th anniversary of "Just Do It." The ad featured professional football player and civil rights activist Colin Kaepernick, best known for taking a knee during an NFL game's national anthem to protest social injustice and police brutality. In white font overlaying a black-and-white, zoomed-in, full-bleed photo of Colin's face, looking directly into the camera, are the words: "Believe in something. Even if it means sacrificing everything."

But what if we took it one step further? What if we shifted the focus from the "something" that Hamilton and Nike reference in their messages and we turned it directly to you?

Let's try it.

If you try to be liked by everyone, you'll be loved by no one—least of all, yourself.

Women are so often told that their lived experience didn't happen, that their perspective is wrong, their opinion is flawed, or that their existence is irrelevant. But when they decide they are not here to win everyone over, to get total buy-in, and to convince every single person that they matter, they are free. They are able to live in a way that is genuinely, authentically, and fully who they are meant to be—flaws, complications, and fuckups included.

But until we make that shift, on the hamster wheel we run. There is no time—or space—to focus on you.

There's always *something* else to do.
There's always *someone* else to see.
There's always *somewhere* else to be.

That is until *you* reign.

It's 6:45 a.m. EST on March 10, 2024. I'm sitting in one of the low-back counter stools at the Airbnb we're renting in Austin, Texas. Four of us are staying here while we attend SX (pronounced "South by"). The South by Southwest (SXSW) Conference provides an opportunity for the global community of creatives to encounter cutting-edge ideas, discover new interests, and network with other professionals who share a similar appetite for forward-focused experiences.

The makeup artist I've hired to do my makeup professionally is applying false eyelashes to my dirty blonde lashes that just don't pop enough on their own. Damn natural lashes.

I hear the footsteps of one of my best friends—Jen Cho—coming from the hallway by her room as I'm obediently looking down during lash application.

"Jennnnnnnnnnnn!" I say as a warm wave washes over me. That always happens to me when Jen enters the room.

"Errrrrrrrinnnnnnnn," Jen coos back. We love each other. It's as simple as that.

She admires my almost-complete hair and makeup.

Yesterday was a whirlwind. Jen arrived at our Airbnb less than 24 hours before, as I was headed out the door with my dear friend Stacy London to make our call time.

Stacy and I were speaking on stage at SX. Our panel was titled "System Failure: Why Women Are Opting Out."

The description of our panel stated:

The current systems (yes, all of them) aren't built for—or by—women. We're here to change that. More women should be running the world. Why aren't we, you ask? The lack of women in positions of power and influence has nothing to do with ability, ambition, or aspiration. It has everything to do with access. So, we're opting out. By disrupting existing industries and creating entirely new ecosystems across media, health, finance, tech, and intersectional gender equity, these businesswomen are on a mission to achieve a true cultural and generational metamorphosis.

I had created, pitched, and landed our stage spot at SX. I felt responsible for marketing our panel and encouraging people to attend. I needed all of this effort to be successful.

And it was.

Or so I thought.

The room was engaged, and women came up to us afterward to thank us for the conversation to share their own personal stories.

As soon as the room was empty, Stacy had to haul ass to the airport to make her flight back to New York ahead of her next obligation. She had flown to Austin, Texas, for a whirlwind 36 hours just to show up for me. That's the kind of friend, sister, and Hype Woman my beautiful, brilliant, beloved Stacy is for me.

Five of my girlfriends, who were hyping me from the audience, piled in for congratulatory hugs.

"Let's go celebrate!" they shouted. "Our girl killed her first SX panel!"

We went up to the rooftop of a nearby hotel and had the most fun and joy-filled afternoon eating, drinking, and letting go together.

Now, here Jen and I were 18 hours later as I prepared to host my second SX panel. (Honestly, what the fuck was I thinking? One is enough. Two is too many. Did I mention that on top of both, I also had planned a Hype Women Soiree, complete with another panel, speeches, and a seated dinner for 120 women?)

I was still recovering from who I had always been.
I was still hustling and grinding myself to dust.
I was still showing up for everyone except myself.

And that's just what Jen is about to tell me.

"How do you feel about your panel yesterday?" Jen asks while cradling a steaming cup of coffee in her hands.

I hop down off the chair, my hair and makeup complete, to join her on the couch.

"I think it was good. Everyone seemed really engaged. And we had a few ladies ask some really powerful questions during the Q&A. I feel good."

Jen nods at me, with understanding.

"Where were you?" she asks in the least judgmental or accusatory or condescending way possible.

It's hard to explain the magic of Jen Cho. She can level me with one look. She can ask a question that calls in decades of conditioning. She can crack me open just when I think I have done an excellent job of Gorilla Gluing myself shut.

"What do you mean?" I ask genuinely confused and curious about where she's headed.

"I mean, where were *you*? Yes, you were on stage and you did a great job and anyone watching wouldn't think otherwise."

She takes a sip of her coffee, and I watch her in slow motion, waiting for the Jen beat to drop.

That's what she does. You're cruising along, bobbing your head to the melody, thinking you know this song and you have your shit figured out. And then, the music pauses for a brief moment and the beat drops. Like, that full-bodied, skin-tingling, soul-crushing, hurt-so-good beat drop that invites you to let go of it all and release all the shit you are so tightly holding in.

She continues.

"I didn't see you up there. I didn't hear you. I didn't feel you. You acted like a moderator who was there to interview Stacy."

I tilt my head. "Well, I was. I was the moderator—there to interview Stacy."

Jen does this closed-mouth, slight upturn of her lips, slow nod thing when she's encouraging you to keep going—to keep digging on the thing you're saying. I know it well, and it has changed my life more times than I can count. I follow her lead.

"At least, that's why I *thought* I was there. It was set up that way. They came to see Stacy."

She does her slow nod thing again. And then she stops and looks me dead in the eye.

"They came to see *you, too.*"

I stop. I replay her words in my head. I inhale deeply. I exhale defeatedly. Fuck.

I did it again.

Now, let me be clear, Jen wasn't knocking Stacy in her comment. This wasn't an "either/or." It was a "both." She wasn't pitting us against one another. Because she's not a mean girl.

A mean girl would have said this:

> *"You were so good yesterday. Do you feel like you were good? Ohmygod Stacy was AMAZING. I mean, she always is. It's so clear why she's such an icon and like a total star. Wow, I just love her. But anyway, you did a really good job interviewing her."*

Mean girls don't give a shit about you. They don't want you to be seen or heard or to grow or evolve. They want you to hate other women, just like they do. They want to stir shit up and create tension and conflict where it doesn't exist. They want you to question yourself and to feel less than. They want to extinguish your light because watching you succeed unearths deep-seeded envy in their veins.

That's not Jen.

Jen is an Unabashed Hype Woman.

It is no coincidence that her last name is Cho and she is my Chief Hype Officer (CHO) for life. (*Trademark!*) Jen sees me in ways that I can't. She unlocks doors in my heart that I have steel-trapped shut with the hope of never having to open them again. She knows who I am at my core. She reminds me of who the fuck I am when I forget.

When Jen looks me dead in the eye and raises an eyebrow, she says everything that needs to be said, without uttering another word.

Main. Fucking. Character. Energy.

I nod back.

"Fuck." I say.

"Yeah," Jen replies.

We both lean our heads back against the couch cushions and stare at the ceiling. Sitting in silence with Jen feels like a warm blanket, a crackling fire, a deep embrace. It's so. damn. comfy.

I turn back to her. "Okay. I got it. I hear you. I receive it. You're right. What the fuck? How am I still doing this? Why do I keep needing to learn this lesson?"

Jen hugs me. She knows all of these questions too well. She's felt them too. The number of hours we've logged traveling through our tortured past together has made us experts at navigating the rocky terrain.

But what's crazy is that the more we've done it, the less rocky it's become. We don't need to go back so often or so far or with such a heavy heart. Now, we can look left and see it and say, "I don't want to go there again."

That's the thing about your most important life lessons. They will continue to show up until you learn them. You will repeat patterns and walk the same path until you see it for what it is, until you feel differently in a situation that seems oh-so-familiar, and until you decide who you want to be.

My next panel starts in four hours.

It's titled "Why You Are an Abortion Beneficiary."

I will be joined on stage by a trio of phenomenal change-agents: my dear friend Dawn Laguens, the chief strategy and innovation officer of Planned Parenthood; Kiki Freedman, the co-founder and CEO of Hey Jane; and Dr. Roopan Gill, co-founder of Vitala Global Foundation.

Jen puts the perfect punctuation on what would become one of the most important conversations of my life:

"I didn't want to have this conversation yesterday. Yesterday was for celebrating, for honoring a milestone. But I also didn't want to wait until after your panel today. Because I know you can show up on stage today in your full power—remembering to use your voice and honor everything you've built that has brought you to this moment."

Goddamn I don't deserve Jen Cho. Okay, okay, main fucking character energy. I *do* deserve Jen Cho—and I am eternally grateful that she is by my side in this lifetime.

If you don't have your Jen Cho, please go find her. She's out there. And please start to walk away and distance yourself from the women who not only don't want to see you shine, succeed, or shed your inhibitions but who actively work against you and your progress and growth.

I'm on stage at SX with Dawn Laguens, Kiki Freedman, and Dr. Roopan Gill. I turn my mic on, look out at the audience, and open our session with these words:

"I've had two abortions over the course of my life. The first, at age 20 at Planned Parenthood in Ann Arbor, Michigan. The second, 20 years later at age 40, married with two children, using the Hey Jane abortion pill in the comfort of my own home. And the reasons I had those abortions is no one's fucking business."

The audience roars. Women shout out "Yes!" with raised arms and vigorous claps.

I was a different person on that second stage than I was the day before.

I remembered to show up.
I remembered to use my voice.
I remembered to be the main character in my own damn life.

I look out into the audience and lock eyes with Jen. They are sparkling with the joy and pride and knowing that can come only from someone who truly understands your journey.

Main Fucking Character Energy does not mean that everything *is* about you. Nor does it mean that you *make* everything about you.

It means you remember that you are the main character in your own damn story. So, you better show up that way.

I often think about the line that Kate Winslet says in *The Holiday*. She's sitting at dinner with the older gentleman played by Eli Wallach.

His character, Arthur, says to her: "You, I can tell, are a leading lady, but for some reason you are behaving like the best friend."

Kate's character Iris responds, "You're so right. You're supposed to be the leading lady of your own life, for God's sake!"

That's it right there.

Main. Fucking. Character. Energy.

I declared it my vibe for 2025. And I hope you declare it for yourself, right now, too.

We sabotage ourselves, sidelining our stardom, riding backseat in a car we should be driving (I mean, damn, we bought and own this thing!) because it's what good girls are told to do.

Don't talk about yourself.
Don't be the center of attention.
Don't be showy.
Defer, defer, defer.

Defer is defined as "to delay something until a later time; to postpone."

And as women, we defer our happiness, our self-care, our prioritizing of our needs, our desires (how selfish!) every single day. Choosing ourselves last is conditional.

"I'll take care of myself when . . ."

It's always just out of reach; not that we're even attempting to outstretch our arms in the direction of ourselves. It's so much easier to focus on everything happening around us—or so we *think* we're thinking. Conditioning is a sneaky bitch that way.

There's always something, someone, somewhere more important than we are—as we stand right here in this moment.

We are taught that being liked by others is more important than liking ourselves.

Let me write that—and ask you to read that—again.

We are taught that being liked by others is more important than liking ourselves.

But it's a trap, and it's meant to silence you.

Here's what I've learned firsthand: if you want to be "liked" by everyone, say and do nothing. You'll fly under the radar, not disrupting or changing a damn thing. You'll exist as quietly and obediently as a clock on the wall ticking time off of each day of your life.

It took me 40 years to outgrow my penchant to be a people pleaser and instead to fully embrace being "likeable enough."

Here's the secret they don't want us to realize: it's an unwinnable game. Being likeable is subjective.

What makes you likeable to one person may make you intolerable to another. Women are not a monolith. And we don't deserve to be condemned for being multifaceted.

I've stopped saying sorry—not for mistakes I've made that deserve reflection or redemption. After all, failing and learning and owning your actions is the only way to evolve and grow.

But I've stopped saying sorry for being myself.

On episode 9 of my *Hype Women Podcast*, published on January 11, 2024, the first anniversary of our Hype Women Movement—Hype Women Day—my dear friend Alexis McGill Johnson, the CEO and president of Planned Parenthood, shares a story with me:

> About six or eight months into my interim role as CEO of Planned Parenthood, one of our affiliate CEOs came to me to say:
>
> "I see you being a little tentative. Just because your title says 'interim' or 'acting' CEO doesn't mean you are not the CEO."
>
> And I had this "aha" moment: you know when you go and visit someone's house—and they have a beautiful guest room and everything is

perfectly pointed? And you fold the towel back exactly as it was and put everything back in its place. The feeling is "I want to look like I wasn't here."

And she said to me, "You need to drive it like you stole it."

When she said it, it went through me; it made me stand up straighter in a way where I recognized that I had *stepped* into power, but I wasn't *standing* in it.

How many of us feel like we are powerless in our own stories? In our own relationships? In our own lives?

We can't let the fear of what others think stop us from existing wholly.

So many of the people we waste our time and energy and spirit on are only extras in the movie of our life. Most didn't even get cast for a role. But you did. Starring role. Main fucking character. The heroine of her own story.

It's time to stand in the spotlight and show the world the woman they've all been waiting to see.

Five Shifts to Main Fucking Character Energy

1. **Determine your worth.** You can't demand that others respect and value you until you respect and value yourself. Deep down, you know what you bring to every room you're in. The people you allow into your life should see it, celebrate it, and sing your praises without envy.

2. **Analyze your energy.** How much of it is spent making other people money, making other people famous, making other people feel good about themselves? Can that be shifted toward you? If yes, start today.

3. **Practice hyping yourself without qualifiers.** Do you always add a "but" or a "I don't mean to talk about myself" after you hype yourself? Please stop. No, but seriously. Hype yourself. And then stop talking. Qualifiers aren't invited to our Main Fucking Character Energy party.

4. **Find your Jen Cho.** Having a friend who sees everything you're capable of and knows everything you're worth is essential to believing it yourself. Let her remind you of who the fuck you are, believe her and then repeat it on repeat.

5. **Own the spotlight.** When you're standing in the light for the first time, it will feel uncomfortable. You will want to push someone else out in front of you. Don't do it. The discomfort will pass. Bathe in the light.

13 | Prioritizing Pleasure

I've had a complicated relationship with pleasure since I was a young girl. My Catholic-infused upbringing instilled shame in me around the topic of sex. And I don't remember *ever* learning about the idea of pleasuring myself. And then, my experience as a woman—who was shown the way of selflessness and sacrifice—learned to think of any kind of pleasure as excessive, indulgent, unnecessary.

Even saying—and now, writing—the word *pleasure* makes me uncomfortable. And I know I'm not alone. Women gather and share our deepest, darkest experiences of trauma and pain. And we do it often. But the actions and experiences that bring us pleasure and joy? Those not only are experienced fewer and farther in between, but they are rarely discussed.

Pleasure doesn't have to be sexual. It can be experienced through tastes and smells and textures and sounds. It's about tapping into your senses—and giving space and time for those senses to be realized. It's about slowing down, taking time, creating space, and being where your feet are.

When we prioritize pleasure, we unlock and unleash the most beautiful and primal parts of ourselves. And it is through that connection to our core that we are able to experience fully. Without it, we walk through life on autopilot.

There is no place where choosing what *feels* good eclipses what *looks* honorable.

There is no room to explore our desire over our duty.

There is no amount of control over our life that will guarantee it all works out.

That is, until we release.

I'm walking to pick up my second grader from school. It's May 6, 2024. I am recording a voice note to send to my book doula, Rea Frey. I could write an entire book that is filled purely with the transcripts of Rea and my voice notes to one another.

Rea is the reason this book is in your hands. Without her, I never would have pulled what was in my heart and mind into a proposal that was worthy of reading—*or* buying. She was with me through it all. She asked me questions I had never considered. She shifted the way I think. My 2024 vibe to take back my body needed my A-team to do it. And Rea is forever part of that squad.

When I was struggling to articulate my vision for this book, I started and stopped writing 100 times, I scribbled words and phrases and bulleted lists on whatever scrap of paper I could find—in the glove compartment while driving, on the back of a receipt in the bottom of my purse during my son's soccer practices, inside of my kids' art notebooks laying on our kitchen island, on the envelope in a stack of bills splayed on the round table in our front room.

I needed to capture what was swirling inside of me.

I needed to get it out of my head and into written form.

I needed to release it from my body.

There was no wanting, no exploring, no pleasure. I was on a fucking deadline—and I was missing it.

That's when Rea texted me "Just give yourself permission to wander a bit first."

What the fuck was she talking about?

Wandering is for people who don't get shit done.
Wandering is for people who have time to waste.
Wandering is for people who are lazy.

Giving myself permission to wander is the work of my life. Twenty-five years of therapy and I am *just* scratching the surface.

I sat with her words and let them penetrate my steely exterior.

Then, I sent her this voice note:

So, I'm walking to pick up my William and I was thinking as I just typed this to you—holy shit. "Permission to wander." What? Is? That? I mean we have this running joke in my marriage—and this was actually a part of my vows—that my husband and I have the exact opposite definition of the best way to get somewhere.

Because to me the best way to get from point A to point B is the shortest, fastest route. It's direct. It's efficient. It gets it done. And Brian is like, "you just go where the wind takes you." He's a wanderer. He wants to explore. He wants to turn down the street that he doesn't know. And I'm like, "This is so fucking inefficient. And what are we even doing and how do we even know what we're gonna come across?" And so—like, wow—it's hitting a little too close to home that this is my exact problem with this process. I'm like, "Okay I need to get this done—like just wrap it up, tighten it up, get it locked,"

And the idea of wandering has always felt indulgent to me. But what's sadder than that, it's felt—what is the right word that I'm looking for—it's felt worthless. Why would I do that? That's a waste. It's a waste. It's a waste of time and energy. So much of my life the past year has been about trying to shift this idea of efficiency and production and output. And instead, thinking more about actually experiencing and enjoying and being in the moment. So this is all just very cerebral for me. Okay, hopefully that made sense. I appreciate you standing by me on this journey.

Our conversation continued through texts, voice notes, and memes of Emma Stone eating ice cream crying and Jennifer Lawrence saying "What do you mean?" three times in a row: at first, incredulous and accusatory; next, pleading and desperate; the last, broken down and broken open.

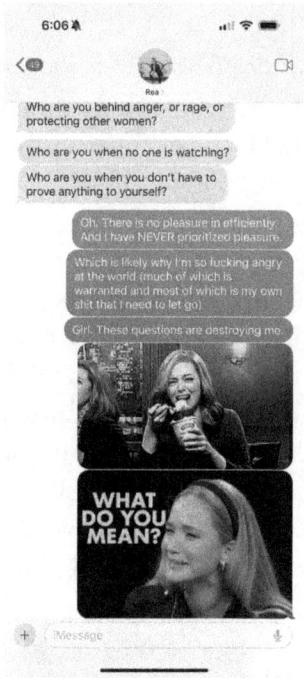

My text exchange with Rea Frey.

It was the perfect depiction of the transformation I was experiencing. Here is the transcript of our combination text and voice note exchange:

Rea:

> You are designed so different from your husband. And once you understand WHO YOU ARE, you look at yourself with a whole new lens.
>
> It completely altered my marriage and parenting my daughter.
>
> I would also ask: Where is the pleasure in efficiency?
>
> Because pleasure is just as important—if not more so—than efficiency.
>
> Who are you when you slow down?
>
> Who are you when you're not being efficient?
>
> Who are you behind anger, or rage, or protecting other women?

Who are you when no one is watching?

Who are you when you don't have to prove anything to yourself?

Erin:

Oh. There is no pleasure in efficiently [sic]. And I have NEVER prioritized pleasure.

Which is likely why I'm so fucking angry at the world (much of which is warranted and most of which is my own shit that I need to let go).

Girl. These questions are destroying me.

Rea:

Oh my God, I don't mean to be laughing at these memes. But thank you for being so vulnerable and honest. So, I too, *never* used to prioritize pleasure. So, I would—you know—wake up at the crack of dawn and go put myself through a brutal workout and restrict my food and work crooked over a computer.

And just like rage, anger and just pissed if people didn't move as fast as me or didn't process things as fast and just go go go and everything's hard and everything's just like volatile.

And I felt enraged a lot of the time and then, through a series of self-exploration and excavation, I really discovered: What am I actually getting out of all of this? And if I'm not feeling good—in my body and in my mind—then how am I going to help anyone or love anyone when I'm just not even giving love to myself? So, I realized I was really self-punishing constantly.

And so, I completely changed it. Very Cliff's Notes version, but: I went from completely plant-based to literally I find pleasure in every bite of food. It's butter and full-fat dairy and grass-fed meat and I'm nourished. For instance, today, I got my work done and I went and took a super long walk with my dog and then went and laid by the pool and finished a book—like read a book—and I'll do that now in the middle of the day.

God, if I can't give myself pleasure—because that's where we get tripped up too, as we expect pleasure from our partner or somewhere else. We expect other people to make us feel good and we outsource instead of self-source and that starts with fucking feeling good—whether that's physically good, mentally good, emotionally good.

If we don't do it for ourselves—and we don't allow the receiving and the softening, which is so feminine. And feminine is also so powerful. But I think, much to your point about your book, we have to sometimes be in our masculine or feel like we do all the time when the feminine is so much more powerful. And the feminine definitely gets shit done. But if you can't receive—and that includes pleasure—then what is it really all about?

So, I really implore you to even figure out what pleasure looks like for you.

What is your relationship to pleasure? What would you like it to be? I mean that's so much more fun now. I'm waking up and thinking: Ok, how can I pleasure myself today? Whether that's an orgasm or going for a swim and laying out in the sun midday. And I don't feel guilty about that. I used to just be run by: how much money am I making? What does my bank account say? How many clients am I booking?

And that's just not why we're here. We're not here for that. And I think just forging that connection with yourself in a stronger capacity— that is not in relation to any of the shit in the matrix or culture or society—when you create that bond with yourself, it just becomes unshakable and unbreakable. And I think that is worth exploring.

Erin:

OK You are a fucking genius and that voice note is completely shifting something in me on this book. So, just know that you are doing your fucking life's work in this role. I hope you realize and recognize your power and expertise and gift.

So, a while ago I went to a shop where I had an akashic reading. And she told me that my journey in this particular lifetime is to shift from being in my masculine to my feminine. And that in every previous life, I have been a man. And I have almost always been, like, on the battlefront, in wars, leading charges, fighting. And so that's clearly in me.

And so, when you just said what you said in your voice note, I started furiously writing something down on a piece of paper: I was. I am. I will be.

I was operating from my masculine because I had to. It saved my life; it protected me; and it actually also helped me break free from people and places that were toxic and traumatic.

What I am is—I am understanding the power of the feminine and fig-uring out how to use new language and ways of living that are softer and not seeing that as weak.

So, what I am moving towards—what I will be—is someone who is standing in my divine feminine power.

I am not there yet. I am so deeply comfortable in my masculine power and I think also when I look back at all of the trauma, I would prefer that certain people are afraid of me and that is what you see in the different chapters—that anger. That message of "this what the world thinks and they hate us"—and all of that is there because I wake up ready to fight.

And so this idea of waking up ready to find pleasure feels like the oppo-site of that. It's not external and proactive and preparatory and ready. It's sitting and experiencing and being and going inward and think-ing about me and that is, that's the journey that I'm on.

Okay, so wow, all right. This is—this is like a big shift for me. And there's also, like, I'll tell you some things tomorrow when we talk—about some experiences I've had with women lately who are like absolutely tapping into that—sort of like, that scarcity. They're always assuming that someone's out to get them and what that energy feels like when it comes towards me now—and how I'm just like "Whoa, whoa, whoa. That's not mine to solve." That sort of journey, as well. Like not taking on everyone else's unresolved shit.

Yeah, this is crazy. So, I'm gonna take a picture of my 2024 vision board that I did because it's something for me to kind of go back to—and sit with and look at again and think about. And it's not surprising to me that you also are interested in me writing the main fucking char-acter energy. Because I think that one is incredibly important as well because part of that is: if I'm always in service to other people and I'm always thinking about what the world needs from me and I'm always deferring, I'm never the main character in my own story. And if I decide to make myself the main character, a lot of stuff is actually gonna fall away and a lot of the things I thought were important to me that I was striving for no longer are. And that's even more confus-ing. So super excited for this metamorphosis that I'm experiencing yet again. But I'm on it, girl. I got it. I got this. I'm gonna pour myself a glass of wine.

My 2024 Vision Board.

When Rea told me that she took a bath in the middle of the day, I almost fell off of the uncomfortable chair I was dutifully working from, inside of my own office, inside of my own house, inside of my own company of one, where no one was watching me.

We're *allowed* to do that?

Who did I need permission from?
Who was I doing this all for?
Who was I ever going to be that felt like I was enough?

One of my favorite movies is the 1989 Dramedy *Parenthood*. There's a scene toward the end of the movie where Steven Martin's and Mary Steenburgen's characters Gil and Karen are talking in their bedroom. She just shared that she's unexpectedly pregnant with their fourth child.

Gil is struggling with his roles as a husband, a father, a provider, a worker.

As Karen tells him she's pregnant, he's getting ready to go coach his son's little league game. The kids are screaming in the house; they're running late. His stress around it all has been building throughout the movie. And you have a feeling that this is the moment when he's really going to lose his shit.

She wants to know what he thinks about having another baby. He tells her that he can't talk about this right now because he has to go coach the little league game.

She says, "Do you *have* to?"

And with deep indignation, he responds:

"My whole *life* is '*have* to.'"

I think about that line all the time. I've said it in my head and out loud hundreds, bordering on thousands, of times over the past 20 years, even more so after becoming a wife, a mother, an entrepreneur, a founder, a business owner.

I have vivid memories of the visceral reaction I would have when my husband asked around 9 a.m. every Saturday morning—in our condo in Chicago, with our two children under three crawling all over me:

"So, what do you wanna do today?"

I felt rage course through my veins, heating the temperature of my body to "just about to blow" status every time.

What do I *want* to do?
What the fuck even *is* that?

Here, I'll tell you what I *have* to do today to keep this family afloat, our lives from falling apart, the world spinning.

My whole *life* is "*have* to!"

God, it was exhausting being so angry. It drained me. I know it drained Brian.

But I didn't know any other way to be. Anger had protected me when softness, trust, and vulnerability had almost destroyed me.

Was there even another way to be?

The short answer is YES.

But it didn't happen overnight. It won't happen in a day for you either. But every day you wake up and decide to do it differently, to prioritize your pleasure over punishing yourself with pain, is a chance at a new way to live your life.

I did it. And I believe you can, too.

I started to develop a new decision-making barometer to measure where I was going to put my time, my energy, my effort, my body: the Could-Should-Would Method.

I ask myself three questions when it comes to who and what I will prioritize.

1. Could I do it?
2. Should I do it?
3. Would I do it?

Let me explain.

Could

"Could I do it?" is about ability. Is this something I am capable of doing? This is purely a skill-based, practical, and logistical question.

For example, could I fly a plane today? Answer: no. I have no training, skillset, or ability to fly a plane.

But, *could* I reorganize my sons' art bins today? Yes. I am capable of doing that.

I will stay with this "art bin organization" example for the next two questions.

Should

"Should I do it?" is focused on strategy. Is this something that has merit, is useful, or helps you achieve a greater goal?

Example: *Should* I reorganize my sons' art bins today?

The answer might still be "yes" based on what's going on in my life. Perhaps this will help them spend more time creating art versus staring at their iPads. Or maybe the clutter of the bins is spilling over into another area, making life a bit more chaotic. Organizing them may prove to be helpful. Therefore, maybe I should do it.

Would

"Would I do it?" asks: If given many choices for how to spend your time would you choose this one? Do you have a desire to do this? Does this bring you pleasure?

Back to the bins. Would I—if given many options—still choose to reorganize my sons' art bins? A big ol' FUCK NO to that.

First, no one cares if I organize them. Second, no one appreciates it. Third, I resent that no one cares or appreciates it. Fourth, I tell my children and husband that I reorganized the bins. Fifth, in response, they don't care or appreciate it. Sixth, in response to their response, I resent them. Seventh, I sit back down, two hours later, with organized bins and unappreciative family members and I'm angry. They read books and played on iPads and did whatever the fuck they wanted. And I—good citizen and productive mother—organized the damn bins that are just going to be dumped out and used and then put back in the wrong place in the wrong way and and and . . .

Do you see what happened here?
Do you recognize yourself in this example—or in one similar to it?
Do you want to know why it happened?

It all goes back to our worth being tied to our service. If we are not staying busy doing things for other people, do we even matter? Are we worthy?

Today, the bins are filled with uncategorized art supplies. And the boys don't know the damn difference. And my husband doesn't feel the burning glare of my soul-piercing stare.

I'm reading a book on the couch, next to a spruce-scented candle, feet up on the chaise, under a cozy, fuzzy blanket.

Brian asks, "What do you wanna do today?"

And I pause, take a sip of my piping hot Americano and respond following a deep exhale, "I would love to do *nothing*."

And because I know when Brian reads this, he's going to say, "Yeah . . . you're still *kinda* doing the bin-organizing, soul-piecing glare thing," I will respond here.

"Yes. But I'm doing it *less*. Right?"

Progress over perfection, people.

Five Shifts to Prioritizing Pleasure

1. **Say the word pleasure out loud, five times.** I'm not kidding. Stop reading and do it. Are you done? Did you do it? Did it make you uncomfortable? Okay, but did it kill you? No. It's time to start getting comfortable with your own pleasure. If you can't say it, you can't do it.

2. **Define what pleasure means to you.** This exercise will take much longer. If you haven't prioritized pleasure in your life for a really long time, you need space to even consider it. Who are you right now? What brings you joy when you're not being judged or evaluated? Start there. Keep going.

3. **Start small.** You don't have to leave your family for a two-week retreat on the opposite side of the world (but you can if you want!). Small acts of prioritizing pleasure—sitting while you drink your morning coffee (instead of running around in the hustle and bustle), closing your eyes when you eat a piece of chocolate, or wearing your favorite perfume today—the one that you usually save only for special occasions—will begin to rewire your brain. Because you're worth it right now, in this moment.

4. **Implement the Could-Should-Would Method.** Instead of jumping right into what's next—running to solve the next crisis or creating a crisis for yourself that doesn't even exist—ask yourself whether you could, should, or would do it.

5. **Spread the love.** Share how you're prioritizing your pleasure with the Hype Women in your life. Encourage them to do the same. Hold each other accountable and enjoy sharing your journeys of pleasure-seeking and prioritization.

14 | Take Up Space

The world tells women to make themselves smaller physically, emotionally, spiritually, financially, professionally. When we don't, the cavalry comes for us to remind us to get back in our cages.

> **It happens in physical spaces.** We make sure we aren't too loud, too direct, too much; we apologize when someone walks mindlessly into us on a crowded train; we concede our path on the sidewalk to an oncoming runner; we opt for a seat on the fringes of the room, instead of at the head of the table; we fold into ourselves in public, shrinking against the ever-expanding presence of the spirit-sucking space around us.
>
> **It happens in metaphorical spaces.** Our voices, lost in the sea of mansplaining; our spirits, dimmed and dwindling from generation to generation; the fire and the light in us, in danger of being completely extinguished.
>
> **It happens in the spaces of our minds.** We question whether we belong in the rooms where we *do*. We believe others when they make us feel small. We kowtow to mean girls who tell us where to sit and how to act and who to be. We question what right we have to take up more space in our own damn lives.

We let the world relegate us to the corner—hidden, dismissed, forgotten.

We become unrecognizable versions of ourselves, as we make ourselves smaller and smaller and smaller and smaller. Until there is nothing left. And into the ether, we disappear.

There's no space to exist in the room where we're standing.
There's no space to try and fail and try again and soar.
There's no space to breathe when the walls are closing in.

That is, until you break out.

I slide my right arm into my favorite blazer: a creamy white, gray, and black crosshatched wool jacket with white silk lining and ornate, gold buttons. My dear friend and ridiculously talented Chicago-based fashion designer Christina Karin created this beloved staple of my wardrobe. When I wear it, I feel powerful. I feel confident. I feel like me. Her clothing does that. *She* does that.

I'm getting ready to have new professional photos taken. The last time I did this was three years earlier, a few weeks before launching my first company into the world. Those photos were taken at The Wing in Fulton Market—a rapidly growing area of Chicago's West Loop neighborhood.

The Wing, as you may remember, was a women-focused co-working space and social club that operated from 2016 to 2022. The Wing had locations in New York City, Washington, DC, San Francisco, Los Angeles, Boston, and Chicago. Founders Audrey Gelman and Lauren Kassan created The Wing to be a "women's utopia." They set out to create a safe space *for* women, *by* women.

After four years of massive success and growth, COVID forced The Wing to shut its locations and shed staff. And then, the house of cards began to crumble. After complaints about how The Wing failed to address racist behavior of its members surfaced and an employee walkout made headlines, Gelman stepped down as CEO in June 2020. A larger co-working company (run by a bunch of white men) eventually bought a majority stake in the startup. Under new ownership, The Wing staged an ambitious reopening of six locations in 2021 that lasted just months.

On August 30, 2022, The Wing shut down permanently.

A *Fortune* piece written by Paige McGlauflin—published on October 7, 2022—told the story: "The rise and fall of the Wing: How a popular women's co-working startup failed despite billionaire backers, a $365 million valuation, and a 35,000-person waiting list."

Paige writes:

> The Wing had tapped into the post-2016 outrage among many American women who were fed up with systems of power built and controlled by the patriarchy. The Wing promised a safe space designed by women, for women. Its libraries were lined with books by only female authors. It offered lactation rooms and daycare services. Its thermostat was always set at a comfortable 72 degrees. It encouraged women to let down the guard that the world forced them to put up. So, when the real-world experiences of members and employees didn't meet the expectations the Wing set out, it wasn't just a matter of bad service or poor employee relations. It felt like a violation of trust.

I had been a woman who founded a company from the booths and plush, high-back chairs and conference room tables of The Wing in Chicago.

The irony of the rise and demise of both companies is not lost on me.

I was a different person in those photos—in that body—taken in that now defunct space. She's still inside of me. But this time, I'm holding and protecting her. I'm not lost inside of her, fighting a battle without reinforcements.

Today, while wearing my favorite blazer, I'm standing in the panoramic suite on the 13th floor of The Robey, a boutique hotel at the corner of North and Milwaukee avenues in Bucktown, Chicago. In three hours, I'm hosting a dinner on the rooftop terrace of The Robey for 22 women. It is my second "Wing Women Dinner."

My best friend Jen Cho is the current CEO of The Wing. She was brought in to fix what was broken; to steer the Titanic clear of the impending iceberg; to put out a fire that she didn't start. After all, she's an overqualified, successful Korean woman with a proven track record of bringing back fledgling businesses from the brink.

It's that "thing" Corporate America does to women of color. We ask them to clean up our messes—with little to no support, resources, investment, or power. And when they do it—because they do it every time!—we tell them that it was all just for show and their tireless work meant nothing to us.

Jen brought me in as a consultant to help realize her vision for a new, more inclusive, intersectional experience at The Wing. This dinner is laying the groundwork for what I would launch with my own company two months later: The Fairway.

The idea for The Fairway came to me almost a year earlier. For my entire career, I had seen men—correction: straight, white men—doing business on the golf course. They've been doing it for 300 years. They're out there for eight hours, on their company's time and dime, drinking Miller Lite from a can, driving around in golf carts and swinging clubs toward little white balls that they send in whatever direction they feel like blasting them. They're giving each other backdoor access to opportunities, talking about investments, and building their generational wealth.

It's an entire business ecosystem that women—and people of color— are not invited into. And if we dare to show up, we're not included. The conversation changes. The doors to opportunities slam shut.

So, I thought, fuck it. We're not going to increase our wealth on *their* fairway. So, let's do it on our own. Let' do it our way. And so, The Fairway was born.

Intimate, inclusive, intersectional dinners of 20 women: a curated mix of Fortune 500 C-Suite; mid- to senior-level leaders across public, private, government, and nonprofit; and founders and entrepreneurs. Because I had experienced firsthand what happens when you bring a room of women who all have the same professional makeup together: it's much harder to do business with one another.

A room of all senior women have been taught to view one another as threats, as competition. They hold their cards close to their proverbial vests, uncertain about sharing—and unwilling to share—their wealth; the scarcity mindset keeps them from seeing the forest through the trees of abundance. Their chief concern was—and always will be—themselves.

A room of all founders and entrepreneurs are pouring all of *their* sweat equity into building and growing their *own* companies. Even if they are willing to support other founders—and so many are—they have very little left to give.

I wanted to center collective wealth building in these rooms.
I wanted to create access to human, social, financial, and political capital.
I wanted to conspire with genuine co-conspirators to create a better world.

I knew that if we brought the right room together for a four-hour experience of supported connection, drinks, and dinner, we could make magic.

In my first three years of business, I've hosted 33 Fairway Dinners and nine Hype Women events in ten major markets: Atlanta, Austin, Boston, Chicago, DC, L.A., Minneapolis, New York, Portland and San Francisco.

For more than 1,500 women—in these spaces we created together—we've increased our collective wealth by more than $33 million.

And there weren't any balls in sight.

But back to June 28, 2022.

On the day of *this* dinner, I'm in between. I'm 89 days out from resigning from my first company. But I haven't yet launched my next company—and my first foray into solopreneurship—Ella: an inclusive ecosystem unlocking women's access to human, social, financial, and political capital.

I brought my dear friend—my incredibly talented forever photographer—Lena Jackson to the suite at The Robey to take my new photos. What transpired over the first 30 minutes of the photo shoot had 30 years all wrapped up in it.

I started out sitting in all of the proper ways I had been taught over the course of my life:

- Hands on my knees with ankles overlapped
- Legs crossed tightly with a smile plastered on my face
- Elbows kept tightly flush to my sides

My 2022 professional photo session, version 1.
Photo credit: Lena Jackson

In every photo, I made myself smaller.
Until I *didn't*.
Something came over me.

Maybe it was the blazer.
Or the faux leather pants.
Or the power heels.
Maybe it was something else altogether—a lioness slowly waking from
  a tranquilized haze.

I decided to sit the way I see men sitting every damn day:

- In *their* photos
- On websites
- Next to me on planes

- At conference room tables
- While being interviewed on stages
- On a damn park bench
- I took up space.
- I let my power show on my face.
- I didn't adhere to the rules of what I had been taught it meant to be "feminine."

This photo was the result.

My 2022 professional photo session, version 2.
Photo credit: Lena Jackson

That exercise has changed the way I show up—and claim my rightful space in this world.

And here's my wish for you: believe that you deserve the same.

Take. Up. Space.

Not because you wished for it.
Not because you've asked for it.
Not because you've earned it.

But because it is inherently yours for the taking.

I slowly unroll my black Gaiam yoga mat with a gold design of lotus flowers and vines and swirls and curves.

I'm in my favorite spot at The Sanctuary.

"My spot" is tucked away in the darkest corner of the yoga studio. There is a 35-square-foot tapestry of all of the signs of the zodiac with the words "The Moon" written in bold capitalized letters hanging on the charcoal-gray-painted wall behind it. Every phase of the moon is represented in a never-ending circle. Two wolves are howling at all of the moons.

I love looking at that tapestry. Sometimes, when I'm in a downward facing dog pose, upside down, I see something new on that wall, a sign I didn't know was there.

But this story isn't about that special spot that I love. It's about taking up space. And it's about what happens when someone asks you to give up yours.

On this particular day, after placing my mat down in my favorite spot, a woman immediately arrives inches from where I've laid my mat. Now, mind you, this room can comfortably hold 12 to 15 yogis in addition to our beloved teacher, Natasha. The class that morning only had five people.

So, why she needed to place her mat inside of *my* space was odd, nonsensical. But then she took it one step further.

She asked *me* to *move*.

She asked me to retreat closer to the wall, further into the corner. At first, I was disoriented because it wasn't a logical request. There was enough space for *all* of us in this room. Hell, we could each take up the space that three people could occupy with all the damn floor space available! So, the fact that she needed me to have less just didn't feel right.

The next thing I did shows the work that I continue to need to do: to be intentional in moments when I'm caught off guard and unprepared. It shows the repeated work required to break my own patterns of diminishing my existence in relation to those around me.

Not wanting to be confrontational—or even to displease this woman I have never seen before in my entire life—I obliged. I moved my mat, I withdrew farther—and further—into the corner.

But then something in me broke. And I couldn't stop the words from escaping my lips:

"Why do we need to all smash into this corner? There's plenty of room in this class. I don't understand why you need me to move."

She was perplexed. How could *I* question *her* direction?

"Well, I need to make room for my friend," she stated back flatly and matter-of-factly.

Her friend, by the way, was the only man attending the class that day. Now, let me be clear: *everyone* is welcome in *every* yoga studio, regardless of gender.

But I will admit that I am most comfortable in rooms filled with women. I am most comfortable in yoga studios surrounded by women. I feel like I can let my guard down, exhale freely, open myself up in a way—physically and emotionally—that I very intentionally close off when in the outside world.

When men enter this space, that changes. It is no longer completely safe. What I'm wearing transforms from the clothing meant to guide my body through the class into an opportunity to be ogled, leered at, visually consumed.

The fact that this woman wanted to take space from me to make more space for her male friend didn't help the tension of the situation.

When I didn't respond to her "rationale" for asking me to move, she looked at me with her head tilted and said, with judgment and condescension, "Are you *okay*?"

This is a classic move of a mean girl. Don't be fooled. It's strategic. They ask you to do something that's inappropriate. And then, when you question it—or say no—they tell you that *you're* the one with the problem. They ask, with feigned, false concern, if something is wrong with *you*.

"Oh, I'm great," I said strongly. And then, I immediately sat down on my mat.

I was so mad at this stupid situation for so many reasons. First, I was mad because this space was supposed to be a safe place for me: a place to exist, free from struggle and strife. But what made me angrier was that I couldn't believe that this stranger had dysregulated my entire nervous system with two sentences—with what might seem to you like a "simple, innocuous, harmless request."

It occupied the space in my head for the first 22 minutes of class.

Goddamnit. I am at yoga to heal, to release, to feel safe. The sanctity and sacredness of that space had been violated. But not just in the moment of the 22-second interaction; in the replaying of the exchange over and over in my head. How much longer was I going to allow mean girls to occupy the space in my mind?

It may look simple from the outside. And I may even look like the villain to you here.

But, when these experiences happen in multiple spaces with multiple people multiple times a day, every week, every month, every year, every decade, it's death by a thousand cuts. What looks like a breeze becomes a hurricane that grinds the toughest steel to dust.

What was most triggering for me was being faced with relinquishing space that I had the courage to claim; with relinquishing space that I inherently deserved; with relinquishing space that my body and spirit occupy.

And aside from the metaphysical, existential piece of the experience (ugghhhhhhhh, why is everything so fucking heavy all the time?), I was pissed that I was being asked to do something that was just purely ridiculous. Again.

A former, longtime therapist of mine, Carolyn, who helped me through some of the most challenging moments of early marriage and motherhood, gave me advice that I still follow today. She said that when a person says something to me that is utterly preposterous—be it absentminded, unintentional, unconscious, tactically targeted, cruel, or spiteful—I have the power to determine how their words impact me.

She told me in those moments to respond with "What an odd thing to say."

Now, the phrase may not always apply directly to the situation—and honestly, you don't even have to say it out loud. It could simply be the mantra you repeat in your mind before you decide to react—or not react.

If I went back to that moment, the morning of my yoga class, when I was asininely asked to take up less space than I deserved, my first thought would now be: what an odd thing to say.

And then before responding with my answer, I would ask a question back to that woman: "There's so much space here. Why do you need me to take up less?"

Taking up space is an act of resistance.
Taking up space is an act of self-love.
Taking up space is an internal revolution.

So, I want you to try it today. Pay close attention to the space you occupy. Notice when someone infringes on what's yours or asks you to relinquish the space where you exist—literally and metaphorically.

Is your instinct or habit or pattern to make yourself smaller? Pay attention to your body language. How do you respond to the way others treat you?

The way you take up space shows the world how much space you're worth.

Spread out.
Expand in every direction.
Take flight.

Five Shifts to Take Up Space

1. **Claim what's yours.** Whether it's physical space in a room or metaphysical space in a relationship, state what's yours and defend it with your life.
2. **Stop apologizing.** When someone walks into you on the street or tells you to move from the rightful place you've claimed, resist the urge to apologize and acquiesce.
3. **Practice expanding.** Pay attention to your body language. Are you hunched over, folding into yourself, making yourself smaller, silencing your spirit? It's time to expand. Stand up right now.

(continued)

(*continued*)

    Spread your arms up and out and your legs strong and wide. Make an "x" with your body. Lift your chin up to the stars. You belong here.

4. **Walk away.** If anyone makes you feel small, get the fuck away from them. They don't deserve you. Not every experience is a challenge to prove your worth. Some spaces don't deserve your energy. Listen to your intuition.

5. **Make space for women.** Taking up space for yourself is strengthened when you make space for women—the right women, Hype Women. Its never-ending ripple effect will change the world. And we will occupy all the spaces we deserve, together.

15

The Goddess of Your Dualities

The biggest moments in my life—the most impactful decisions I've made—can be categorized by whether I was leading with my masculine or feminine energy. I always felt like it was truly a binary choice. That I was divided.

The masculine was for my outside world. I needed to be hard-hitting, all-knowing, full-throttle at all times. Don't let them see you sweat or cry or falter. Dominance meant success. Failure was not an option. I needed to care less. Move on. Let it go. Get it done.

The feminine was for my inside world. I could be softer, more thoughtful, unsure, afraid. I listened to my intuition. I had room to see signs, to feel deeply, to live expansively. Failure meant courage. Growth was the only option. I was able to care more. Stay here. Let go. Become undone.

Everything on the other side of 40 has been about nuance, about context, about dualities. I am never one thing or another all the time. I contain a multitude of complexities. It is in the tension of my dualities that my strength lies.

When women realize that no part of them is ever gone and no options for them are ever off-limits, the Goddess of their Dualities appears. She is the one who will change the world—but most importantly, *she'll change yours*.

But first, we must travel through the lines of defense meant to strip away the layers of complexity that lay beneath our surface. The world doesn't want a *complicated woman*. It can only handle *simple and easy*, which we both know you've never been.

There is no space for both sides to exist.
There is no safe place for your dualities to be exposed.
There is no lid that can contain the rising tide of the ocean inside of you.

That is, until you overflow.

The Devout Masculine

In fifth grade, my nickname was "The Terminator."

Cute, right?

I was tough. I played sports with all the boys during recess while the girls talked in whispers on the fringes of the blacktop. I stood up for kids who were being bullied or dismissed. I physically put my body in front of kids who were being targeted, in the middle of a fight. I was a playground vigilante. The biggest reason I acted this way was because of my deep sense of justice. It's always been in me. I am a protector.

But I now realize that I also acted this way as a line of defense. If I made sure everyone knew I was indestructible—if they were maybe even a little afraid of me—I thought I was less likely to get hurt. It was the way I thought I could best protect myself.

Without being fully conscious or intentional, I've lived the majority of my life with my devout masculine energy out in front.

Energy is genderless. While we've been taught that "masculine" is associated with men and "feminine" is associated with women, it's just not true.

When you read this next part, I want you to very intentionally read it as a description of *energy*, not *gender*.

—

According to ChatGPT:

Masculine energy refers to qualities, behaviors, and characteristics traditionally associated with masculinity. It's not necessarily tied to gender, as everyone has both masculine and feminine energy in varying degrees. Masculine energy is typically associated with action, structure, logic, and drive. It often represents a more assertive, goal-oriented, and outward-focused approach to life.

Some common traits of masculine energy include:

1. **Leadership:** Taking charge, providing direction, and guiding others.
2. **Focus and Determination:** Staying goal-driven and pushing toward a specific outcome.
3. **Discipline:** Being consistent, organized, and committed to responsibilities.
4. **Problem-Solving:** Approaching challenges with a practical, analytical mindset.
5. **Strength:** Often tied to emotional, mental, or physical resilience.
6. **Action-Oriented:** Emphasis on doing, achieving, and creating tangible results.
7. **Protective Nature:** A desire to safeguard others and provide stability.
8. **Confidence:** Trusting one's ability and decisions.

What makes masculine energy unique is how it expresses itself differently in each person, depending on personality, culture, and life experiences.

—

While my masculine energy has helped me in so many ways, standing fully in it and forgetting to embrace the other parts of me has limited my success—and my happiness.

It's made me closed off.
It's made me meaner.
It's made me aggressive.
It's made me inflexible.

It's made me reactive.
It's made me volatile.
It's made me cold.

But the "it" of this masculine energy is not an all-powerful, unstoppable force puppeteering my body. It's *me*. I was doing all of those things. And I was letting what I thought the world wanted me to be grab the wheel of a car I should be driving.

I didn't need my masculine energy to stop existing or to fully disappear. But I did need to get control of it. To wield it in a way that worked for me, rather than consuming me to the point where I couldn't breathe.

🐺 🐺 🐺

The Divine Feminine

I've always been drawn to—and connected with—women. As the oldest, first-born daughter of a single mother (also an eldest daughter), I grew up surrounded by women. I have one sister. All six of my cousins are girls. I played on all-girl sports teams for 12 years. I was a Brownie and then a Girl Scout. I was on the executive board of my sorority Alpha Chi Omega at the University of Michigan. I wrote poetry and drew and painted and made friendship bracelets and listened to emo music. The feminine energy in my life was off the charts.

Energy is genderless. While we've been taught that "masculine" is associated with men and "feminine" is associated with women, it's just not true.

When you read this next part, I want you to very intentionally read it as a description of *energy*, not *gender*.

—

According to ChatGPT:

Feminine energy, like masculine energy, refers to a set of qualities and traits that are often associated with femininity, but can be embodied by anyone, regardless of gender. It's typically seen as more receptive, nurturing, and fluid in nature, offering a balance to the more action-oriented or assertive qualities of masculine energy.

Here are some core aspects of feminine energy:

1. **Nurturing & Compassionate:** Feminine energy is often linked to care, empathy, and emotional support. It's about creating harmony, offering unconditional love, and being present for others in a deeply compassionate way.

2. **Intuition & Sensitivity:** It's associated with a strong connection to intuition, gut feelings, and emotional awareness. Feminine energy is more attuned to the subtle currents of life and often leads with heart over logic.

3. **Creativity & Flow:** This energy is deeply connected with creativity, inspiration, and the ability to be in the flow of life. Feminine energy can express itself through artistic endeavors, spontaneous action, and adapting to change.

4. **Receiving & Surrendering:** Feminine energy involves being open to receiving, whether it's love, support, or information. It's about surrendering control and allowing things to unfold rather than trying to force them.

5. **Emotional Expression & Vulnerability:** Feminine energy tends to honor emotional expression and vulnerability, embracing the full spectrum of feelings without judgment. It's a space for depth, connection, and authenticity.

6. **Collaboration & Community:** Rather than seeking dominance or independence, feminine energy often values collaboration, community, and connection with others. It nurtures relationships and fosters interdependence.

7. **Grace & Softness:** Feminine energy can also express itself through grace, gentleness, and softness—whether in movement, speech, or approach to life.

Just like with masculine energy, feminine energy isn't something that's limited to women. Everyone can tap into it, and most people will experience both masculine and feminine energy to varying degrees throughout their lives.

—

It's no surprise to me that I founded two companies focused on women.

It's also deeply indicative of my conditioning, my operating system, my growth, and my healing that I co-founded my first company because I didn't believe I was good enough to do it alone; and that I solo-founded my second company, because I finally believed that I was.

My journey over the course of my 20+ year career deepened the divide of my masculine and feminine sides. I felt as though I had to show up as two different people in two different places for two different end goals.

I associated my feminine side with my personal experiences with women and my internal experiences with myself. And I was fully stuck in my masculine side when it came to business, work, money, and interactions with men.

The playground vigilante became the justice warrior.

This common binary categorization limits us in our lives and our interactions. We lose the power of the nuance when we silo off parts of ourselves and don't allow them to meld together.

When you read the previous descriptions of the "masculine" and the "feminine," how did you feel?

Did you see yourself in one more than the other?

Do you want to see *more* of yourself in the one that you've been ignoring?

Did you judge the characteristics of one more than the other?

And can you accept that that judgment is your conditioning, not your truest belief?

Were you repelled by the description of one?

And do you want to uncover what lies beneath *that* feeling?

What if we were never, ever just one thing?

What if an entire ocean and universe exists inside of you?

🦋 🦋 🦋

The Goddess of Your Dualities

Everything good in my life has come from a place where my feminine and masculine energies joined together to create something magical; where I was not limited, boxed in, pigeonholed to one way of thinking, of feeling, of being.

Too much salt in a recipe makes you desperate for water.
Too much sugar makes your brain ache.
But the right mix of both? Addicting.

Women are not a monolith. *You* are not a monolith.

You will never be all of one and none of the other.
You will always feel the tension between who you were and who you are becoming.
You will sometimes feel lost as you navigate the in-between.

That's okay. *You're* okay. Keep. Going.
It took me 40 years to have the space to recognize, accept, and embrace this truth. And when I did, I began operating at a higher frequency and vibration than I thought was even possible.

According to @liveyourimpossible on Instagram, there are seven tells that you are vibrating at a higher frequency.

Signs of a High Vibration:
1. People stare at you.
2. Kids like you.
3. Animals feel safe around you.
4. Strangers tell you their life stories.
5. The room's energy shifts when you walk in.
6. You irritate toxic people by being authentic.
7. People envy you, and you don't know why.

Oh, that hits. Check, check, check.
And that word "envy." It's a heavy one.

My brilliant therapist Sarah said something to me a few years ago that I think about all the time. Many of you have probably heard me say it or seen me write it. And while these aren't the technical definitions according to Merriam Webster, *that* dictionary was created by two white dudes, brothers Charles and George, in 1831. So, I don't know, maybe some of these locked-in definitions could use some updating?

Here's what she said:

Jealousy is when you want *something* that someone else has. It can be a healthy motivator to work toward achieving that goal, acting as inspiration for aspiration.

Envy, on the other hand, is when you don't want *someone* to have what *they* have. It is driven by resentment, spite, and malice.

Do you have women in your life who envy you?

Who look pained through forced smiles when you share your success?

Who respond with "how great for you" when your hard work pays off?

Who publicly "applaud" you but talk shit behind your back?

You do. We all do. These are mean girls. And we don't have to put up with their shit for another damn day.

As you *step* into your full power and you then *stand* in it, shoulders back, chin up, feet planted firmly on the ground, it will stir up unresolved feelings in those who have yet to do the work, who have no intention of looking inward, or who are not here to learn and evolve and grow.

It took me 40 years to finally feel safe and secure enough in myself to become the Goddess of My Dualities and to hold them in each hand with equitable care, support, strength, and compassion.

Here's what I now know is true:

I am fiercely independent *and* deeply loyal.

I am a devoted mother *and* a selfish woman.

I am sensitive *and* tough.

I am careful *and* carefree.

I am a Hype Woman *and* I have Hype Women.

I play it safe *and* I take risks.
I follow the rules *and* I break them.
I am concerned *and* courageous.
I am a builder *and* a disruptor.
I work hard *and* I rest.
I seek joy *and* I create it.
I am empathetic *and* I have boundaries.
I embrace my masculine *and* my feminine sides.

My power lies in my dualities.
So does yours.
Our strength, as women, lies in the constant calibration of our dualities. And it is in our life-long journey to achieve daily equilibrium that we come home to ourselves; that we remember who the fuck we are.
You know who you are.

Stop hiding it.
Stop running away from her.
Stop letting others steal her spirit from you.

Today is the day that you not only *step* into your power but you stand tall in it; that you own it; that you know everything you are and everything you were meant to be is right here, right now, in this moment.
When a butterfly flaps its wings alone, it makes a breeze.
But when hundreds of butterflies, thousands of butterflies, millions of butterflies flap their wings together, they change the weather pattern on the opposite side of the world.
They become a *heri*cane.

Individually, we make a breeze.
Collectively, we create a *heri*cane.

The *heri*cane is *in* you. And we'll have your back, every step of the way.

Five Shifts to Becoming the Goddess of Your Dualities

1. **Embrace your divine feminine.** This side of you is not weaker or less important. It is the truest, most powerful part of your being. Honor her.

2. **Acknowledge your devout masculine.** This side of you is not stronger or more important. It is the truest, most powerful part of your being. Honor her.

3. **Worship the Goddess in you.** Test out when and where your masculine and feminine energies serve you best. Recognize the societal conditioning that makes you view one as more worthy than the other. It's a lie. Your power lies in your dualities.

4. **Do it differently.** What worked for you 5, 10, or 20 years ago may no longer work for you today. Honor what you had to do—and who you had to be—in order to survive. And recognize that it may be time to change.

5. **Be gentle with yourself.** This is not a simple task. It will be uncomfortable and even painful along the way. Becoming undone and piecing yourself back together takes time. And care. Please give her all the love she deserves.

16 | Where We're Headed

We all carry the history of our ancestors in us: the experiences of our parents as children and the dreams of our parents as they raised the children we once were. It's a life filled with so much potential—and what can also feel like immense pressure.

Rules of law and families and systems were all created by someone.

Sometimes that person looks like us, understands who we are, and has lived through experiences in the way we've had to navigate our own.

Many times, none of that is true.

So, how do we stop following rules in our homes, our families, our communities, our companies, in any and all of the systems that surround us, and inside of structures intentionally built to ensure we crumble?

You may not want to hear this, but the answer is: we break them.

It's not always possible.
It's rarely met with anything but resistance.
It's never easy.

But it's the only way out.

You can start in small ways. Within the four walls of your home and the space inside of your family and friendship circles.

You can build to bigger efforts, going back generations in your family, your community, your country.

You can join others to create collective Movements that shift history, change laws, and impact the planet.

And sometimes, the biggest changes don't come from what you *do*, but instead, from what you *don't* do; what you refuse to perpetuate, duplicate, commiserate.

It is in the protecting of your peace that you regain your strength; that you fill a reservoir reared barren by the constant depletion of your lifeforce; and that you able to create—and exist within—the space to remember who the fuck you are, to discover what it is exactly that you want in this life.

Protecting your peace doesn't mean you ignore the truth and pain and tragedies of the world. But it does mean that you are not solely responsible for fully feeling, caring for and holding them 24 hours a day, 365 days a year.

This has been the work of my life. And it required the undoing of the blueprint I was birthed into the world bearing on my soul.

Generational trauma, after all, runs deep.

—

According to ChatGPT:

Generational trauma, also known as intergenerational trauma, refers to the transmission of trauma from one generation to another. This can happen in a variety of ways, often unconsciously, where the effects of trauma experienced by one generation—such as abuse, war, displacement, or systemic oppression—are passed down to subsequent generations. This can influence the emotional, psychological, and even physical well-being of children, grandchildren, and beyond, without direct experience of the original trauma.

The trauma can manifest in several ways:

1. **Psychological and emotional effects:** Children may inherit coping mechanisms, emotional responses, or patterns of behavior

that reflect the unresolved trauma of previous generations. For example, someone who grew up in an environment of emotional neglect or abuse may develop attachment issues, anxiety, or depression.

2. **Behavioral patterns:** Trauma can affect the way individuals relate to others. For example, someone from a family with a history of addiction or violence may be more likely to engage in similar behaviors.

3. **Physiological effects:** Some research suggests that trauma can affect the genetic expression or epigenetics of descendants, potentially influencing things like stress responses, immune system function, or susceptibility to certain health conditions.

4. **Cultural and societal influences:** Trauma can also be transmitted through societal and cultural narratives. For instance, communities affected by systemic racism, colonization, or forced migration may experience collective trauma that is passed down culturally and may shape identity and social behaviors over time.

The cycle of generational trauma can be broken through awareness, healing, and therapeutic interventions. Addressing the root causes of trauma and providing individuals and communities with the tools to process and heal from it can help prevent its transmission to future generations.

—

Trauma lives in our bodies, passed from one generation to the next, stored in our genetic code, the sequence of our DNA. It creates the blueprint for our beliefs about humanity. It's ever-present just under the surface and deeply unseen at a cellular level.

Over the course of your life, you will be—or will become—a person who takes on the responsibility of your own generational trauma.

Over the course of your life, you will know and love people who choose to do the same.

Over the course of your life, you will encounter those who allow the past to consume their present and determine their future—and you will be faced with the decision to absorb the side effects that are hurled your way or to acknowledge that their work is not yours to do and you must let go of them to save yourself.

This is hard stuff. This is really messy. This is a way of walking through the world that so many avoid at all costs. And it will stir up deeply uncomfortable emotions in others because you've decided to face yours, within yourself.

I have been the black sheep of my family, questioning, challenging and removing patterns, traditions, and people that no longer support my healthy, healing life.

I have been the black sheep of my marriage, ungracefully walking the tension of the tight rope between domestic, dutiful wife and ferociously, independent woman.

I have been the black sheep of my friends, refusing to take the bait—or assume the guilt—of a scoreboard relationship that conditionally measures my every move, while also holding firm that friendship does, in fact, live on a two-way street.

I have been the black sheep of my companies, speaking up—and out—in spaces that were not built by, or for, me and didn't know what to do with me when I stopped falling in line.

How do you sustain long-term relationships, friendships, partnerships, and marriages when they began at a point in time when you were a different person?

As a 42-year-old woman who has moved to entirely new places every two to four years for the majority of my life, I know the challenge that comes along with building community; with creating foundation; and with growing and sustaining connection in the face of ever-increasing absence, distance, time, space, and change.

Relationships, friendships, partnerships, marriages—they survive only if you're willing to break and then put yourself back together and if others are willing to let you break and then help you pick up the pieces. Anyone who wants you to stay the same—to stay stuck in a version of yourself that you have outgrown—isn't in it, with you, for the long haul.

And while that may feel devastating to realize in the moment, while it may shake up and shift your world as you knew it—and as you thought it would always be—you *will* survive.

Some people, places, and programming are meant to exist in our lives for a finite amount of time. They help us learn lessons, to better understand

ourselves, to heal and to grow. But if they can't grow with us, we will outgrow them. And we must accept that our time has ended. We move forward,
without them.

My mom tells the story about how her mother always used to stand in
their kitchen with one leg bent, the heel and arch of her foot resting on her
opposite inner thigh.

It's one of her most vivid memories.

Funny enough, I have the same memory of my mother standing in our
kitchen still wearing her navy-blue uniform skirt—undone from the waist
up. Her cream-colored silk slip is out in the open, exposed, while her uniform shirt lays tossed on a nearby chair—her thick, curly crown of crimson
locks released, flowing wildly around her shoulders.

We always called this stance "flamingo"—because it resembled the infamous one leg balance of the perfectly pink wading bird.

My body has been finding this position a lot lately. Sometimes in a yoga
class, sometimes standing in my own kitchen, but most surprisingly when
I've been lying in bed.

It's a very different feeling when you do it without the full weight of
your body, the full weight of the world.

What my grandmother and my mother and I have been doing for
decades—what our bodies have been drawn to stand in—is, I've come to
realize, "tree pose."

—

According to ChatGPT:

The **Tree Pose** (called *Vrikshasana* in Sanskrit) is a foundational standing posture in yoga that symbolizes balance, strength, and groundedness. Its
meaning can be explored on multiple levels:

1. **Physical Meaning**
   Balance and Stability: Tree pose strengthens the legs, core, and
   stabilizing muscles while improving overall balance. It represents
   finding steadiness even when facing challenges.

Rootedness: Like a tree rooted in the earth, the pose encourages grounding and connection to the physical world.

2. **Symbolic Meaning**
   Growth and Resilience: The posture mimics the structure of a tree, rooted firmly yet reaching upward. It symbolizes personal growth, resilience, and the ability to stay grounded while striving for greater heights.
   Unity with Nature: Standing in tree pose can remind practitioners of their connection to nature and the importance of harmony with the environment.

3. **Mental and Emotional Meaning**
   Focus and Concentration: Maintaining the pose requires focus and mental clarity, reflecting the need to center the mind and block out distractions.
   Inner Strength: It teaches patience, self-awareness, and confidence in one's ability to remain stable despite external or internal disturbances.

4. **Spiritual Meaning**
   Balance of Energy: Tree pose symbolizes the balance between opposing forces—roots grounding into the earth while the arms stretch toward the sky. It can represent the integration of body, mind, and spirit.
   Grounding in the Present Moment: In yoga philosophy, *Vrikshasana* encourages mindfulness and living fully in the present, just as a tree exists naturally in its environment.

5. **Practical Lessons from Tree Pose**
   Patience and Practice: It reminds us that balance comes with practice and that it's okay to fall as long as you keep trying.
   Flexibility in Life: Like a tree sways in the wind without breaking, the pose teaches adaptability and grace under pressure.

—

We've been practicing stillness, strength, and growth for generations. And we've each done it in our own way.

My grandmother, wearing her nurse's uniform, standing in her kitchen, making dinner

My mom, wearing her Coast Guard uniform, standing in our kitchen,
reading the newspaper
Me, wearing a loose-fitting tank top and sleep shorts, lying in my bed,
weightless, feeling everything

Our family tree is shifting.

The original roots are still firmly planted, but new branches have grown,
new leaves have appeared, and new seeds have fallen from blossoming flowers and started the cycle of life all over again.

A new set of roots is taking hold beneath the layers of time.
A new tree is growing above the surface.
A new life is being created.

It doesn't exist in the shadow of the original, but next to it, side by side,
growing at different paces, in different ways, for different reasons.

It is its own tree.
It grows its own branches.
It blooms when it wants to.
It sheds leaves when it needs to.

I believe that my grandmother did the best she could, with the tools
that she had.
I believe that my mother did the best that she could with the tools
that she had.
I believe that I did the best I could with the tools that I had.
And my hope, my determination, and my steadfast commitment is to
keep refining those tools by throwing out the ones that are broken, fixing
the ones worth repairing, and adding new and different mechanisms to
meet me in this current moment, to build the bridge to what's next, and to
create space for who I'm meant to be.

I forgive my grandmother. She did the best she could.
I forgive my mother. She is doing the best she can.
I forgive myself. I am doing my best.

As this book comes to end, you begin again.

On May 6, 2024, I drew three columns on a piece of paper.

At the top, I wrote "was," "am" and "will be."

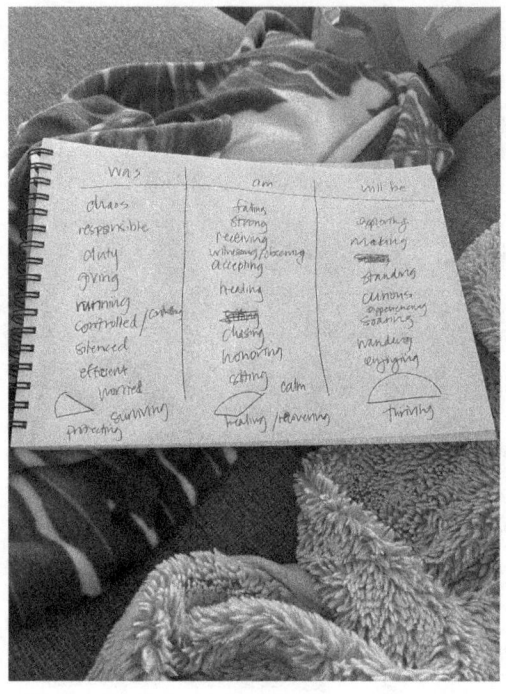

My metamorphosis.

Under the first column, "was," I wrote:

- Chaos
- Responsible
- Duty
- Giving
- Running
- Controlled
- Controlling
- Silenced

- Efficient
- Worried

I drew a one-third-full fuel tank gauge. Under that, I wrote "protecting/surviving."

Under the second column, "am," I wrote:

- Failing
- Strong
- Receiving
- Witnessing
- Observing
- Accepting
- Healing
- (I wrote, and crossed out, "sitting.")
- Chasing
- Honoring
- Sitting
- Calm

I drew a two-thirds-full fuel tank gauge. Under that, I wrote "healing/recovering."

Under the third column, "will be," I wrote:

- Exploring
- Making
- (I wrote, and crossed out, "sitting.")
- Standing
- Curious
- Experiencing
- Soaring
- Wandering
- Enjoying

I drew a full fuel tank gauge. Under that, I wrote "thriving."

My favorite part of this image is seeing the struggle I had with the word "sitting."

I first wrote it under "am." But when I started to write the "will be" column, I felt like it belonged there. So, I crossed it out and wrote it under "will be." Then I realized—no, no, no. What I *will be* is "standing." And what *I am doing* right now is "sitting." So, scratched that off the "will be" column and back under the "am" column she went.

Sitting—being—is what I am working to embrace the most, in this moment.

When I wrote out this new roadmap for my nervous system, I was honest with myself. And now, I want you to do the same.

I want you to take all the validation, all the inherent truths, and all the beliefs and all the hope that has fueled the fire throughout these pages and decide your way forward: a clear, outlined path to wake you up to your power.

Get out your piece of paper, write your three columns, and fill the page with your truth.

Because while your power may have been taken by others, or lost along the way, it is never, ever fully gone. It's always inside of you.

It's time you reclaim it.

So where do we go from here? Wherever the hell we want to.

It's time to break the spell. Maybe you've already broken it.

We know who the fuck we are.

And soon, the world will, too.

Bibliography

Addiction Center. "How Growing Up with Alcoholic Parents Affects Children." addictioncenter.com, August 22, 2024. https://www.addictioncenter.com/alcohol/growing-up-alcoholic-parents-affects-children/. Accessed 1 February 2025.

Adelson, Judith I. "Contemporary family systems approach to substance abuse." *Forum on Public Policy: A Journal of the Oxford Round Table*, Spring 2010. *Gale Academic OneFile*, link.gale.com/apps/doc/A252191861/AONE?u=anon~7a16d06d&sid=googleScholar&xid=013d0dec. Accessed 1 February 2025.

Adult Children of Alcoholics. "The Problem" adapted from "The Laundry List." *Adult Children of Alcoholics*, 2014. https://adultchildren.org/literature/problem/. Accessed 1 February 2025.

Angelou, Maya. *A Song Flung Up to Heaven*. Random House, 2002.

Bennet, Jessica and Daniel Jones, Miya Lee and Anya Strzemien, "Together." *New York Times*, June 12, 2020. https://www.nytimes.com/2020/06/12/style/modern-love-coronavirus-living-together.html. Accessed 1 February 2025.

Black, Claudia. *It Will Never Happen to Me: Growing Up with Addiction as Youngsters, Adolescents, Adults* (2nd edition, revised). MAC Publishing, 2001.

Bowie, Rachel. "So Long Mean Girls, 2023 Is the Year of the Hype Woman." *PureWow*, March 6, 2023. https://www.purewow.com/money/why-the-hype-women-movement-is-now. Accessed 1 February 2025.

Center for Disease Control and Prevention. "Adverse Childhood Experiences (ACEs): Preventing early trauma to improve adult health." CDC.org,

August 23, 2021. https://www.cdc.gov/vitalsigns/aces/index.html#:
~:text=61%25%20of%20adults%20had%20at,health%20problems%20
across%20the%20lifespan. Accessed 1 February 2025.

Coffey, Clare and Patricia Espinoza Revollo, Rowan Harvey, Max Lawson,
Anam Parvez Butt, Kim Piaget, Diana Sarosi and Julie Thekkudan. "Time
to Care: Unpaid and underpaid care work and the global inequality crisis."
Oxfam, January 20, 2020. https://policy-practice.oxfam.org/resources/
time-to-care-unpaid-and-underpaid-care-work-and-the-global-
inequality-crisis-620928/. Accessed 1 February 2025.

Einstein, Albert. "Quotable Quote." Goodreads. https://www.goodreads
.com/quotes/987-there-are-only-two-ways-to-live-your-life-one.
Accessed 1 February 2025.

Frost, Robert. "The Road Not Taken." Poetry Foundation, 1915. https://
www.poetryfoundation.org/poems/44272/the-road-not-taken.
Accessed 1 February 2025.

Gannon, Emma. X platform, May 13, 2020. https://x.com/emmagannon/
status/1260495435468341249?lang=en. Accessed 1 February 2025.

Gatta, Frances and Amber Felton. "What Is Karma?" WebMD, October 2,
2024. https://www.webmd.com/balance/what-is-karma. Accessed 1
February 2025.

Gough, Christina. "Size of the wellness market worldwide from 2017 to
2023, with a forecast to 2028." Statista, Nov 28, 2024. https://www
.statista.com/statistics/491362/health-wellness-market-value/.
Accessed 1 February 2025.

McGill Johnson, Alexis. "Hope." The Hype Women Podcast, Episode 9.
January 11, 2024. https://open.spotify.com/episode/4z4H9MKtyapQ
CnLuXqhblH?si=ed0ce7eaa38f4c3b. Accessed 1 February 2025.

McGlauflin, Paige. "The rise and fall of the Wing: How a popular women's
co-working startup failed despite billionaire backers, a $365 million
valuation, and a 35,000-person waiting list." *Fortune*, October 7, 2022.
https://fortune.com/2022/10/07/the-rise-and-fall-of-the-wing/.
Accessed 1 February 2025.

Mediadata. https://www.medidata.com/en/life-science-resources/medidata-
blog/women-in-clinical-trials-history/?utm_source=chatgpt.com.

National Association for Children of Addiction, "Important Facts." NACOA
.org, 2024. https://nacoa.org/important-facts/#:~:text=More%20than%

2028%20million%20Americans,tend%20to%20run%20in%20families. Accessed 1 February 2025.

National Institute of Health. "The Curious Case of Baby Formula in the United States in 2022: Cries for Urgent Action Months after Silence in the Midst of Alarm Bells." National Library of Medicine, December 2022. https://pmc.ncbi.nlm.nih.gov/articles/PMC9734447/. Accessed 1 February 2025.

nymag.com. https://nymag.com/intelligencer/article/trauma-bessel-van-der-kolk-the-body-keeps-the-score-profile.html?utm_source= chatgpt.com.

O'Toole, Peter as the voice of Anton Ego. Pixar's *Ratatouille*. IMDB, 2007. https://www.imdb.com/title/tt0382932/characters/nm0000564. Accessed 1 February 2025.

psychologytoday.com. https://www.psychologytoday.com/us/blog/beauty-sick/202308/what-happens-when-children-think-girls-are-bad-at-math?utm_source=chatgpt.com.

Roosevelt, Theodore. "Citizenship in a Republic" speech. The American Presidency Project, April 23, 1910. https://www.presidency.ucsb.edu/documents/address-the-sorbonne-paris-france-citizenship-republic. Accessed 1 February 2025.

Statista Market Insights. "Beauty and Personal Care Worldwide." Statista, November 2024. https://www.statista.com/outlook/cmo/beauty-personal-care/worldwide. Accessed 1 February 2025.

Stewert, Rebecca. "Two Students File Sexual Assault Complaint Against Ad Industry Consultant in Cannes." *Adweek*, September 3, 2024. https://www.adweek.com/creativity/cannes-lions-students-sexual-assault-complaint/. Accessed 1 February 2025.

Straits Research. "Medical Aesthetics Market Size." Straights Research, October 11, 2024. https://straitsresearch.com/report/global-medical-aesthetics-market#:~:text=The%20global%20medical%20aesthetics%20market,period%20(2025%2D2033). Accessed 1 February 2025.

The Economist Editorial Team. "Shrek 5: the headhunters." *The Economist,* February 7, 2020. https://www.economist.com/graphic-detail/2020/02/07/shrek-5-the-headhunters. Accessed 1 February 2025.

Ward-Glenton, Hannah. "Meet the woman who invented a whole new subsection of tech set to be worth $1 trillion." MSNBC, March 6, 2023.

https://www.cnbc.com/2023/03/06/meet-the-woman-who-invented-
a-whole-new-subsection-of-tech-set-to-be-worth-1-trillion.html.
Accessed 1 February 2025.

Wezerek, Gus and Kristen R. Ghodsee. "Women's Unpaid Labor Is Worth
$10,900,000,000,000." *New York Times,* March 5, 2020. https://www
.nytimes.com/interactive/2020/03/04/opinion/women-unpaid-labor
.html#:~:text=The%20value%20of%20this%20shadow,of%20unpaid%
20work%20across%20genders. Accessed 1 February 2025.

ypulse.com. https://www.ypulse.com/article/2018/04/12/teen-girls-are-
less-confident-than-boys-its-affecting-their-futures/.

Acknowledgments

To Brian, you are my sunrise and my sunset—forever by my side for every beginning and every end. Thank you for allowing me to cocoon and dissolve, so many times; for creating the space for me to reemerge as someone completely different and new; and for standing before, beside, or behind me every step of the way. There is no one else I would rather do life with than you. Thank you for loving me unconditionally. I, unconditionally, love you. Forever.

To Will, you are my sun. You show me that anything—and everything—is possible. Thank you for choosing—among your cosmically infinite possibilities—me to be your mother. You have more courage, strength, resolve, empathy, determination, enthusiasm, and intuition than most people 10 times your age. I am a braver person because of you. Where there's a Will, there's a way. I love you more than the universe.

To Charlie, you are my moon. You show me a more magical world through your brilliant big brain and your soul-piercing sapphire eyes. Thank you for choosing—among your cosmically infinite possibilities—me to be your mother. Your creativity and freedom of expression enhance and expand everyone's life around you. I am a bolder person because of you. I love you more than the universe.

To Lincoln, the best dog on planet Earth. You have made the last decade of my life better simply because you exist. Thank you for waking up with me between 4 and 5 a.m. every morning for months as I wrote this book—and for checking on me every 20 minutes the day I submitted my manuscript. Lincy, I couldn't have done it without your love and support. My couch always has been, and always will be, your couch. Forever. I love you.

To my mom, my first and fiercest Hype Woman. Without you, I don't exist. You showed me how to be a justice warrior, an ambitious woman, a ferociously protective mother, a compassionate friend and to never take "no" as the final answer, to always believe in myself, and to never give up. Learning from—and leaning on—one another as I became a mother and a woman over 40 has been one of the great joys of my life. You started out as my North Star. And then, you gave me the gift so few mothers, parents, mentors, or leaders have the courage and humility to release: you encouraged me to become my own. Thank you. For everything. I love you.

To my sister, my universe expanded the day you were born. You were my first friend, and there is no one who could ever take your place. Thank you for walking through the world with me. I love you.

To my dad, choosing to heal and move forward is a path I hope we both travel, together. I love you.

To Jamie Lee Curtis, the OG Unabashed Hype Woman. The universe had plans for us long before our paths crossed. That's the thing about soul sisters. They continue to meet, lifetime after lifetime. I'm so grateful that I get to do *this* life with you. Forever in solidarity. I love you.

To the women who have been with me on my darkest days and brightest nights: Ambika Pai, Amanda Boyle, Asia Star Day, Bliss Lau, Carrie Herschman, Danielle Wight, Devan Hanna, Isabella Yani, Jen Cho, Michelle Stuntz, Neha O'Rourke, Nicci Morris, and Stacy London. I am standing today because of you. Thank you for being my best friends and sisters for life.

And included in this group, a special shout-out to my University of Michigan college girlfriends of 20+ years: Sallie (Taylor) Benson, Erika (Waddell) Barrett, Katie (Towl) Khouri, Amy (Jaick) Gottlieb, Alexis (Waldor) Zager. We have been through so much together. Thank you for never leaving my side. I love you eternally. 1020 for life! Brown Jug for life! AXO is the only way to go! Love and ITB! GO BLUE! xoxo, Erin Trainer (Turner)

To Carrie Herschman: yes, you deserve two acknowledgments. You have seen me at my lowest—and not only did it not scare you, it made you fight for me harder. You were the second person to read my manuscript. And in what was, yet again, an incredibly intense and vulnerable experience, you made me feel both held and free. You protected me and have given me the strength to keep going time and time again. This book is better because you traveled the journey with me. Thank you for being one of my best friends—and the greatest fucking lawyer on the planet. I love you.

To my cousins Jessica Casillas, Tara Donohoe, Christine Donohoe, Elizabeth DiCrosta, Amelia Jaffe, Sarah Donohoe, and Rachel Donohoe: let's keep choosing to break the cycle. I love you all forever.

To the Hype Women in my life who have made me—and the world—better: A'shanti Gholar, Abby Hayes, Alex Yewon, Alexis McGill Johnson, Alexis Voss, Allyson Felix, Amy Cross, Amy Naughten, Andrea McBride, Arlan Hamilton, Ayana Parsons, Blessing Oyeleye Adesiyan, Bonnie Wan, Brenda Cumby McGee, Brittany Gooden, Brooke Skinner Ricketts, Caitlin Armstrong, Carol Fabrizio, Caroline O'Halloran, Carolyn Versical, Chani Nicholas, Chanté Thurmond, Charlie Salgado, Cherie Animashaun, Chloe Jackman, Christina Cue, Christina Karin, Cindy Gallop, Colleen Bordeaux, Dana Mahina, Dawn Laguens, Diana Lyman, Diana Weymar, Dr. Roopan Gill, Dr. Samantha Conrad, Dr. Tana M. Session, Elaine Rocha, Ellen Gallerini, Ellen McGirt, Emily Tisch Sussman, Erin Davis, Erin Kopeny, Erin Matray, Erin Vilardi, Eve Rodsky, Gayatri Agnew, Gretchen Carlson, Hillary Hittner, Hitha Palepu, Holly Azulay, Ije Jemie Nwabueze, Imani Moore, Jac Gamache, Jeannine Adams, Jen Fisher, Jennifer Paulson, Jennifer Treat, Jenny Nguyen, Jess Clifton, Jess Smith, Jessica (Kimbrough) Meunch, Jordy Brooks, Jotaka Eaddy, Judee Ann Williams, Julia Larkin, Julia Pemberton, Kacy Fleming, Karine Jean-Pierre, Kate Galecki, Kate Kelley, Katie Klumper, Katie Powell, Kiki Freedman, Kimberly Bernhardt, Kym White, L'Oreal Thompson Payton, Laura Correnti, Laura Forman, Lena Jackson, Lindsay Stein, Lisa Sun, Lori Avdoian, Mallory Waxman, Margaret Richardson, Mariah Hancock, Mariel Espejo, Martha Plimpton, Mary Beth Canty, Mary Beth Ferrante, Mecca Benitez, Meggie Palmer, Megs Shah, Melanie Scroggins, Melanie Whitney, Melissa Hobley, Meredith Klein, Michelle Akers, Mina Black, Molly Morter, Molly Segal, Monica Austin, Morgan Fisherman, Munawar Ahmed, Natasha Palmisano, Nathalie Walton, Nicole Hawthorne, Patti Rockenwagner, Randi Matthews, Rebecca Minkoff, Renata, Robin McBride, Rosanne Donohoe, Sali Christeson, Sam Katz, Sarah Spain, Sarah Hardy, Sarah Krcmarik, Sarah Mitchell, Shannon Schuyler, Soledad O'Brien, Sophia Bush, Stephanie

Nadi Olson, Sukhi Sahni, Suzy Richard, Tamika Hawkins, Tauna Dean, Thekla Brumder Ross, Tori Dunlap, Tracey Halama, Trish Heusel, Trish Lindo, Vitale Buford, and Vivian Dewey. I deeply grateful for—and love—you all.

To Rea Frey, my dear friend and book doula: without you, this book doesn't exist. I love you.

To Frank Weimann, my agent. Frankie, I knew in the first three minutes of our first call that you were my person. Thank you for believing me, for saying "fuck you" to the naysayers and for the hours we've spent swearing and laughing on the phone together.

To Victoria Savanh, my brilliant editor. Where do I even begin? You saw a book in me before I did. Thank you for your commitment to women authors, for never giving up on me, for taking a chance on a first-time author, and for showing up with such sisterhood and solidarity. Your hype has healed me in more ways than I could ever repay you for. This is just the beginning of our journey together.

To my team at Wiley, who has had my back from day one: Trinity Crompton, Jeanenne Ray, Michael Friedberg, and Purvi Patel. Thank you for believing in me and for shepherding my book every step of the way.

To my developmental editor Julie Kerr, thank you for receiving, honoring, and celebrating my manuscript (and me!) with compassion. You gave me the space to show up authentically and saw how much of myself I poured into writing this book. And thank you for only recommending I remove "fuck" six times. It means more than you fucking know.

To my PR team at Smith Publicity: Marissa Eigenbrood, Sandy Smith, and Janet Shapiro, I'll never forget our first New York lunch. It was pure magic as I know our work together will continue to be.

To the men who understand that Hype Women is a noun *and* a verb: Brad Levison, Carlos Butler-Vale, Dante Pannell, Dave Sessions, Jordan Acker, Kevin McGarvey, and Richard Flatau. Thank you for showing up for me time and time again.

And to Hype Women, everywhere, who are changing the world, waking up the sleeping giant within you and remembering who the fuck you are: we are in this together. Individually, we make a breeze. Collectively, we create a *heri*cane. LFG.

About the Author

Erin Gallagher is the CEO and founder of HYPE WOMEN, an inclusive ecosystem hyping women to remember who the fuck they are. Karma is their currency. And through deposits and withdrawals of human, social, financial, and political capital, Hype Women are building a better world for—and by—women. She is the author of *Hype Women: Breaking Free from Mean Girls, Patriarchy, and Systems Silencing You.*

Erin is a LinkedIn Top 100 Influencer, Top 10 DEI Voice (#5), and one of the Top 200 Most Powerful Women on LinkedIn, and she wrote one of the 100 Most Influential LinkedIn Posts of the Decade.

She grew the previous company she founded, Have Her Back, from becoming global holding company Interpublic Group's first equity investment in a majority women-owned business (ever . . . in its 93-year history) in 2019 to earning the recognition from Fast Company as one of the World's Most Innovative Companies of 2022.

She began her career at Servicemembers Legal Defense Network, a nonprofit legal services watchdog dedicated to ending discrimination/ harassment of military personnel affected by the "Don't Ask, Don't Tell" policy (which they ultimately achieved).

Erin spent her almost-20-year corporate career leading global marketing, business development, branding, and communications for agencies and global brands.

She's counseled the White House, Fortune 100 C-suite, and senior leaders at some of the world's biggest and best brands and companies (from LinkedIn to United Airlines to Carhartt to McDonald's). In 2019, she was honored as a PRNews 2019 "Top Women in PR."

Through her work forging relationships with changemakers and leaders who believe in the power of diversity, equity, inclusion, and access, Erin has become (as one global CMO so succinctly put it) "the not-so-secret weapon so many leaders count on to drive real change . . . she knows everyone."

As the creator of "The Fairway"—inclusive, intersectional, intimate dinners of women who desire transformation—Erin makes space for women to do business. In its first three years, Erin has hosted 33 Fairway Dinners and nine Hype Women events in ten major markets: Atlanta, Austin, Boston, Chicago, DC, L.A., Minneapolis, New York, Portland and San Francisco.

For more than 1,500 women, she's increased their collective wealth by more than $33 million.

Erin is also the founder of the Hype Women for Harris Coalition— recognized by Vice President Kamala Harris and Oprah Winfrey at Oprah's 2024 "Unite for America" global event—where she spent all 100 days of VP Harris's presidential campaign dedicated to getting her elected.

Since writing her Unabashed Hype Women post on January 11, 2023, that went viral globally, she has created the media platform hypewomen. com, featuring the Hype Women Brand Market and the Hype Women Book Collective.

Erin is also the producer and host of the *Hype Women Podcast*, which as of January 2025 has produced 23 episodes featuring guests such as Aisha Tyler, Ambika Pai, Alexis McGill Johnson, Allyson Felix, Arlan Hamilton, A'Shanti Gholar, Chani Nichols, Demi Moore, Gretchen Carlson, Jamie Lee Curtis, Representative Jasmine Crockett, Jenny Nguyen, Jess Smith, Karine Jean-Pierre, Kiki Freedman, LaTosha Brown, Molly Ringwald, Monica Padman, Retta, Robin McBride, Sheryl Lee Ralph, Soledad O'Brien, Sophia Bush, Stacy London, Yvette Brown and many more.

Index

A

Abortion, 212, 213
Abundance mindset, 71, 234
Addictive families, 13–17
Adelson, Judith, 14
Adrenal fatigue, 149
Adult Children of Alcoholics, 16
Adverse childhood experiences (ACEs), 16–17
Aerial yoga, 155–158
Alchemy, 161–205
    believing in yourself, 162–165
    and butterfly symbol, 162, 166–167
    at Ella, 202–204
    in entrepreneurship, 178, 192–202
    at Have Her Back, 192–202
    of "Here's the Problem" manifesto, 173–177
    of "Progressive Workforce" pilot, 186–189
    on quest for equilibrium, 170–173, 189–192
    science and magic in, 161–162
    shifts to become an alchemist, 205
    and working for someone else, 178–192
    for working mothers, 166–173, 189–192
Alcohol use and alcoholism, 13–17, 137–144
Alone, feeling, 43. *See also* Solitary confinement
"Alone Together" feature, 94–97
Angelou, Maya, 39, 107
Anger, 221–223, 227, 229, 240
Anxiety, 152–153
Apologizing, 215
Attachment difficulties, 150
Authenticity, 208. *See also* Main character energy

B

Bard, Carl, 126
Be Her Jamie bag, 71

Belcher, Nancy, 136
Believing in yourself, 118–125, 184, 193–194, 207–208, 231
Benioff, Marc, 185
Bennett, Jessica, 96
Black, Claudia, 14–15
Blame, 56, 58
Bodily autonomy, 132
Body, relationship with, 107, 112, 129–131, 145. *See also* Taking back your body
Bodywork, 150
Boundary setting, 5, 98
Bowie, Rachel, 74–76
Breastfeeding mothers, 44–49
Breathwork, 150
Brown, Brené, 97
Building bridges, 60–62
Burning bridges, 53–62
    by confronting harasser, 56–60
    healing effect of, 58–60
    historical advice about not, 53–54
    operating in inequitable paradigms vs., 60–61
    and sexual harassment, 54–60
    shift to building and, 61–62

C

Calming rituals, 21–23
Cardinal zodiac signs, 112–113
Chaotic environments, 11–27
    in addictive families, 13–17
    difficulty replacing, 19–23
    due to divorce, 12–13
    effects of lifelong exposure to, 11–12
    in families, 12–18
    Family Hero role in, 15–16

273

Chaotic environments (*continued*)
  going in as response to, 112–113
  hypervigilance in, 17–18
  lessons from Saugatuck about, 23–26
  shifts to move from, 26–27
  in workplace, 18–19
Chemistry, blurred lines of, 161
Chernin, Ari, 30
Childhood experiences:
  in addictive families, 13–17
  adverse, 16–17
  buttery symbol in, 162, 167
  in chaotic environments, 11–18
  desire to serve yourself first, 82–83
  with masculine and feminine energy, 244, 246
  with mean girls, 30
  of parentified children, 155
  with prioritizing pleasure, 219
  with "tracks" in education, 162–165
Cho, Jen, 108, 202, 208–213, 233–234
Choices, ripple effect of, 67–69
Chronic pain, 149
Closed circles, 30–31
Community, building, 256
Compensation, decisions about, 195
Complicated women, 244, 249
Compton, Trinity, 120
Could-Should-Would Method of decision
    making, 228–229
COVID-19 pandemic, 84–91, 94–97,
    139, 186, 232
Criticism, 42–43, 72–73, 89–94, 98,
    123, 238–241
Curtis, Jamie Lee, ix, 3, 63–76, 78–79

D
Day, Asia Star, 64, 65
Disintegration, 20–21
Dissociation, 43, 132–133, 149
Divorce, 12–13
Domestic violence, 180, 181
Dualities, holding, 5–6, 243. *See also* Goddess
    of Dualities

E
Eaddy, Jotaka, 102
Education system, "tracks" in, 162–165
Efficiency, valuing, 221–223
Einstein, Albert, 146
Elektra Health, 135, 136
Ella, 75, 77–78, 202–204, 235
Entrepreneurship, 178, 192–202

Envy, 249–250
Equilibrium, 167–172, 186–188
Equitable leadership, 186–188
Everything Everywhere All at Once (film), ix, 63,
    65, 71, 74–75
Exercise, 137, 147–148, 154–158
Experimentation, *see* Alchemy

F
Failure, being set up for, 191–192
The Fairway, 78, 202, 234–235
Family Hero role, 15–16
Fashion, 145–146
Fast Company, 199
Feminine energy, 224, 225, 243–244, 246–248
Femtech, 135–136
Fight or flight response, 11
Five archetypes of women, 34–38
Flashbulb memories, 13
"Flooding" tactic, 104–105
Forgiveness, 258–259
Freedman, Kiki, 212, 213
Freedom, 158, 197
Frey, Rea, 122, 220–226
Frost, Robert, 191
Future, connecting past, present, and, 156–158

G
Gannon, Emma, 98
Gastrointestinal issues, 149
Gelman, Audrey, 232
Generational trauma, 5, 98, 253–259
  breaking the cycle of, 1–3
  forgiveness to end, 258–259
  letting go to heal, 255–257
  manifestations of, 254–255
  responsibility for ending, 255–256
  rule breaking to end, 253–254
  and tree pose, 257–258
Gill, Roopan, 212, 213
Girls, self-confidence of, 83, 163–164
Giving up your space, 238–241
Goal, wins on path to, 144–146
Goddess of Dualities:
  core aspects of masculine and feminine
      energy, 244–247
  leading with binary energy vs. embracing,
      243–244, 248
  shifts to become, 252
  vibrating at higher frequency as, 249–251
Going in, 18, 101–113, 225
  and fund raising for Harris campaign,
      102–105, 108

going through situations vs., 101–102, 110–111
at lunar eclipse, 112–113
shifting to, 113
and 6-D Strategy of mean girls, 105–107
to stop toxic white women, 108–110
and trusting yourself, 107
Golin, 168, 172–173, 178–192
Gough, Christina, 132
Grief, 110–111, 118

H
Habits, mindless, 137–144
Hamilton, Alexander, 207
Harris, Kamala, 102–108, 110
Harris Victory Fund, 102, 104
Have Her Back, 5, 18–20, 77, 78, 152, 192–202, 233
"Have to" mindset, 18, 226–228
Healing, 58–60, 78, 150
Healthcare, 133–137
Hemophilia A, 185
Henderson, Alessandra, 135
"Here's the Problem" manifesto, 173–177, 180
Hey Jane, 212, 213
Higher frequency, vibrating at, 249–251
Hormone replacement therapy (HRT), 136
Hsu, Stephanie, 69
Hypervigilance, 17–18
Hype Woman Day, 215
Hype Women:
    being your own, 75–76
    as cultural phenomenon, 72
    defined, 63–64
    feedback from, 211
    in karmic transformation, 118–120, 125
    shifting to being, 70
    shifting your spend to, 110
Hype Women for Harris, 108
Hype Women Movement, ix, 63–80
    anniversary of, 215
    backlash against, 72–74
    Rachel Bowie's article on, 74–76
    Jamie Lee Curtis's support for, 66–68, 71–74, 76, 78–79
    and Ella, 77–78
    events, 78–79, 210, 235
    image that inspired, 64–65
    media interest in, 71–72
    metamorphosis in, 3
    ripple effect of choices made in, 67–69
    scope of, 6–7
    tending seeds of, 69

"Unabashed Hype Women" post, 63–68
and Unabashed Hype Women shirt, 69–71
Hype Women Podcast, 215

I
Ideas, generating, 178
Immune system suppression, 150
Inequitable paradigms, 60–61
Infant formula crisis, 45
Instagram, 64, 66–67, 96, 97, 108, 141
Intergenerational trauma, *see* Generational trauma
International Women's Day Event, 180–181
Intuition, 1, 68, 103–104. *See also* Going in
Isabel's Eatery (Saugatuck, Mich.), 24–26
Isolation, *see* Solitary confinement

J
Jackman, Chloe, 78–79
Jackson, Lena, 235–237
Jealousy, 250
Johnson, Alexis McGill, 215–216
Jones, Daniel, 96
"Just," softening messages by using, 104

K
Kaepernick, Colin, 207
Karin, Christina, 70, 71, 232
Karmic transformation, 112, 117–127
    and definition of karma, 117
    mean girls and Hype Women in, 118–119
    shifts to, 126–127
    of writing this book, 119–126
Kassan, Lauren, 232
Kerr, Julie, 124–126

L
Laguens, Dawn, 212, 213
Lawrence, Jennifer, 222
Leadership:
    with binary energy, 243–244, 248
    equitable, 186–188
    main character energy for, 215–216
    not questioning, 31–32, 177
    support for equilibrium, 189
    telling the truth to, 181–182, 190–191
    women in, 175, 182–188, 190–191
Lee, Miya, 96
Likability, 207–208, 214–215
LinkedIn, 44, 97
    message to harasser, 57–58
    post on breastfeeding, 44–48

LinkedIn (*continued*)
    post on equilibrium, 167–172
    post on sexual harassment, 58–60
    "Unabashed Hype Women" post on,
        63–68, 75, 130
@liveyourimpossible, 249
London, Stacy, 97, 209–211
Lunar eclipse, 112–113, 118
Lurie, Ann and Robert H., 185

M
McGlauflin, Paige, 233
Main character energy, 207–217, 225
    believing in yourself, 207–208
    failing to bring, 208–213
    and likability, 214–215
    shifting to, 216–217
    at SXSW Conference, 208–214
    for women in power, 215–216
Masculine energy, 224, 225, 243–246, 248
Maternity leave, 173
Mean girls, 2, 29–41, 75
    adult and child, 30
    breaking free from, 40–41
    challenging, 239–240
    closed circles of, 30–31
    credit taking by, 178
    cutting off access for, 38–40, 106–107
    effects of living under, 29–30
    feedback from, 211
    five archetypes of women, 34–38
    flooding by, 104
    in karmic transformation, 118–119
    shifting spend away from, 109–110
    6-D Strategy of, 105–107
    toxic white women as, 108–110
    and trauma bonding, 32–34
    and workplace abuse of power, 30–34
Memories, flashbulb, 13
Merriam, George and Charles, 250
Metamorphosis:
    and butterfly symbol, 162, 166–167, 172
    charting your own, 260–262
    children and, 157
    to serving yourself first, 99
    shock at others', 190
    stages in, 3–4
    to stop abandoning self, 4–5
MeToo movement, 175
Mindfulness, 150
Mindless habits, 137–144
Misogyny, medical, 133, 134

Mission, 195–196
Mistakes, by entrepreneurs, 192–193
Modern Love column, 94–97
Mood disorders, 150
Moss, Kate, 146
Motherhood:
    alchemy for working mothers, 166–173,
        189–192
    breastfeeding mothers, 44–49
    connecting past, present, and future
        in, 156–158
    during COVID-19 pandemic, 94–97
    "have-to" mindset in, 227
    quest for equilibrium in, 167–173,
        186, 189–192
    and serving yourself first, 82–91
Mother's Day trip to Chicago, 82–91
Muscle tension, 149

N
National Association for Children of
        Addiction, 16
National Football League (NFL), 207
National Institutes of Health (NIH), 45, 133
National Sexual Assault Hotline, 59
Nelson, Danielle, 197–198
Nervous system, trauma and, 11, 148
New York Times, 94–97
Nike, 207
The19th, 108–109

O
O'Rourke, Neha, 21

P
Palm Springs, Calif.-198, 197
Parentified children, 155
Past, connecting present, future, and,
        156–158
Patriarchy, 2, 29, 172
Patterns, repeating, 212
Peace, protecting your, 254
Perimenopause, 136, 148
Permission to prioritize pleasure, 220–226
Planned Parenthood, 212, 213, 215–216
Play, 155–158
Pleasure, *see* Prioritizing pleasure
Postpartum depression, 47, 151
Post-traumatic stress disorder (PTSD), 13, 149
Power:
    abuse of, 30–34, 54–55

inequitable systems of, 57, 60–61
of toxic white women, 109–110
women in, 215–216
Predator archetype, 34–35
Present, 153, 156–158
Presidential election (2024), 102, 108–110
Pretender archetype, 35–36
Prioritizing pleasure, 219–230
and Could-Should-Would method, 228–229
discomfort with, 219–220
"have to" mindset vs., 226–228
making progress at, 230
and play, 155–158
seeking permission for, 220–226
shifting to, 230
PR News, 178–179
Problem solving, 101–102
Progress, making, 23, 230
"Progressive Workforce" pilot, 186–190
Projector archetype, 36
Promoter archetype, 36–37
Protector archetype, 37–38

Q

Quitting, 18–20, 99, 201

R

Ray, Jeanenne, 122
Rebirth, 201–204
Reitman, Catherine, 89
Relationships. *See also* Burning bridges
letting go of outgrown, 99, 255–257
unresolved trauma and, 150
Responsibility, for ending generational
trauma, 255–256
Roan, Chappell, 143
Rockenwagner, Patti, 78
Roles, entrepreneurs' decisions about, 195
Roosevelt, Theodore, 73
Rose, Emily, 71
Rule breaking, 157, 253–254

S

Salesforce, 185
Satir, Virginia, 14
Saugatuck, Mich., 23–26
Savanh, Victoria, 119–123
Scarcity mindset, 225, 234
Self, abandoning, 1–2, 4–5, 33–34, 81, 83, 98
Self-care, 23, 91–92, 214–215. *See also* Serving
yourself first

Self-confidence, 83, 163–164
Self-criticism, 43–44
Self-definition, 3
Selfishness, 5, 90, 214
Selflessness, 81–82
Self-loathing, 129–132
Self-worth, 1, 21, 33, 98, 118–125, 194, 229, 241
Serving yourself first, 1, 81–100
abandoning self vs., 4–5
and "Alone Together" feature, 94–97
author's childhood thoughts on, 82–83
effects of, 97–100
within families, 82–91
messages about selflessness, 81–82
Monday after Mother's Day tradition, 91–92
Mother's Day trip to Chicago, 82–91
others' negative reactions to, 89–91
shifting to, 100
in your career, 92–94
Sexual harassment, 54–60, 151
Shame, 2, 47–49, 56, 74, 90, 97, 132
SHREK executive search firms, 55
Silent Generation, 14
Sitting in stillness, 152–154, 200, 262
6-D Strategy, 105–107
Sobriety, 140–144
Solitary confinement:
for breastfeeding mothers, 44–49
in roles assigned to women, 43–44
sharing to break, 48–49
shifts to escape, 49–50
Somatic memory, 149
South by Southwest (SXSW)
Conference, 208–214
Space, claiming, *see* Taking up space
Spotify, 117
Start date, for new endeavor, 195
Stewert, Rebecca, 56–59
Stockholm Syndrome, 32, 33
Stone, Emma, 222
Strzemien, Anya, 96
Stuntz, Michelle, 202
Swift, Taylor, 117
"System Failure" panel, 208–212

T

Taking back your body, 129–159
being at war with your body, 129–130
celebrating wins along the way, 144–146
connecting past, present, and future, 156–158
exercise, 147–148, 154–158
finding the right healthcare, 133–137

Taking back your body (*continued*)
   freedom in, 158
   and mindless actions/habits, 137–144
   releasing stored trauma, 148–154
   shifts for, 159
   as vibe of the year, 130–132
   women's difficulties with, 132–133
Taking up space, 231–242
   demonstrating your worth by, 241
   at Ella, 235
   with The Fairway, 234–235
   messages for women about, 231–232
   others' responses to, 238–241
   in professional photo shoot, 235–238
   shifting to, 241–242
   at The Wing, 232–234
Talk therapy, 111, 150, 221
Teachers, impact of, 164–165
Tin, Ida, 135
Toxic people, 29, 49, 53–60, 108–110
Trauma, unresolved, 148–151
Trauma bonding, 2, 32–34, 58, 60, 109
Tree pose, 257–258
Trump, Donald, 109, 175
Trusting yourself, 103–104, 107
T-Shirt Deli, 70

U
"Unabashed Hype Women" post, 63–68,
   75, 130
Unabashed Hype Women shirt, 69–71
United States Coast Guard, 17
"Unite for America" event, 108
University of Michigan, 54, 137, 165, 246
Unpaid labor, 1–2, 85, 186–187
Unresolved trauma, 148–154

V
Vision, mission and, 195–196
Vision boards, 130, 225–226
Voss, Alexis, 108
Vulnerability, 227–228

W
Wandering, 221–226
Wegscheider-Cruse, Sharon, 14
Weight loss drugs, 136–137, 140
"White Women: Answer the Call" virtual
   event, 104–108
"Why You Are an Abortion Beneficiary"
   panel, 212–214
Wiley, 119–124

Winfrey, Oprah, 108
The Wing, 202, 232–234
Winona, 136
Wins, celebrating, 144–146
Win With Black Women (WWBW), 102
Women:
   believing accounts of, 173–177, 180
   complicated, 244, 249
   departure of, from workplace, 173–176,
      208–212
   domestic violence against, 180, 181
   five archetypes of, 34–38
   going through, messages about, 110–111
   in leadership, 175, 187, 190–191
   medical research excluding, 133–134
   navigating roles assigned to, 43–44
   in power, 215–216
   power of collective change by, 251
   selflessness, messages about, 81–82
   serving yourself first, messages about, 99–100
   shaming and blaming of women by, 59
   spaces occupied only by, 239
   support for Harris from, 102–103
   systems silencing, 2
   taking back body, difficulties with, 132–133
   taking up space, messages about, 231–232
   toxic white, 29, 108–110
   unpaid labor by, 1–2, 186–187
   viewing, as competition, 39, 64, 73, 74,
      234–235, 250
Women of color, corporate treatment of, 234
Work–life balance, 172
Workplace experiences:
   abuse of power, 30–34
   of alchemy, 178–192
   blurred lines of personal and professional,
      167–172
   of breastfeeding mothers, 44–49
   chaotic, 18–19
   of entrepreneurship, 178, 192–202
   quest for equilibrium, 170–173, 189–192
   serving yourself first in, 92–94
   of sexual harassment, 54–60
   of taking up space, 232–235
   for women of color, 234

Y
Yeoh, Michelle, ix, 3, 63–66, 70–75
Yoga, 154–158, 239, 240, 257–258

Z
Zodiac signs, cardinal, 112–113